Indian Booker Prize Winners on India

Edited by

Supriya Shukla
Neeru Tandon
Chhaya Jain
R.P. Pradhan

ATLANTIC

PUBLISHERS & DISTRIBUTORS (P) LTD

Published by
ATLANTIC
PUBLISHERS & DISTRIBUTORS (P) LTD
7/22, Ansari Road, Darya Ganj,
New Delhi-110002
Phones : +91-11-40775252, 23273880, 23275880, 23280451
Fax : +91-11-23285873
Web : www.atlanticbooks.com
E-mail : info@atlanticbooks.com

Branch Office
5, Nallathambi Street, Wallajah Road,
Chennai-600002
Phones : +91-44-64611085, 32413319
E-mail : chennai@atlanticbooks.com

ISBN 978-81-269-1846-1

Printed in India at Nice Printing Press, A-33/3A, Site-IV,
Industrial Area, Sahibabad, Ghaziabad, U.P.

Preface

India today is the cynosure of all eyes. Whether it is India shining or India suffering, she continues to entice the world. Literary artists across the globe are irresistibly drawn to probe into the labyrinthine depths of the India of yesteryears and the present times. Likewise, Indian English writers are persistently exploring and treating artistically the multiple conceptions of India and Indianness. This marketing is attracting the attention of the West. The emerging dominance of Indian English writing has made its presence felt in the world of Booker fiction. The Indian recipients of the celebrated Man Booker Prize have rendered kaleidoscopic narrations about their own nation weaving together fact and fiction, realism and fantasy laced with their own imagination and vision.

The book comprises a collection of 26 essays by literary luminaries and eminent scholars who have earnestly discussed, debated and probed into the various facets of the Indian Booker Prize winners, their perceptions and projections of their own country and the question of the West being enamoured by Indian English fiction. These essays are their deliberations on the topic of the National Seminar organised by the Dept. of English, V.S.S.D. College, Kanpur on "India in the Fiction of Indian Booker Prize Winners".

Recipient of the Sahitya Academi Award and the Commonwealth Poetry Award, a leading figure in Indian English poetry, a poet with a powerfully developed social conscience, Keki N. Daruwalla proffers a candid, categorical and critical analysis of the 'varied and dynamic' imaginations of the award-winning novelists and their presentation of the Indian reality. Evaluating their works on the basis of four decisive factors—imagination, history, language and metaphor—Daruwalla offers a liberal and progressive view towards creative artists who, he opines, hold every right to having their own visions and projecting them.

An erudite scholar and former Vice Chancellor of Utkal University, Prof. G.K. Das's thought-provoking article questions the intrinsic merit of the Booker Prize winners of India. He unflinchingly declares that writers like Rushdie and Adiga have used India for their own gain. Their focus is not on delineating "India's past or present history or a vision of her future' but on marketing India as a "saleable merchandise". However, Prof. Das considers *The God of Small Things* a masterpiece belonging to a different league of fiction wherin Arundhati Roy has depicted the Indian family and society being impacted by external pressures. Using the metaphor of "cooking India" he explains, "What I should like to stress, however, is that the motive for writing a narrative of India today in its best sense has almost come to be synonymous with one's appetitive urge for eating and drinking, a totally hedonistic exercise."

Dr. N.M. Nigam, Dean, faculty of Arts and Convenor (English) of CSJM University and principal, M.M. College, Kanpur gives an in-depth overview of the "Image of India in the Works of Booker Prizes". Furnishing a detailed analysis of each novel, she however, posits several meaningful questions regarding the negative image of India being flaunted by Indians to international readers. Dr. Nigam suggests that writer should be wary and cautious about the way they present their country and not give a lopsided view.

Dr. Supriya Shukla, convenor of the "National Seminar on Booker Prize Winners of India" and HOD (English), V.S.S.D College Kanpur, enumerates the wide range of thematic concerns of the Indian Booker Prize winners and their fictional and realistic presentations of the Indian subcontinent whereby they emphasize the need to evolve an egalitarian society. The novelists seem to be obsessed with portraying the malaise gripping their country and the people so that they are unable to emerge from the slough of inadequacies that have engulfed their nation for an indeterminate length of time. Dr. Shukla compares the writings of international bestsellers by foreign authors who have visited India, lived in Indian conditions and yet have presented a rounded and holistic picture of the country.

Dr. Neeru Tandon in her research paper "The Making and Marketing of Booker Prize" tells the story of the inception of Booker Prize in a very interesting way. She discusses at length the role of publishers and market tendency regarding the Booker Prize winning novels. She also mentions the Man Booker Dozen, The Booker International Prize and Booker of Booker Prize. Dr. Tandon writes we all know that within no time the authors "selected for long list and short-list, become the stars for the reading public".

In a comprehensive study of the "Reconstruction of Supressed Histories in India", Dr. P.C. Pradhan delves into Naipaul's search for an Indian identity and his representations about India. Naipaul's position as an outsider and insider and his "European-centric mindset" are the factors responsible for his myopic vision of his ancestral land. However, Naipaul's frustration is justified as he earnestly desires Indians to be more progressive which alone can eliminate their woes and travails.

Describing V.S. Naipaul as a "nomadic intellectual in a postcolonial world", Dr. Neeraj Kumar poignantly and compellingly reveals Naipaul's predicament of being in exile. In his essay "An Area of Darkness: A Postcolonial Overview" he reiterates that it is his homelessness and rootlessness that makes Naipaul adhere to a dark and pessimistic vision. This displacement forms the crux of his creative talent.

Manisha Mathur has highlighted the Rushdie phenomenon and enumerated the strong presence of Bollywood in his novel *Midnight's Children*. Rushdie has been quite dismissive of Bollywood, Hindi films nevertheless figure prominently in his novel. The manifestations of Bollywood are often playful and despite the mocking tone, he seems to revel in the loudness, vitality and popularity of Hindi films in India.

Dr. R.N. Rai has drawn our attention to a glaring issue of gender inequality presented by Arundhati Roy in her novel *The God of Small Things*. The novel may be regarded as a protest novel as it surfaces her unforgiving anger against the age old rotten systems and social hypocracies. "Man is free to do whatever he likes but no freedom is granted to a woman. If something is prohibited for a woman, how can it be desirable for man?"

Dr. Chhaya Jain's article pinpoints the sensuous imagery present in *The God of Small Things* with extraordinary linguistic inventiveness. Arundhati Roy's novel surpasses all in narrating incidents very tenderly, craftily and in a highly poetical manner. It is a fascinating experience to focus on the text's play with the imagery which is pre-eminently sensuous.

Dr. Bhupendra Pratap Singh Chauhan has delineated different aspects of human nature that emerge from the novel—love, madness, hope and infinite joy. All sections of the novel showcase the reflections of secret passion and frustration, fears and forbodings, dreams and reality.

Dr. R.P. Pradhan's paper refers to the ongoing conflict between the "high and the low" in *The God of Small Things*. The conflict is caused by segregating a section of society for being untouchable. The novelist raises her powerful voice against the evils of discrimination on caste and gender. In the end, the readers find themselves sympathising with Ammu and Velutha who bear all sorts of tyranny and tortures.

Dr. Reena Mitra has underlined the new social, political and cultural challenges that have come to the fore in the fiction of the writers of Indian diaspora. Kiran Desai, unlike the majority of writers living abroad, portrays both life in India and the life of Indian Americans, settled in the USA with a rare sureness of touch. She has demonstrated effectively the erosion of identity in the lives of Indian immigrants—the affluent and the successful as well as the poor and the hunted.

Dr. Sarvajit Mukherji has raised some pertinent questions regarding the damages done to the natural world by human activities. *The Inheritance of Loss* poses such questions which need serious pondering and eventually the appropriate solutions. The growing urbanization is a serious threat to the Nature.

Dr. Soumen Mukherjee has highlighted the suffering of the poor and the powerless as portrayed by Kiran Desai who is a careful observer of behaviour. The character of the cook, Panna Lal represents all those marginalised individuals who work like donkeys because they accept it as their destiny. This passivity of the powerless men leads them to self-negation and self-abasement.

Dr. Anita Bhela has advocated to give a Bakhtinian reading to the novel *The White Tiger*. Mikhail Bakhtin's ideology of the traits of the novel gets exemplified by Adiga's text. The novel presents a multi-languaged world where we come across the differing voices of the masters and servants, servants and other servants, masters and their masters.

Dr. S.K. Arora has pointed out that the mindset of Aravind Adiga, if not anti-religious is not certainly religious. The paper brings out the deep-rooted anger of Dr. Arora who finds one thing common among Booker Prize winners that they all sell India in the West-sponsored sale, and get the gold, awards and rewards.

A.S. Rao and P.K. Sharma are of the opinion that Adiga, in the novel, is primarily interested in shooting at the dark side of contemporary Indian society. For that purpose he divided India into India of darkness and India of light. He strongly opines that it is almost impossible to bring justice and equality for the commoners.

Lt. Anjita Singh in her article on *The White Tiger* has given a vivid explanation of India's class struggle. The novel is apparently straightforward. It gives a dazing account of the realities of the life of India's poor. The sharp and satirical eye of the narrator draws the reader into dark regions of our country.

Anshul Chandra in her article on Adiga describes the innermost thoughts of a driver, a real Indian who dreams to be a rich man.

Krishna Singh endeavours to analyse the political-social and cultural consciousness in Kiran Desai's *The Inheritance of Loss* and Aravind Adiga's *The White Tiger*.

Smita Verghese in her article on *The Inheritance of Loss* illustrates the problems of alienation. The fact of real life is that the worst part of war, unrest, uprising, is that life goes on.

Dr. Charul Jain has projected the similarity between the Booker Prize winning novels of Arundhati Roy and Aravind Adiga because in both the cases India is presented as a nation that is full of sadness, agony and desperation yet is attractive to the imagination and in being so is also mysterious and saleable.

Dr. Vipin Kumar Singh seeks to compare and contrast the ways Kiran Desai and Adiga adopted in their Booker winning novels to represent the voices of the subaltern.

Dr. Sunita Sinha endeavours to focus on the various trajectories of masculinities that the two eminent Indian Booker winner women novelists, Arundhati Roy and Kiran Desai, present in their respective Booker winning novels.

Dr. Jaya Kapoor has referred to the political aspects in *The God of Small Things*. The primary focus is on the Communist rule in Kerala.

Writing is a process to unhinge a person. With this in mind we hereby present the articles of different scholars in the form of a book. We hope this presentation will serve the purpose of examining and understanding India and Indian society better through the lens of Booker winners. The book will be useful for the students and teachers of English Literature.

Editors

Contents

Preface *iii*

1. Booker Prize-Winning Novels by Indian Writers 1
   –Keki N. Daruwalla

2. Representations of India in (Booker) Award Winning Fiction 9
   –G.K. Das

3. Image of India in the Works of Booker Prizes 18
   –N.M. Nigam

4. The India of the Indian Booker Prize Winners 30
   –Supriya Shukla

5. The Making and Marketing of the Man Booker Prize: An Inside Story 42
   –Neeru Tandon

6. Reconstruction of "Suppressed Histories" in India: *A Wounded Civilization*: V.S. Naipaul's Search for an Indian Identity 55
   –P.C. Pradhan

7. *An Area of Darkness*: A Post-Colonial Overview 84
   –Neeraj Kumar

8. Blurring Distinctions Between 'High' and 'Low': Bollywood and Rushdie's *Midnight's Children* 93
   –Manisha Mathur

9. Roy's *The God of Small Things*: A Search for Female Identity — 99
–R.N. Rai

10. Sensuousness in *The God of Small Things* — 112
–Chhaya Jain

11. Theme of Human Nature in the Novel of Arundhati Roy *The God of Small Things* — 118
–Bhupendra Pratap Singh Chauhan

12. Segregational Trait and Social Exclusion in *The God of Small Things* — 126
–R.P. Pradhan

13. Reverberations of the Diasporic: Kiran Desai's *The Inheritance of Loss* — 133
–Reena Mitra

14. Losing the Inheritance: An Ecocritical Reading of *The Inheritance of Loss* — 139
–Sarvajit Mukherji

15. Panna Lal's Tryst with Destiny in *The Inheritance of Loss* — 145
–Soumen Mukherjee

16. *The White Tiger*: A Bakhtinian Reading — 155
–Anita Bhela

17. Aravind Adiga's *The White Tiger*: An Anti-religious Text — 165
–Sudhir K. Arora

18. Aravind Adiga's *The White Tiger*: An Overview — 176
–A.S. Rao and *Pawan Kumar Sharma*

19. An India of Light and an India of Darkness: Reality Check in Adiga's *The White Tiger* 180
–Anjita Singh

20. Reflection of India in Aravind Adiga's *The White Tiger* 189
–Ansul Chandra

21. Politico-social and Cultural Image of India in Kiran Desai's *The Inheritance of Loss* and Aravind Adiga's *The White Tiger* 195
–Krishna Singh

22. India—Constructed or Incidental 210
–Smita Verghese

23. Booking the Booker: Re-Presenting India to the Western Gaze 220
–Charul Jain

24. Subaltern Voices in 21st Century Indian Fiction: A Study of *The Inheritance of Loss* and *The White Tiger* 231
–Vipin K. Singh

25. Situating Masculinities in Arundhati Roy's *The God of Small Things* and Kiran Desai's *The Inheritance of Loss* 240
–Sunita Sinha

26. The Failed God of Small Things: Political Aspects in *The God of Small Things* 251
–Jaya Kapoor

List of Contributors 259

1

Booker Prize-Winning Novels by Indian Writers[1]

Keki N. Daruwalla

The subject, I must confess, sounded a bit odd to me first, for one would be hard put to find a common strand in the five Indian novels that have won the Booker Prize. The subject is also a measure of what a star struck people we are. Having sat in some award-doling juries, one knows that often there is nothing much to choose between the prize winner and the other short-listed writers. We get star struck by actors, models who walk the ramp, TV anchors who walk the scam ramp or the terror ramp *a la* 26/11, or the Kargil ramp. Flash bulbs would start exploding if even a TV anchor were to walk in here. This goggle-eyed worship of stars and pseudo stars reflects on the Indian's insecurity.

We need to consider how and why fiction in English written by Indians has taken the Western readership, if not by storm, at least by a strong gale. Perhaps we could date it to 1981 when *Midnight's Children* won the Booker Prize. The book of course was great, apocalyptic, fiercely original in its technique with a mix of history and magic. And the magical realism was not a pastiche, not a derivative of the Latin Americans. The narrative was kaleidoscopic. A slew of books, many of them very good, followed, taking the same line—Vikram Chandra and Mukul Kesavan to mention just two, both very talented and self-assured novelists. But I am not here to trace things chronologically. The first question we need to ask is what was the dramatic change from the thirties, when R.K. Narayan, Raja Rao and Mulk Raj Anand wrote? By the standards and the style of the thirties, surely these three pioneers could not be despised. Yet they needed the intervention of people like Graham Greene and E.M. Forster to even get published.

I feel that the most accessible and entertaining novelist India has produced is Manohar Malgonkar. Yet you will never find a book by him in a bookshop today. His copyright is held by publishers in their twilight, to put it mildly. Or publishers have sadly forgotten him.

I feel that the main reason why the Indian novel has taken off is that it now reflects the myriad and multi-faceted Indian reality. And the Indian reality is mind-boggling in its contradictions, its complexity and its tremendous diversity. Sky scraper and slum, corruption and crime, the mafia and Maharishi Mahesh, Rajneesh and the Ramdevs, Sadhus who declare they are going to walk on water, millions of tons of surplus grain and starving millions, changing of place names—Chatrapati this and Chatrapati that, this Sena and that Sena, terrorism and the counter-terrorism of the state and its alleged atrocities, all jostling together. The politics of caste and intrigue and vote grabbing, not forgetting money grabbing—all this has its own entertainment value. So has the combination of cinema and politics, as in Tamil Nadu. Along with this, thank God we have people who hark back to values, segments that still believe in non-violence and simplicity and Gandhiji. Where else can a novelist get such a storehouse of raw material?

As an aside may I venture to say that the inner response of a writer should be as dynamic, diverse and complex as the reality he or she faces. For after all what is creativity (let's restrict it to fiction) if not a response to the reality around us. Whether our responses are as complex and intricate, or not is a moot point.

I have talked elsewhere of the fact that fiction has its own, what for want of a better word, I would call 'determinism'. I talked about "the remorseless logic of circumstance, the slow buildup of tension, the past illuminated by a flashback and in turn throwing light on the future, like the spurt of a match in a hall of mirrors".

Stendhal said, "A novel is a mirror walking along a main road." It is a measure of how far we have drifted from the nineteen century votaries of realism that fiction today is judged by how much, or rather how imaginatively it has moulded and changed reality to its ends. Rushdie has talked of magical mirrors.

A sizeable part of our reality would be our history, starting with the Partition, 1962, then 1965 and the war with Pakistan, the liberation of Bangladesh, the JP rebellion or revolution (it had both elements) and the Judgment and the Emergency—the Pakistanis, the Khalistanis, Bhindranwale and his atrocities, the dithering manner he was tackled and then the Blue Star. We have assassinations galore from M.K. Gandhi to Rajiv Gandhi, and the exotic and the esoteric go hand in hand, with blood and crime and intrigue. So one of the questions before Seminarists here would be to evaluate how these novelists have negotiated the past. We should not forget Henry James's dictum that "It takes a great deal of history to produce a little literature." My rider to that would be that fascinating history should produce fascinating literature.

The third element is the language. We do not have a patois. The Indian novelist in English cannot bring out the different inflections and pronunciations, dialects and intonations that differ from district to district in our Indian languages. Yet our speech rhythms in English, the way we speak half a sentence in Hindi or a local language and half in English, is unique. Novelists have brought that in, while poets have not been able to.

Lastly, metaphor, the staple of poetry, sometimes takes a look in. *Midnight's Children* is an ingenious and a wonderful metaphor. If Manto's *Toba Tek Singh* is a spatial metaphor, the mad man dying on no man's land between India and Pakistan, Rushdie comes up with that temporal metaphor, the exact moment that separates colonialism from freedom, colonialism from post-colonialism, and undivided India from a fractured partitioned country. And Saleem Sinai is born at that precise moment of India's, rather South Asia's tryst with destiny, if we are to believe Pandit Nehru, or *yeh shab-gazidah sahr, yeh dagdar ujala*, if we believe Faiz Ahmad Faiz. As metaphor and symbolism goes, you cannot easily beat Rushdie's novel.

So, arbitrary as it seems, the yardsticks for evaluating these four fine novels boil down to four elements. Firstly, how the Indian reality comes through the alembic of the writer's imagination. What have they done with it.

Secondly, if history comes into play, as it does conspicuously in *Midnight's Children* and *The Inheritance of Loss*, how it is handled. What does the writer do with it, with the conveyor belt of national or regional events? Does the narrative differ radically from reportage, or not? Is the discourse meaningful?

Thirdly, does the writer use language as a magic wand rather than as a truncheon? Does language lift the narrative to a different plane? Three of the novels (all except Adiga's *The White Tiger*) pass this test. There is poetry in what Arundhati Roy and Kiran Desai write, and for Salman Rushdie, language becomes an invention, an eminently successful laboratory experiment.

Lastly comes metaphor, and while it is glaringly spot-lit in *Midnight's Children*, one cannot say it is non-existent in the other novels. Arundhati Roy's novel is also a metaphor in its own way on family, caste and also class. Life and love and landscape are seen through the eyes of a child. It reminds me of a scene in Satyajit Ray's *Shatranj ke Khiladi*, where the invading British army with a gun mounted on a caparisoned elephant is shown through the eyes of a half frightened, half wonder-struck eyes of a gawking child. The novel almost becomes a metaphor on life and landscape, on Kerala itself. Though the novel dabbles in politics, it never turns into a political tract.

But the real metaphor in *The God of Small Things* lies in the "oneness" of the non-zygotic twins, Rahel and her twin brother Estha. On the very first page, Rahel wakes up giggling at Esthappen's funny dream. She remembers the taste of the tomato sandwich which he has eaten. Midway through the book Estha stops talking. Speaking of a character Larry McCalsin, the author writes, he could not be expected to understand that "the emptiness in one twin was only a version of quietness in the other. That the two things fitted together."

The other overpowering current is the falling away of caste taboos before the call of the flesh. On page 176, we have Ammu watching her child Rahel in the arms of Velutha, the toddy-tapper. He looks up and catches Ammu's gaze. "Centuries telescoped into one evanescent moment. History was wrong-footed, caught off guard. Sloughed off like an old snakeskin. Its marks, its scars, its wounds from old wars, and the walking backwards days all fell away. In its absence it left an aura, a palpable shimmering that was as plain to see as the water in a river...." It could not be more beautifully put. These are among the first intimations of the torrid affair that is to take place between the two.

She can castigate when she wants to. Comrade K.N.M. Pillai's son does painting and plumbing for Dutch and German embassies. One also notices impish irony. "A small tin sign on a big banyan tree said for VD sex complaints contact Dr O.K. Joy" (151). We have children's jokes. When Ammu starts babbling in her sleep during her noon siesta, Estha says: "It's an afternoon-mare" (217).

I have already given my brief views on Rushdie's acclaimed novel. It is too complex for a short analysis. In my view, *Midnight's Children* and *The God of Small Things* are in a league by themselves, and a cut above the other two. (I am not talking of V.S. Naipaul's *In a Free State* here.)

I do not think anyone can take up all four books in any detail. I would like to deal at some length with Kiran Desai's *The Inheritance of Loss*. The novel starts bleakly—but there is no law against a bleak start. We are told about the death of Sai's parents and then we have the Judge, Sai's grandfather being robbed of his guns by the Gurkhaland thugs. Yet the way the novel is plotted at the start, Sai's journey to Kalimpong (very reminiscent of an Anita Rau Badami's novel, where also a girl loses her parents abroad and comes to her grandparents in India) is a bit airy fairy. A Parsi called Mistri marries a Gujarati. This Mistri gets selected for a USSR Space Programme to pilot a spaceship, but he and his wife get squashed by an Indian bus. Symbolism? Irony, or ironic metaphor, or all three? She won't let us forget the central word "loss". I thought this bit was sloppily contrived. In Gujarati lingo we would say *kai dhar poochroo nathi* which translates as 'neither tail nor torso'.

Then there are jibes at Convents on pages 29 and 30 which any ex-Convent School girl can make. I get a lot of verse manuscripts—many of them by ex-convent School girls. Kiran Desai's mother, master of bleak plots, rather master of bleak overhangs on almost non-existent plots, wrote better.

When I had read the book first I was bowled over by the language in the first sixty pages. No longer so. It is amazing what a second reading does to a book. I noticed cliches this time: "Death whispered into Sai's ear", "life leaped in her pulse", "her heart plummeted" all on page 30 describing how they "corkscrewed on to Darjeeling".

Among the characters, the Judge is stereotyped to the *n*th degree, the Brown Sahib of yore, the butt of both the Indians and the Brits. He can neither stand his wife, nor soup being served after the main course. The Brits must have chuckled over the prim Gujarati justice. The ICS were quite sophisticated. Here the Judge is shown as rustic. I found nothing noteworthy about Sai and Gyan either. Their affair was also tawdry. Biju is a cook, and though his fate is a bit pitiable, and he is shown as the typical Indian servant who cannot adjust abroad, and eventually is robbed of all his savings, his character is not lit up with any word or action of his.

With the nomenclature she belittles her own characters at times—Lola and Noni, Uncle Fatty and Father Booty. I did not see the humour in this either. Father Booty is thrown out, fine. But he made cheese. Sai, "marooned during the curfew, sick about Gyan, and sick with the desire to be desired", still hoping for his return, is "bereft of her former skill at solitude". Fine passage this (250). Sai goes to find Gyan and confront him in his rundown Nepali quarters. What do they talk about, this Nepali Master and the granddaughter of an ICS Judge? Cheese and chocolate, if you please.

Moreover, is this the way to tackle a political movement in a novel? You will say but she is writing a novel not a political tract. But within the first six pages the Gorkhaland thugs come and rob the Judge of his hunting rifles. And was this tawdry affair between a sixteen-year-old school girl (Sai) and her twenty-year-old Nepali master (Gyan) the opening that Kiran Desai found fit to get an entry into the Gorkhaland movement? On page 272, Kiran Desai says: "The trouble was he (Gyan) had tried to be a part of a larger question, tried to be part of politics and history." So does Kiran Desai, as also the novel, but like Gyan they are not a part of it, the larger political question. If you were writing a novel about the French Revolution, how would you go about it? Would one write of totally inconsequential characters, living out their rat-like existence in garrets? Wouldn't the shadow of the guillotine and Robespierre and Danton be around even as a backdrop? Not that Gorkhaland and the Bastille can be talked of in the same breath.

On page 303, Nehru is being welcomed at a railway station and we have Congressmen eating scrambled egg on toast! Come on! Has she ever seen Congress workers, the four anna paying walahs? But then do you judge fiction according to how it conforms to reality on the ground? I would rather not answer the question.

Finally, a word about the earliest of the Booker prize winning novels, V.S. Naipaul's *In a Free State*. That was won by a West Indian and not an Indian, let us be clear about that. Here Naipaul plays with the genre itself, as only a master would dare to do. In a way, the novel is split into what one could at a pinch call two stories followed by a long fictional travelogue. And these are sandwiched between a prologue and an epilogue, which are again both travelogues, one dealing with a tramp on a ship and the other a piece on Egypt. One admires Naipaul's audacity.

The first section "One of Many" details the life of an Indian servant/cook taken to Washington, paid next to nothing and made to sleep in something resembling a cupboard. (Both Kiran Desai and Adiga deal with similar situations it may be noticed.) He is appalled that *hubshis* ("this wild race") live in America in such numbers! He switches masters and goes to

Priya (a name strangely given to a male). It ends with him marrying a *hubshi* woman.

In the next section, "Tell Me Who to Kill" Naipaul is on home ground—West Indian poor brothers coming to England and trying to survive. It is reminiscent of his lovely novel *The Mimic Men* (1967). The characters tail as in the first story and come to no good. The third section "In a Free State" the tables are turned. It's the whites, two English persons Bobby and Linda are driving back from the capital of an African country called Collectorate, to their cubby hole which is called "Compound". (Sir Vidya leaves me disappointed with the names he gives to places and countries.) The drive in Bobby's car is eventful—they even drive past the scene of the King's murder by the President's soldiers. This time it is the whites who fail in Africa, they cannot adjust. In one dialogue, Linda says: "You go out driving with Sammy Kisenyi...(he) later reads a paper on broadcasting at the conference. He's lifted whole paragraphs from T.S. Eliot, of all people. You say nothing about it, you can't say anything about it. Outside you encourage (the Africans) and encourage. In the compound you bitch about them." And Bobby tells her "It's their country. But it's your life." And later makes it clear that the Europeans came "for the freedom" (225).

One cannot go on and on. Enough to say that each novel is a strong piece of fiction, each can stand scrutiny. The imaginations at work are varied and dynamic. Most of the novels paint a bleak picture the characters do not seem to prosper. The Indian reality is bleak, but not that bleak. But each creative artist has a right to his or her vision. We need to salute the novelists who have, through the prism of their imagination, held a mirror to the Indian reality as they see it, and yet transformed it into excellent fiction.

NOTE

1. I must confess, I have not touched upon V.S. Naipaul, a tremendous writer, merely because it escaped my mind that he had also won the Booker Prize. One thinks of him more as a Nobel Laureate.

2

Representations of India in (Booker) Award Winning Fiction

G.K. Das

How are we to evaluate works of literature/culture and their authors? By the status and money value of the awards they may have received or by what they intrinsically contain and stand for? That plainly is the central concern of this paper, in special reference to the Booker awarded Indian authors.

The highest and most covetable literary award is the Nobel Prize founded by Alfred Nobel. Nobel was a visionary and benevolent altruist. His own view of the award he founded was based on both material and ideal (transcendental) considerations. A Nobel Laureate in his judgment should have 'conferred the greatest benefit to mankind'. That manifestly was the central testament of faith in Alfred Bernard Nobel's Will. A Nobel laureate in the field of Literature, in particular, should likewise have produced a 'most outstanding work in an ideal direction'. A statutory requirement of the Nobel Foundation is also a book should deserve consideration for the Nobel Prize in Literature if it in 'form and style, possesses literary value'. (Emphasis added)

The criterion 'The greatest benefit to mankind' sounds pure Benthamism—the utilitarian philosophy of 'greatest good of the greatest number' that Jeremy Bentham propounded, which laid the foundation of industrial and technological development in Britain, Europe, and North America.

Subsequently, that philosophy came to be used to support of the policy of imperial expansion and to justify the political fallacy that the empire existed for the good of the subject peoples. This fallacy stood exposed in course of time, however, by mounting resistance to imperialism by countless people across the world. By the same apparently altruistic consideration, a Nobel Prize winning book, however outstanding, say Doris Lessing's *The Golden Notebook* (1962), could simply not be assumed to have 'conferred the greatest benefit to mankind'. The fact that Lessing's fascinating book came as a late bloomer (2007) to the list of Nobel Awards could be an indication of genuine misgiving about its merit. Lessing herself was aware of the shortcomings of her magnificent work. Written with the purpose of giving 'the ideological feel' of the mid-century, *The Golden Notebook* was set among socialists and Marxists and the 'great debates' of our time; it did not show an 'ideal direction', however, as Hermann Hess's *Siddhartha* (1922/1954), for instance, had shown.

That brings us to yet another important conditionally—that most outstanding book in question must be in 'an ideal direction'. Several of the award winning books, judged strictly by this criterion, should indeed have failed to qualify. Tagore's *Gitanjali* (1912) or Golding's *Lord of the Flies* (1954) that stood the test are among the admirable exceptions no doubt.

Judging whether a literary work points to an ideal direction is not easy, for it is not easy to define what truly is 'ideal'. One comes, here, from the material to the domain of the transcendent. However, well-produced, dazzling in ideas, and richly invested for a book may be, Dan Brown's *The Da Vinci Code* or *The Lost Symbol*, for instance, does in no way show an ideal direction, although it surely has may have given pleasure to millions of readers all over the world. (Giving pleasure is also doing good to people.)

I do not mean to imply that the 'material' is in any way inferior to the 'transcendent', or *vice versa*. Neither do I hold the view that the material is the base to subculture; the transcendent to high/ideal culture. To me, both plains of perception/interpretation/assessment are important. But the moral value (in the sense Sartre uses the term) of any work of literature/culture to a large extent does get conditioned by the nature and quality of the motivation behind it. The social/political/aesthetic value of the Nobel Prize and the plethora of Booker Awards funded with private capital and used by large for huge monetary profits to some (no doubt) distinguished individuals and groups of vested interests in the publishing industry today, is an eminently debatable matter.

Coming to the Booker Award, it no doubt is a prestigious recognition given to distinguished writers of chiefly of the (British) Commonwealth and several eminently gifted writers, e.g. Salman Rushdie, Arundhati Roy, Kiran Desai, and Aravind Adiga have received it.

On the whole, Booker Award winning fiction on India has been a remarkable feat to have happened around the new millennium: never before was India presented in such delicious variety of recipe and with such minute skill and cleverness. Ruth Prawer Jhabvala's *Heat and Dust* (1975) was made with a recipe of such iridescent and inscrutable glamour which in Joseph Conrad's cryptic words could be summed up as the 'fascination of abomination': Prawer's narrative deftly serves the reader on a platter all three stages of the author/narrator's 'Indian experience'—mystique, real, and surreal. *Heat and Dust* indeed set the trend in India of Booker fiction; the fiction of the consumer, by the consumer and for the consumer.

Sponsored by the Booker Prize Foundation from the profits of the Booker Prize Treading Ltd., the phenomenon today apparently is 'one of the world's most coveted literary prizes', as Anjali Thomas of the largest-selling Times News Network once put it.

That all companies are run for profit is a truism not for Conrad alone but in global business, anywhere. The investment company Man Group is an independent registered 'charity'. We need not ask the question for whose 'profit' it is run, though that is an eminently debatable point. Looking at the best side of the consumption domain, however, the present paper inquires into the geniuses of a variety of representations of India in the more recent Booker Award winning fictions, especially the India-related novels of Salman Rushdie, Arudhati Roy, Kiran Desai and Aravind Adiga. The subheading above 'Cooking India: the Fusion Trend' is an adaptation from Kiran Desai's characteristic opening passage in chapter Twenty-four of her Booker novel *The Inheritance of Loss*: "In the Gandhi Cafe, the lights were kept low, the better to hide the stains. It was a long journey from here to the fusion trend, the goat cheese and basil samosa, the mango margarita. This was the real thing, generic Indian..." (145).

It will be noticed that the cook in Desai's novel, like the fool in a Shakespeare play, is a very remarkable figure. He oversees the prime motives and actions and sees things that others do not always see and thus plays a key role in the unfolding of the domestic comedy from the very beginning:

> Sai, sitting on the veranda, was reading an article about giant squid in an old *National Geographic*. Every now and then she looked up at the Kanchenjunga, observed its wizard phosphorescence with a shiver. The judge sat at the far corner with his chessboard, playing against himself....
>
> Here, at the back, inside the cavernous kitchen, was the cook, trying to light the damp wood. He fingered the kindling gingerly for fear of the community of scorpions living, loving, reproducing in the pile....
>
> Eventually, the fire caught and he placed the kettle on top, as battered, as encrusted as something dug up by an archaeological team, and waited for it to boil.... (Ch. One, 1-2)

Adiga's subaltern-hero and narrator in *The White Tiger* is a *halwai*, maker/vendor of sweets. A typical product of postcolonial consumerist new India, Balram *halwai* is a rootless, garrulous, down to the earth man who *a la* Herzog is engaged through the novel in constructing long and intimate letters addressed to the Chinese Premier Jiabo, as he is addressed, relating his story and India's. His hilariously boastful and subversive narration clearly is designed to deflate the euphoric current notion that independent India is steadily on its way to becoming a superpower along with her spectacularly successful neighbour China.

An able go-getter Balram *halwai* has found the job of a town driver of India's new national doll of a Honda City that he knows is by far superior to the Maruti Suzuki. Shrewder than the cook in Desai's *Inheritance*, he can tell you precisely what the relative advantages and disadvantages of each car are. The Honda City is a smart and beautiful modern car, "with all the necessary comforts: a speaker system, A/C, nice glossy leather seats, and a big stainless steel spittoon in the back". The Maruti is "a small, simple fellow, a perfect servant to the driver; the moment you turn the ignition key, he does exactly what the driver wants him to do" (62).

In Balram *halwai's* perception, the democratic republic of India gives the consumer a choice that the Peoples Republic of China does not give. In religion there is choice. In liquor too: Black Dog Full bottle 1530/-, Teacher's 1030/-, half 530/-, Vat 1210/-. And so, of course, in the brothel: Indian, Foreign, Nepalese partners available to suit different fancies, habits, tastes; at different prices. Balram *halwai* knows it all, is a good guide and has 'enacted on the same bed' in fertile, consumer-friendly, postcolonial India's wasteland.

It is not corruption or crime, but a way of life. Choose what you want to do. The choice is yours: cheat, loot, murder and get on in life, whether you live in Laxmangarh, Varanasi, Dhanbad, Bangalore, or Delhi. One moves from place to place not by Karma, but by choice, and Balram knows this too well.

Tradition dies hard in India but you also have to modernize. Never mind if you end up only as a 'half-baked Indian'. 'The readiness is all.' That's what Adiga's subaltern protagonist Balram *halwai* is meant to stand for, in contemporary India/world, in a converted and convoluted Shakespearean sense.

Like the GNLF story and associated details, the endless partying, and the showings-off on the BBC or the CNN of newly rich family styles in Kiran Desai's *Inheritance of Loss*, what the city bosses do or not do to Balram *halwai* and the like of him in *The White Tiger* is but peripheral, like the icing on a plum pudding. The gripping central story is that of Balram *halwai*, who is such an extraordinarily impressive success in selling himself in the market; he is the white tiger in the cultural jungle that is postcolonial India.

Adiga's spiritual progenitor is Rushdie. They both, materialist in their reading and interpretation of history, are believers in a fabulist rather than moralist view of literature and the arts. The focus in their work is not on India's past or present history or on a vision of her future, but on her saleability, on how best India will sell, in the home and the global market. It is not on the making of a new India: it is instead on the art of their self-making as writer. It is also on the very intelligent and efficient technique of packaging of India as saleable merchandise. Both use India in their own way and interest and to their gain.

The representation of India in both *Midnight's Children* and in *The White Tiger* is of the nature of a master cartoon and is as real or unreal as a cartoon is in relation to an original. And since no one can conclusively pronounce which precisely is an original or real image, it is the cartoon that safely encapsulates the subjectivity in the act of perception/ reconstruction of the image and therefore it cannot be questioned.

Likewise, no single situation or episode in *The White Tiger* or in *Midnight's Children* can be ruled out as fake or a falsification. There are numerous exaggerations no doubt but every exaggeration points to a fact.

It should not be difficult to see how close the art of cartooning is to that of cooking. Both arts are age-old and are meant for creating and providing pleasure and enjoyment of the senses. A good cartoonist, like a good cook, has the taste of a connoisseur. They both have expert knowledge of the properties of the object and ingredients they want to use and they also well understand the mind of the subject who they intend to serve. Adiga and Rushdie as also Kiran Desai are adept in the culinary art and in the art of cartooning. Kiran Desai's Gandhi Café is as central a motif in *Inheritance* as is Rushdie's Pioneer Café in *Midnight* or Adiga's Connaught

Place or the Rooster Coop of ten thousand years of history, behind the Jama Masjid in Old Delhi, in *The White Tiger*, it is all so very exotic and tempting to the reader-consumer whether she is a visitor or a resident in India.

The metaphor of cooking that I use to describe the genius of the award-winning writer about India today is not intended to denigrate the spark of any particular product. I see the brilliance and enjoy the product. What I should like to stress, however, is that the motive for writing a narrative of India today in its best sense has almost come to be synonymous with one's appetitive urge for eating and drinking, a totally hedonistic exercise. Consider for instance a characteristic passage from the 'Snakes and Ladders' chapter in *Midnight's Children*:

> "What is left in this India?" Reverend Mother asked, hand slicing air. "Go, leave it all, go to Pakistan. See how well that Zulfikar is doing—he will give you a start. Be a man, my son—get up and start again!"... Reverend Mother sat at the head of the dining table, doling out food...while, in the kitchens. Mary Pereira took the time to prepare, for the benefit of their visitors, some of the finest and most delicate mango pickles, lime chutneys and cucumber kasundies in the world.... Reverend Mother doled out the curries and meatballs of intransigence, dishes imbued with the personality of their creator: Amina ate the fish salans of stubbornness and the birianis of determination.... (189-90)

Rushdie is superb in his reproduction of domestic scenes and conversation. In *Midnight's Children*, politics as a theme is not as engaging as the domestic and community themes are, as those are in a good Dickens novel. The global reader is unlikely to be so much interested in Rushdie's 'chutnified' version of history of the subcontinent, or his narration of the small politics of independent India or account of the court case by Indira Gandhi against certain defamatory statements in *Midnight's Children*. Instead she gets really drawn to India more by Rushdie's genius as a master cartoonist or a chef who can so ingeniously cook a feast of India out of small bits and pieces of the changing lifestyles of the people: in their homes, workplace, clubs and restaurants. Whether in poverty or in plenty, Indians seemed to make their new-gained freedom and exhibited an exuberance of the will to live and to do things as they liked.

Turning to yet another masterpiece among the Booker novels on India, i.e. Arundhati Roy's *The God of Small Things* (1997), one is greatly struck by the exquisitely delicate texture of the narrative that reads like a fascinating homespun fable. More than any of the three novels discussed above, Roy's novel seems to me the least laboured and the most telling saga of an Indian home in its full sense and bewildering complexity. It poignantly unfolds as a story of family bonding and conflict in their most natural shape and flow. The narrative is uncompromisingly neutral in tone and it therefore succeeds in creating due solicitude and empathy where needed. It shows how the old Indian family and social systems are crumbling under external power and pressures with no *bona fides* of their own.

The twins Estha and Rahel come to learn "how history negotiates its terms and collects its dues from those who break its laws". The siege of the small private enterprise of 'Paradise Pickles' under the Marxist regime is an illustration of how absurd it could get for political ideologues in power "to govern a people and foment revolution simultaneously" (67).

People live a full and contented life by their own ideas and family and social equations, not by superstructures of power planted from above. That is what was beginning to happen in neocolonial independent India. Arundhati Roy's homemade fable *The God of Small Things* by giving recognition and social space to the outcast and downtrodden is an attempt at redefining national priorities amidst a state of cultural vacuity. That gives her work its true strength and distinction in my view.

The God of Small Things in many ways does stand outside of the category of market/award motivated fiction that I have discussed earlier. The exception may lend strength to the hypothesis I have tried to build in the paper.

REFERENCES

Adiga, Aravind. *The White Tiger*. Noida: HarperCollins, 2008.

Desai, Anita. Sahitya Akademi Fellowship Acceptance Speech, New Delhi: Sahitya Akademi, 2007.

Desai, Kiran. *The Inheritance of Loss*. New Delhi: Penguin Books, 2006.

Gopal Priyamvada. *The Indian English Novel, Nation, History and Narration*. New Delhi: OUP, 2009.

Jhabvala, Ruth Prawer. *Heat and Dust*. London: Futura Publications, 1984.

Mukherjee, Meenakshi (ed.). *Rushdie's Midnight's Children: A Book of Readings*. New Delhi: Pencraft, 1999.

Naik, M.K. and Narayan Shyamala (ed.). *Indian English Fiction: A Critical Study*. New Delhi: Pencraft, 2009.

Roy, Arundhati. *The God of Small Things*. New Delhi: IndiaInk, 1997.

Rushdie, Salman. *Midnight's Children*. London: Vintage Books, 2006.

3

Image of India in the Works of Booker Prizes

N.M. Nigam

V.S. Naipaul, Salman Rushdie, Arundhati Roy, Kiran Desai and Aravind Adiga are the five Indian novelists who have brought glory to the nation by being awarded Booker Prize. They have been instrumental in drawing international attention to the literary creations by Indian writers. India and Indians feel proud of their achievements on international level. India exhilarated in the glory of international recognition when Rabindra Nath Tagore received Nobel Prize for Literature. India again emerged victorious when Prof. Amartya Sen got Nobel Prize for Economics. These writers, poets and intellectuals crossed the boundary of the nation and by the dint of their powerful feelings, powerful thoughts and powerful fiction our writers have several times, bagged these prizes and showed the world that howsoever unsystematic, topsy-turvy, power teeming millions we may be but we are throbbing and pulsating with life. India—popularly known to be the land of snake-charmers, naked saints; half-naked bodies bathing in the river Ganga; a land of crowded fairs, full of dirt and squalor—is India with multi-cultural civilization. It is an old civilization that has survived million mutinies; it is a land of Mahatma Gandhi who got India free without shedding a single drop of blood. It is a land of festivals, traditional modes of living where a veil-covered face matches with a jeans clad girl. India, with its society, culture, tradition, living style, its good or bad customs; with its declared and undeclared codes of conduct is India in all its glory. The orthodox as well as liberal society; lives side by side the serious or farcical scenes occurring off and on in life only and the richness of its existence.

The image of the people of India with their multi-cultural, multi-religious and multi-lingual texture and its depiction in the works of these writers widely differs.... India, with all its glory and beauty seems to be missing in the works of these writers.

The litterateurs are the ambassadors of the nation to which they belong. The world, today, has become a global village with the use of Internet and computers—facilities of translation have become hi-tech hence the images and ideas travel East. This increases the responsibility of the writers. It also becomes important from where are they writing and what are they writing.

Many Indian Booker Prize winner writers live outside India. Their visits to India are casual. Their casual visits, formal welcomes and the locations actually visited by them become windows through which they look at their own country and evaluate it.

Their assessment also depends on the history narrated to them. Certainly, the experience and first-hand knowledge of these writers differs from those who have first-hand experience of India; know deeply about India and its age-old civilization and are deep-rooted in its culture and tradition. Such writers know well the pulse of the people, their creativity, their spirituality and underlying beauty of life—and its great traditions. Writers like V.S. Naipaul can never understand. India and its depiction in the works of Booker Prize winner writers raises a question as to their deep understanding of the nation. The image of India in their works also questions their deep understanding of India's civilization, tradition, culture and spirituality that have withstood the shocks and attacks of foreign invaders multiple times and despite bearing hardships of slavery through the centuries its culture and traditions still lie intact.

Centuries of subjugation and colonial rule subdued India's freedom of expression. The credit goes to Indian Booker Prize winner writers that India's voice is being heard in the developed world. It is through their works that Indian authors have been internationally acclaimed and Indian life got reading public in the West.

V.S. Naipaul is the first Indian to be recognized by Booker Prize. He is a voluminous writer and some of his works reflect Indian life. He is thrice-shifted Indian but India and its culture drew him to India several times and he made a genuine effort to match the stories that he had heard about India and his first hand experience of India. Naturally, nostalgic memory did not conform to real life experience. He got frustrated at the dirt, squalor, cheating, political upheavals and orthodox beliefs gnawing at the roots of this great civilization. He revolted against the sight of Indians tied down to meaningless rituals and taboos. The religious fanatical also comes under his sheathing attack. Naipaul, in his first visit to India in the year 1929 was shocked to see famine-stricken India and heaved a sigh of relief that he was not living in India (lack of education, lack of job opportunities drew his attention). Naipaul knew about long years of slavery that India had undergone. He interprets the religious fervors as the only refuge that Indians had. Having lost their identity, Indians could not come up with an independent identity—Religion, according to him, was the only identity. Naipaul observes:

> Indian identity was not something developing or changing but something fixed, an idealization of its own background, the past it felt it had first lost. Identity was related to a set of beliefs and rituals. Acknowledgement of the gods, a code and entire civilization.

V.S. Naipaul openly criticizes lack of basic infrastructure in the country. He observes that when there was no system of sanitation, no restroom facility, and no shelter for the homeless, no supply of food and water to the hungry, how can India be called a great civilization. He calls the theory of great civilization a trick only to befool the names.

On the other hand, V.S. Naipaul appreciates the contribution of the British to upliftment of India. He says: "An India which has really been trampled into the dust by the centuries of illiterate, brutal, conquerors, religious fanatics was not able to pick itself up...but I think the British contribution really was quite benign." Naipaul, in an interview, speaks about picking up India as a subject for his novel *An Area of Darkness*. He says that he had been close to India in his upbringing. He had faint memories of India's freedom movement. His book *An Area of Darkness* (1964) criticizes India's poverty and inability to deal with problems of poverty, caste system, superstitions, cruelty and hypocrisy. Naipaul openly criticizes Indian political leaders as they had no sensitivity towards the sufferings of its peasants and masses in his books *India: A Wounded Civilization* (1977) and *India: A Million Mutinies Now* (1990).

Naipaul has been appreciated by Western critics for his unabashed description of Indian reality. Joseph Lelyveld observes:

> The most notable commitment of intelligence that post-colonial India has evoked...he is indispensable for anyone who wants seriously to come to gropes with the experience of India.
>
> *An Area of Darkness*
>
> *A Wounded Civilization*
>
> *A Million Mutinies*
>
> India Through V.S. Naipaul's Eyes.

15 July, 2006 views two comments Rachael Kohn.... V.S. Naipaul in 2001.

> I recently visited India for the first time, and found myself in the poorest and reputedly most dangerous state of Bihar in North-east India. What I encountered there in the early rainy season was human degradation and suffering on a scale that simply defied any easy explanation or remedy. For this kind of life was not confined only to poor states, but was there on the road

side of Delhi, shanty towns that seemed to rise out of mud. V.S. Naipaul blatantly criticizes India in his works.

Salman Rushdie received Booker Prize in the 1981 for his novel *Midnight's Children*. The novel focuses upon the emergence of post-independent India and hangover of colonialism. It showcases the transitional phase of India from colonial rule up to the period of Independence. The novel analyses deeply the historical events of pre- and post-partition India.

Salman Rushdie holds the view that the children born in the midnight of independence possess a special telepathic power. He comments on the expectations of Indians who saw the free morning of 1947 on 15th August. People, in their joy of freedom, had entirely forgotten that there lay lots of troubles in independent India. They could hardly encompass that administration of free India was like a Pandora's Box. The individuality of the nation, with its diversity had to come to terms. There were lots of challenges before the leaders of this newly independent nation like political, religious, linguistic, cultural differences looked askance at the new leaders who, for centuries, had no experience of ruling as they had been ruled by Muslims and then by the British.

Salman Rushdie delves deep into these problems and describes them in his novel *Midnight's Children*. The book is almost a saga of Indian history.

The novel centers on the 'Emergency' declared in the country by late Mrs. Indira Gandhi. He hints at the dictatorial, dynastic rule of that time. The atrocities committed under family planning scheme, anti-encroachment drives in Delhi with its merciless demolition of slums under the name of the beautification of Delhi find place in the pages of this novel. Salman Rushdie weaves the story of Midnight's Children and their dreams. His view is that the sensitivity, dream and creativity with which Midnight's Children were born got a severe jolt by these atrocities. People were shocked to see the new and cruel face of independent India during emergency. The fantasy of free India got a severe blow.

Saleem Senai, who represents the entirety of India, struggles to contain all of India within himself. His personal story is crammed with the themes and stones of his country. The whole book is an allegory about modern India. The child named Saleem, born in the midnight remains confused between two religions, Islam and Hindu. His experience is quite similar to Muslims living in India who have respect and love for Pakistan, while living in India, the hero of the novel lives at one place and longs for another.

Midnight's Children has been called: a dense, discursive epic of post-independence India. The novelist, in an allegorical form, records the troubles, tribulations, cultural conflicts and communal differences along with regionalism cropping up as challenges in post-independence India.

Arundhati Roy won Man Booker Prize in the year 1997. She has vividly and beautifully portrayed class and caste antagonism in Indian society. Arundhati Roy has been a minute observer of class and caste conflict. She weaves the story of her novel *The God of Small Things*, around these conflicts prevailing and dominating the cultural fabric of Indian society. These prevail upon the values of humanity, love and compassion. The themes picked up by Arundhati Roy are the exploitation of weaker section of society and dalits. Class consciousness is also predominant. The poor are taken to be Dalits. Police represents the power group. The novel is a saga of human sufferings in the name of caste, class and politics. The deprived, the untouchables and the poor are born to suffer. The novel offers no hope of betterment for them.

Ammu and her children—though belonging to upper caste—are treated cruelly by Kochamma because they were not rich and Ammu was a divorcee. Besides since the very beginning Ammu did not lead a respectable existence, she never went to school. The family did not care to educate her and paid no attention to her marriage. She eventually gets married but after the birth of Estha and Rahel she is divorced. Since she was uneducated she could not manage for her maintenance on her own and was compelled to come back to Kochamma who does not appreciate their stay in the family.

Constant admonitions and neglect of Ammu and her children draws the attention of Velutha who is a dalit. He showers love and affection on the children and as a result draws a fond look from Ammu too. Velutha responds to the fond eye of Ammu and there starts a new journey of an affair with Velutha. While Ammu is driven by a chemical pull towards the well-built physique of Velutha she does not realize that she was crossing the threshold of class-bound and caste-bound society. That she was breaking the rules of upper caste society. Baby Kochamma hates this relationship and uses her position to teach a lesson to Ammu. Ammu's relationship with Velutha to Baby Kochamma was a disgrace to the family. Velutha belonged to a class where people could not even talk to him without covering their mouth lest the breath of the dalit might pollute them. Velutha and the likes were called Paravans. Hence, a relationship between upper caste Ammu and lower class Velutha should not exist at any cost. Baby Kochamma uses her power and influence to average Velutha for this crime. When Sophie Mol dies Baby Kochamma implicates Velutha and reports against Velutha at the police station.

Arundhati Roy, here, highlights the unjustified ways of police-actions, without investigation of any kind, without making an effort to dig into the reality. The cruelty with which Velutha is beaten crosses all the limits of human understanding. An excerpt will substantiate the point:

> They realized that man beaten was Velutha. They heard the thud of wood on flesh. Boot on bore on teeth, the muted crunch of skull on cement. The gurgle of blood on man's breath when his lung is turned by the jagged end of a broken rib. (*The God of Small Things*, 308)

Velutha is killed brutally because he was poor and untouchable. Ammu is called a prostitute for having relationship with an untouchable. The policeman does not even touch her—rather he strokes at her breast with a stick—Velutha is woken up with boots.

The image of India in *The God of Small Things* is that of a nation which has still not come to terms with modernity. Age-old evils of casteism, untouchables, class-differences and power games continue to spoil the beauty of its civilization. Velutha and his ultimate fate is an example of rampant corruption, high-handedness of police and rejection of love on the basis of caste and class discrepancies. His horrible fate demonstrates that system is higher than human emotions. Patriarchal domination, poverty, class and caste struggles, conservative attitudes and authoritarian social systems of India have been highlighted in this beautifully narrated story of South India.

Kiran Desai got Man Booker Prize for her book *The Inheritance of Loss* in the year 2006. Though she does not live in India, yet she has strong connections with India. Being daughter of Anita Desai, the celebrated novelist delving deep into psyche of woman, Kiran Desai possessed the grains of creativity in her since her childhood. Kiran Desai is a natural storyteller and must be appreciated for her art and narration. Her debut novel *Hulla Ballu in a Guava Orchard* presents India coloured in all its age-old customs, dirt, filth, corruption, insincerity and blind beliefs. But the descriptions are in a humorous vein. The novel is an example of her ability of minute observation and understanding of the day-to-day comedy of life. One small example will suffice to prove the point:

> Barbed-wire fence, that had been erected about the post office compound, to establish it as a place sacred to official order and duty. Naturally, the barbed wire fence was not entirely intact, for the residents of Shahkot, never ones to respect such foolish efforts, had set to work as quickly as they could to dismantle this unfortunate obstruction. All about their own houses and in their gardens and courtyards, they discovered a sudden need for wire. (*Hulla Ballu in a Guava Orchard*, 27)

The image of India in her novel *The Inheritance of Loss* too is not much different but it is on a higher scale and in the background of political upheaval. The backdrop is the majestic foothills of Himalayas. The novel again shows the illogical ways of Indian society.

There are people who wish to stick to colonial past and then there are people who wish to break through the colonial style and warned to have their own way of life.

The Cambridge-educated retired judge symbolizes colonial past. He does not want to change. He still loves hunting and eating imported biscuits and is happy when he keeps dozens of servants (again a colonial trait). The forces of modernization fail in to impress this retired judge.

Kiran Desai picks up the examples of colonial practices in the form of the Brahmin cook and in the lifestyle of villagers. She writes:

> Women walked by myth firewood on their heads, too poor for blouses under their saari. (*The Inheritance of Loss*, 30)

She hints at poverty and also makes a dig at the lack of infrastructure in India. She draws scene of people defecating on the sides of railway lines. It was early in the morning and railways tracks were lined with rows of bare bottoms. Close up they could see dozens of people defecating on to the tracks rinsing their bottoms with water from a can (*The Inheritance of Loss*, 30).

Such details not very important to describe might seem interesting to the foreign reader. Purdah System—no more popular in India, finds a place in Kiran Desai's book, she writes: "Bomanbhai's own wife and daughters, however, were kept carefully behind the high walls of haveli...the strictness of this Purdah enforcement increasing Bomanbhai's honour in the community" (*The Inheritance of Loss*, 89).

The characters leave no stone unturned in commenting upon the statements of political leaders.

Lola, in the novel *The Inheritance of Loss* comments upon Nehru like no Indian would ever do, "This state-making", Lola continued, "biggest mistake that fool Nehru made" (*The Inheritance of Loss*, 128).

They comment on Indira Gandhi too, "Indira Gandhi maneuvered a plebiscite and all Nepalis who had flooded Sikkim voted against the King. India had swallowed the Fewel coloured Kingdom who, blue hills they could see in the distance..." (*The Inheritance of Loss*, 128).

Some post-colonial traits are also observed in the use of words like Bhai, Dekho, aisa hai, Biju Beta, endoo (*The Inheritance of Loss*, 95).

Police, similar to the description in the novel of Arundhati Roy, in Kiran Desai's *The Inheritance of Loss* comes under-criticism. The atrocities committed on simple innocent people have been sensitively described. Kiran Desai—in the following excerpt, hints at the lackadaisical, faulty and cruel style of police action.

> Someday later the police picked up a miserable drunk for the crime. The drunk was a customary sight lying oblivious to the world in a ditch by the side of the market road. The more he screamed the harder they beat him: they reduced him to a pulp, bashed his head until blood streamed down his face, knocked out his teeth, kicked him until his ribs broke.... (*The Inheritance of Loss*, 226)

The image of India in the works of Kiran Desai is that of a country which suffers from maladministration, chaos. Fundamental India, in her works, is a land of Sadhus, idlers and self-seeking politicians, dirt, filth, poverty, lack of infrastructure are the malaise that hamper the growth of nation to international standards.

The recent recipient of Man Booker Prize is Aravind Adiga whose maiden novel *The White Tiger* was acclaimed world-wide. The novel is the journey of an ordinary taxi-driver to the corridors of corporate world. The problems of urbanization and related corruption and creeping insensitivity dominated the pages of the novel. Issues like class consciousness, corruption, lack of public amenities, dirt, filth, illiteracy, poverty and resultant frustration of the youth have been highlighted.

Sudipta Dutta observes, "...Aravind Adiga's debut novel, which throws a light on India's vast area of darkness, cuts through clutter like no other."

The novel points out the problem of big cities, i.e. the problem of migrant labor Munna, in Adiga's novel. *The White Tiger* represents the migrant labor who leaves his village and arrives in the city to take up the job of a taxi driver. Rural India, it has been hinted in the novel, still suffers from poverty and illiteracy.

Aravind Adiga divides India into two parts. One part of India is advanced and rich in basic infrastructure. This is the IT belt, of India where youth from all over the country want to live as jobs are available in this part. As against this part of India there is the dark belt and this is the cow-belt, or so-called BIMARU states of India, namely Bihar, Madhya Pradesh, Assam, Rajasthan and Uttar Pradesh.

Munna belongs to the deprived section of society and is a Dalit. He becomes rich overnight after murdering his master. He becomes the owner of taxis. He violates all codes of social conduct and achieves success by committing the murder of his master. Munna used to look up to the riches, luxuries and wife of his master with lured eyes "Looking at him, I made discoveries. Firstly, you could 'talk' on a mobile phone to someone in New York—just by punching on its buttons. The wonders of Modern Service never cease to amaze me" (142).

Influx of population from villages leads to several evils. Besides, the city becomes overcrowded, the villagers do not have sense of sanitation and use a make shift house for cooking, washing and other utilities. Morally too, they bring degradation as their eyes are flooded with the glittering lights of the city, they find riches and their riches allowing and have strong desire to lead the life the rich are leading. Such desires result in theft and murder and this is what we find in Aravind Adiga's novel *The White Tiger*. Adiga also shows India as a land of such employees who do not possess a sense of duty and cheat the innocent public at every step.

The problem of overpopulation in the lower class brings with it allied problems. The beggars, the novelist says, have eight to nine children and do not know their names even. These are the dark areas. The novel focuses on the emergence of lower class and their hunger and desires. The menial class, though spends time in doing day-to-day ordinary chores have a violently throbbing heart full of ambition to lead a life equal to that of their masters. While trying to fulfill their desires means hardly matter.

All authors included in the Indian Booker list are not based in India except Arundhati Roy and Aravind Adiga. Salman Rushdie lives in U.K., V.S. Naipaul is thrice shifted from India, Kiran Desai has been brought up in U.K.

The India in their imagination or in real experience may widely differ and their approach is likely to be that of an N.R.I., very charming seen from nostalgic point of view the sweet memories recollected from the stories narrated by grandma or collected from reports of newspapers or through movies. Hence, while analyzing the depiction of India in their works one has to be cautious regarding the windows through which these writers are looking at India and referring to it in their works. Is it the image of India of old time or is it that of a developing country struggling with its deep-rooted problems and trying hard to emerge as a strong, awakened and powerful nation? Whether the image of India being presented to the world is of its tradition, culture and spirituality or is it just to draw the attention of the world towards its poverty, illiteracy, corruption, thoughtless action, and communalism, casteism and class differences? Do they want to show India as a country where no rule of law exists and where there is chaos everywhere? The lurid details of human anatomy that sometimes border on pornography are described to draw the Western press to publish a book.

4

The India of the Indian Booker Prize Winners

Supriya Shukla

Indian English writing has come to be recognised as a viable, vigorous and self-generating vehicle for the expression of Indian sensibility. As the most society-oriented genre, the novel illustrates the true history of mankind and of nations. It represents the changing phenomenon of life and reality artistically. As a work of art it manifests the social, political, spiritual and cultural ethos of the people of the existing society. Pointing out the artistic significance of the novel and the inter-relation between novel and society, Michel Zeraffa observes:

> The novel is the first art to represent man explicitly as defined historically and socially.

Novelists who are able to blend artistically fact and fiction, realism and fantasy elucidate and expose the nerve of a nation and its people. Literary writers have been writing about their own nations generating an image and position for their country. They can use their art either to glorify their nation, misrepresent their nation at times and also probe into the dialectics of their nation to redress prevailing social vices.

With the world becoming a global village Indian writers are increasingly becoming popular. It has been rightly remarked, "If you track the Booker over the last seven years, there has always been an Indian connection—whether it was

Yann Martel writing a book based on an Indian story, or Indian authors being shortlisted." The emerging dominance of Indian English writing is unquestionable making its presence felt in the world of Booker fiction. The fact that five Indian writers have been crowned with the coveted Man Booker Prize in almost every decade since its inception in 1968 is ample testimony of the growth of Indian English from a sapling to a strong rooted tree in full bloom. Known for their fecundity of thought and fertility of imagination Indian novelists have been continuously experimenting with new thematic concerns and innovative writing techniques. They have used "imaginative fiction as a social art in order to communicate the human angst...impacted by industrialisation, market economy, rise of individualism, quest for selfhood and conflicts arising out of societal or systemic exploitation". They have achieved distinction by presenting the diverse manifestations of the rich and valuable Indian heritage authentically and artistically. It is imperative therefore to talk about writers who have been bringing laurels for our country.

The Booker Prize has been attributed with such exceptional magnitude that while we Indians, sometimes tend to pay little heed to the National prizes for literature awarded to notable authors in our own country, discussions about the Booker long-list and short-list continue for months together. This makes it difficult to accept the argument that the Booker Prize is not so important for Indians.

Sir Vidiadhar Surajprasad Naipaul being the first Booker Prize winner of Indian ancestry in 1971 pioneered and heralded India's arrival on the international literary firmament. Hailed as one of the Masters of modern English prose and doing India proud by being the 7th Indian to have been awarded the Nobel Prize in 2001, Naipaul is unarguably one of the greatest living writers in English. He has acquired a persona that is a blend of grandeur and iconoclasm, of fear and distance, of subversion and provocation. His judgements—whether on the sacred monuments in literature or on Islam have angered the traditionalists as well as the left-liberal commentarial. His terrifying sense of inquiry, his dispassionate search for the truth continues to be mistaken for cold-bloodedness. Still the master of intuition and sceptical of political ideologies, Naipaul remains surrounded with an aura of ruthlessness. India imagined is replete with golden memories but India in reality is for him as he himself opines,

> ...the India of poverty and an abjectness fearful to imagine.

Naipaul felt that his roots lay in India but feels alienated from India as the myth created by his forefathers is shattered with his visit to India. He is shocked at the squalor, poverty, corruption, the sloth and simplicity of the citizens, the shackles of tradition, filthy display of religiosity and the chaos prevailing in the country.

An Area of Darkness (1964), *India: A Wounded Civilization* (1964) and *India: A Million Mutinies Now* (1990) present an infernal and appalling image of India indicating that India is not a tourist attraction but a place where angels fear to tread.

However, along with decay, dejection, rebellion and mutinies, Naipaul notices a deep and vibrant consciousness of wholeness and humanism, growth and restoration and a renewal which he had earlier denied to India. There is a great moral to his life's work and that is that the human comedy will come out all right because all said and done, intellect is more powerful than vicissitude and wickedness. Despite his terrifying honesty he does see redemption for India in the profound and vibrant consciousness of humanity.

Salman Rushdie's magical feat that created ripples in the literary world by achieving a hat trick of winning the Booker Prize in 1981, the Booker of Booker in 1993 and the best of Booker in 2008 makes him the intellectual vanguard of Indian English Fiction. *Midnight's Children* stamped an indelible mark on the minds of its readers and became a trend-setter in Indian English fiction writing. Rushdie's kaleidoscopic narration profiling India's transition from the British colonialism to independence initiated debates on multiculturalism, postmodernism, postcolonialism and the multiple conceptions of India and Indianness. Rushdie problematizes India perhaps following the mind-reading of V.S. Naipaul or postmodernist literary theorists though he does not present a cynical image of India like Naipaul has done.

The novel is a literary response to a series of real life situations that have been cleverly fictionalised through allusions, disguised as well as direct, to the country's recent as well as not so recent past. The novel has an epic sweep covering about six decades in the history of the Indian subcontinent. At the fictional level, it depicts the events and experiences in the lives of three generations of the Sinai family. *Midnight's Children* does not reveal the movement of history in vividly realised concrete occurrences in a chronological order. It projects the kind of fuller historical truth that incorporates the social and historical reality of the times as interacting with, and affecting, the life of the individual, that is, chiefly the protagonist himself who undoubtedly represents the author.

Rushdie assiduously weaves a complex web of parallels between the life of the protagonist and that of the nation. The novel depicts the writer's quest for identity, his desire to 'belong' somewhere and to discover where he belongs, his urge to know how he came to be what he is and how he came to be where he is. Throughout the novel, the author gives multiple conceptions of India and Indianness. Rushdie is very much a product of what modern India is all about—multiplicity, plurality, incompatible realities and different faiths.

> Contemporary novels are the mirror of the age, but a very special kind of mirror that reflects not merely the external features of the age, but also its inner face, its nervous system, coursing of its blood and the prompting and conflicts which sway it.

It was Rushdie who realized this in the true sense. The novel presents certain phases of history in the course of which the world and the human nature have undergone radical and irrevocable changes.

Arundhati Roy, the first Indian woman writer to win the Booker Prize in 1997, is a novelist with a social commitment. Her rendition of her native country stems from her own worldview. In an interview published in the August 1999 issue of *Frontline*, she argues,

> As far as I am concerned, whether the protest is about nuclear weapons or Big dams on the Narmada, what one is fighting for is nothing less than a worldview, a way of seeing. *The God of Small Things* is a worldview. What all these works have in common is that they attempt to analyse power and powerlessness.

Focusing on the small things that become victims of state, society and the sheer will of the unthinking powerful, she feels that a genuinely broad secular outlook is the only remedy for the social malaise tormenting our nation. The novel in the end emphasises that we need a non-sectarian approach in individual as well as in national life. The ultimate religion is humanity which is the best of all religions. The goal of a human being ought to be become a "lovable human being".

Arundhati Roy does not subscribe to conventional views. She is a non-conformist who cannot be identified with one or other trend without reservations. She wants a saner world based on reason which permits individual freedom, takes due regard of natural instincts and shuns violence.

> *The God of Small Things* represents all those people who are victimised by the forces of history, dead convention, false pride and respectability, the tyranny of the state and the politics of opportunism and andro-centric order.

The novel also highlights gender issues, masculinity and its cultural context.

> Literature often reflects the cultural notions and viewpoints of its period, and that encompasses attitudes towards women: their status, their roles, their expectations. Roy, through *The God of Small Things* is strongly advocating less misogynous mentality, one which would protect women's legal rights and see to their access of education and other opportunities for individual self-development. *The God of Small Things* indicates that violence against women in general, and

domestic violence in particular, is intricately linked to real or perceived fulfilment of masculinities.

The subordination of women in India is due to the patriarchal system which has empowered men. Women are assigned the task of procreation and home-making. As daughters they are supposed to be married off, and as a divorced wife she is inexistent. Not only has Roy has shown the need for education and awareness for women's rights in her novel, she has also stated her belief of the need to break traditional views. Roy's novel is a multilayered, hybrid text presenting the legacy of colonialism, the impacts of modernity and globalisation and gender politics of the Indian post-colonial society.

The new millennium brought fresh laurels for Indian English fiction with two young authors being honoured with the Booker Prize for their respective novels.

Kiran Desai, the young and vibrant daughter of Anita Desai emerged on the Indian English fictional scene in the late 1980s and created a distinct place for herself in the galaxy of Indian women novelists. However, she shot into fame and won international acclaim with the publication of her Man Booker Prize winning novel *The Inheritance of Loss* (2006). The novel has two strands of narrative—on the one hand, it deals with the social, political and economic problems of the people of contemporary society in India and on the other, the social and psychological problems faced by Indian immigrants in America and England. The novel is undoubtedly a perceptive social commentary on modern dichotomies found in contemporary society.

Being a product of intercultural forces herself Desai's personal, social and cultural sides of her personality are very much influenced by expatriate sensibility. Settled in the US, Kiran Desai explains *The Inheritance of Loss* "tries to capture what it means to live between East and West and what it means to be an immigrant". She feels it is the loss of family, love, immediacy of a culture that is the Indian experience of migration, expatriation, of striving to succeed abroad yet yearning for an increasingly imaginary homeland. She has problematized the issues about home, homeland, diaspora and belongingness by treating these from multiple angles. Her novel throws light on the tribulations of Indians who leave their homeland for foreign shores with high hopes of fulfilling their dreams in a land of plenty, whether or not they have legal documentation. Biju, the protagonist's abject condition in the US is due to his illegal status. Reaching US on a tourist visa, Biju stays on even after his visa expires. Kiran Desai provides a vividly shameful picture of the desperation and craze of Indians to enter the US. This diasporic journey across the nations and from one region to another within the nation itself entails various travails associated with it.

Desai's characters lead lives of dislocation—physical, psychological, emotional, ancestral and political—both in the alien land and homeland.

Kiran Desai's extraordinary novel manages to explore with intimacy and insight contemporary issues of globalization, multiculturalism, economic inequality, colonial neurosis, gender bias, racial discrimination, fundamentalism and terrorist violence. Despite being set in the mid-1980s it seems the best kind of post-9/11 novel. Discussing the plethora of thematic concerns in the novel Ragini Ramchandra opines:

> Made up of various strands the novel presents not merely a kaleidoscopic picture encompassing different countries, continents, climates, cultures, peoples, their struggles and their conflicts, their dreams and their frustrations but also a mature understanding of life itself at various levels.

Aravind Adiga's Booker Prize winning debut novel, *The White Tiger* that rocked the literary world showcases India from two different perspectives.... India of Light and India of Darkness. Adiga's focus is on the latter. The novel explores the realities of two Indias exposing the repercussions when there is a collision between the two. *The White Tiger* is a scathing attack on India's age-old, deep-rooted economic disparity. Adiga blatantly and brazenly lashes out at the still-prevailing multiple social evils of corruption endemic to Indian society and politics, religious tensions and the deep divide between urban progressiveness and regressive rural set-up. For him India represents a fragmented civilization. He reconstructs the image of India that has witnessed the collapse of ethical edifice of national structure. Right from the beginning he presents an ironical picture of two contradictory worlds colliding at one point. The protagonist, The White Tiger introduces himself as an entrepreneur who lives in Bangalore—the technology hub and confesses,

> And our nation though it has no drinking water, electricity, sewage system, public transportation, sense of hygiene, discipline, courtesy or punctuality does have entrepreneur. (11)

What is different in Adiga's novel from those of his peers is that he lays bare the seething discontentment of the underprivileged sections of society, the unabashed rage and fury of the have-nots for the haves, that is looming large as a threat for the haves. It is a dark comedy of the Indian predicament. Uma Mahadevan Dasgupta remarks:

> The voice of Dark India—the underclass that is, intelligent, savagely funny and quite unforgettable—it is also a voice of anger and protest, and it is almost completely unsentimental. It is a voice that seeks out and understands the power of beauty.

The novel can also be assessed as a social manifesto that attempts to dismantle the discrimination between the "Big Bellies and Small Bellies" (64) and evolve an egalitarian society. Adiga's defence against the unflattering portrayal of India thus hints at social reform. He analyses and explains,

> At a time when India is going through great changes and with China likely to inherit the world from the West, it is important to highlight the brutal injustices of society. That's what writers like Flaubert, Balzac and Dickens in the 19th century did and as a result England and France are better societies. That's what I'm trying to do—it's not an attack on the country, it's about the greater process of self-examination.

-Adiga's self-examination does seem to be promising.

Self-analysis is one-way of reforming and bringing about a change in society. Literary artists are not only observers of life, they become necessity thinkers about life with a vision of a better society and a better world. Thus, they seek to change the world around them through their works of art. As Amitabh Roy rightly states,

> Novels devoid of a serious view of life are generally ephemeral. Mostly they do not survive their authors. To be lasting a novel requires some seriousness, depth and power. The novel must show a sound knowledge of human nature, a keen insight into motives and passions.

Great novelists have written with a specific purpose and their attempts have not only succeeded but have brought glory to them.

It is true that recent Booker Prize winners from India hold a mirror to realities we as Indians refuse to accept and choose to ignore. Nevertheless, they have tried to present the negativities present in the Indian socio-economic milieu. Their portrayal of India cannot be dismissed as a negative portrayal rather they are realistic presentations of problems which need to be addressed and redressed. Mulk Raj Anand, an epitome of India of the twentieth century, the man with a social vision also reflected the social injustice and exploitation in his books with the aim to reform. He attacked evil of all sorts, and, like G.B. Shaw sought to convert people to his viewpoint in his fiction of revolt. For him political freedom without transformation of hearts was meaningless.

However, the question that comes to the mind of Indian readers is that why do Western publishers appreciate books by Indian authors which most Indians are unsympathetic to? Occasionally, fierce debates erupt which convulse the entire literary world regarding the Indianness of the Indian English writers and their presentation of India in their works of art. Does the India of Darkness appeal to writers more or is it a gimmick to capture the attention of the West? With Vikas Swarup's novel turned film *Slumdog Millionaire* creating history by winning the Oscar in eight categories and with films like *Lagaan* and more recently *Peepli Live* being nominated for the Oscar the question that comes to mind is that does the darker side of India have a sadistic appeal?

On the flip side, it is strange but true that several international bestsellers authored by foreign writers have projected India in a different light. A reading of the 2002 Booker Prize winning novel *Life of Pi*, which is soon to be adapted into a film not only reveals the extensive research of the Canadian author Yann Martel but through his Indian protagonist he also explores issues of spirituality and practicality. Piscine Patel, the hero is a non-conformist—he is a Hindu, a Muslim and a Christian who comes to recognise the benefits of each religion. Isn't this a wonderful portrayal of India's secularism and pluralism? The latter part of the novel shows his heroic struggle for survival when he is shipwrecked and finds himself on a life boat with a bunch of animals including a royal Bengal tiger for 227 days!

Similarly, Elizabeth Gilbert's autobiographical bestseller *Eat, Pray, Love*, and recently released Hollywood film has a complete section of around 250 pages entitled Pray on India in which the novelist showcases India as a land of spiritualism and peace promoting and advocating a stress-free existence. She recounts her own ennobling experience of practising meditation and Yoga during her stay in an ashram in India...thus presenting a holistic picture of our country.

"India is on the move" ...remarked U.S. President Mr. Barrack Obama during his recent visit to India, clearly indicating that India is a developing nation. Similarly, entrepreneur-turned-technocrat and presently chairman of The Unique Identification Authority of India, Nandan Nilekani who feels that inclusive growth is the new mantra for India, believes that, "India is transitioning from a large rural, agriculture-based economy to a modern, entrepreneurial 21st century economy faster than any nation before it", so why should urbanisation, technological advances, expansion of energy, increased literacy, the fast-growing economy—all of which is happening at the same time in India not be endorsed? Besides with 459 million young Indians between the age of 13 to 35, almost 30 per cent of the total population of the country which is estimated to reach close to 574 million by 2020 as per an *India Today* Report, isn't it time to focus on a youth-driven democratic India? It is time writers bring to the forefront their heightened imaginative faculties and weave stories of the kind of society the youth want, the sort of political ideology they wish to support and their dreams of combining excellence with innovation as well as simultaneously publicise and highlight the achievements of the country. Such kind of positive writing can also initiate reform and a change in attitude.

Every committed writer seeks to change the world around oneself. That requires an ideal or a vision of a better society or a better world. Such writers are endowed with a vision and imagination and speak forcibly about certain convictions. Indian Booker Prize winners, whatever their strengths and weaknesses may be have evinced keen interest in their country, its past and its present which reveals their nationalistic spirit and their concern. Through their literary manifestations they have urged the need to bring in corrective measures in the prevailing socio-political and economic conditions. Like all rational Indians they wish for a change that can not only transform the country into a liberal, progressive, tolerant and egalitarian society but that can fulfil the fundamental needs and rights of its citizens providing food shelter and security to every Indian. Once that is done a holistic and inclusive evolvement is bound to follow.

REFERENCES

Adiga, Aravind. *The White Tiger*, New Delhi: Harper Collins Publishers, India with India Today Group, 2008.

Bookbrowse.com 23 Oct. 2008.

Dasan, A.S. *The Rains and Roots: The Indian English Novel Then and Now*. Mysore: Global Fellowship Academy, 2006.

Dasgupta, Uma Mahadevan. *Frontline*, November 7, 2008.

India Today, November 6, 2010.

Moore, Henrietta. "The Problem of Explaining Violence in Social Sciences", *Sex and Violence: Issues in Representation and Experience*, Eds Penelope Hervey and Peter Crow. Routledge, 1994.

Ramchandra, Ragini. "Kiran Desai's *Inheritance of Loss*: Some First Impressions". *The Journal of Indian Writing in English*, Vol. 36, No. 1, Jan. 2008.

Bakhtin. *Reading A Novel*, Penguin, 1971, 18-19.

Roy, Amitabh. *The God of Small Things: A Novel of Social Commitment*, Atlantic Publishers, 2005.

Sharma, R.S. and Talwar, Shashibala. "Arundhati Roy's *The God of Small Things*", *Critique and Commentary*, New Delhi, 1998, 43.

The Sunday Times of India, New Delhi: Oct. 19, 2008.

Zeralta, Michel. "The Novel as a Literary Form and as Social Institution", *Sociology of Literature and Drama*, Eds. Elizabeth and Tom Burns. Harmondsworth: Penguin Education, 1973.

5

The Making and Marketing of the Man Booker Prize: An Inside Story

Neeru Tandon

While going through the history of Booker Prize I came to know of a very interesting story regarding the inception of Booker Prize. The Booker Prize can trace its origin, through an unexpected twist or turn of the thought process of a Scotsman called Jock Campbell (later Lord Campbell of Eskan) who in 1945 became Managing Director of the Booker Company. This factual story also relates to James Bond and the attainment of political freedom in Guyana. I was keenly interested in knowing the history of Booker Prize. How the idea must have occurred to the person who created the history is really what I wanted to explore. I consulted all the documents available like Wikipedia, interviews of judges, articles by concerned publishers and officials of Booker Group. Whatever I could gather is worth sharing.

Jock Campbell is known for transforming Booker from a typical colonial business into a prospering enterprise. Then soon this imaginative individual extended Booker's business into rum marketing, food distribution, engineering, shipping and other activities in the United Kingdom. How exactly the things had taken shape and came into existence runs like this: "One day, Jock learned that Ian Fleming, an old friend and golfing partner, had been given not much more than a year to live.

Over a drink at the 'nineteenth hole', Fleming sought Campbell's advice about securing his estate for his family by selling his interest in the James Bond novels. Income tax at that time, at Fleming's level of income, was almost equivalent to confiscation. Jock recommended a merchant bank, but in his bath next morning thought to himself: 'Wait a moment. I know a knowledgeable tax accountant and a tax lawyer. Couldn't Booker make something of this?' The consequent deal was to the substantial advantage of both Ian Fleming and Booker private limited company and to the substantial disadvantage of The Exchequer. This was the beginning of Booker's 'Authors' Division' which, taking advantage of a loophole in the UK Finance Act, soon added to its portfolio the copyrights of a galaxy of writers, including Agatha Christie, Dennis Wheatley, Georgette Heyer Robert Bolt and Harold Pinter.[1]

As Tom Maschler relates elsewhere, The Booker Prize took its inspiration from France's Prix Goncourt who was referred by *Le Figaro* as the 'French Booker'. Jock Campbell, who was known for his wide and voracious reading, worked on this project along with a number of young executives. The one common factor was their interest in business and their intellectual interest in academics. As a young man, Campbell was respected for his outstanding ability in solving Torquemada's crossword puzzles in *The Observer*. It was noticed by Torquemada's widow who engaged him to edit a book of his 112 best puzzles. She knew that the investments in the Author's Division will make very high returns and surely it will turn into a commercial gain.

Initially, the prize was sponsored by Booker and the Publishers Association. Financial support was given by The Booker Company and Publishers Association was there to guide academic and intellectual affairs. From the beginning, the Management Committee was a mixture of Booker nominees and publishers. Gradually, representation became more formal, with two publishers, hardback and paperback; an author; a librarian; a bookseller; plus Booker directors and executives.

The Committee's main tasks were to frame and revise the rules, and to choose the judges each year.

The official site of Booker Prize states, 'The prize was originally known as the Booker-McConnell Prize after the company Booker-McConnell began sponsoring the event in 1968, and became commonly known as the "Booker Prize" or simply "The Booker". When administration of the prize was transferred to the Booker Prize Foundation in 2002, the title sponsor became the investment company Man Group, which opted to retain "Booker" as part of the official title of the prize. According to the guiding principles of the prize, it would be a cash award (at the start £5,000; today £20,000) for the best novel in the English language, written by a Commonwealth or Irish citizen, and published in the UK. Secondly, there would be five judges as a rule, one of whom would be Chairman. Every title submitted would be considered by all the judges. The judges were to change each year, so that a wide spectrum of views and interests were secured.'[2]

In 1971, the administration of the prize transferred to the National Book League (which, since 1986, has been known as Book Trust) with its Director—later, Chairman—Martyn Goff as the Administrator. Martyn played an important role at Management Committee meetings, raising points for discussion and decision through his great and wide reaching connections with the literary world among authors, publishers, media, critics and academia. He used to invite people to be judges or chairman of the Booker Prize committee. And finally the Committee decides whom to invite as judges and chairman for the following year.

For Booker prize a novel was a 'substantial and unified work of fiction'. Time to time many changes have been introduced in the policies and rules. People who were interested in the field were aware but things were not known to general public. The rules of the Booker changed in 1971; previously, it had been awarded retrospectively to books published prior to the year in which the award was given. In 1971 the year of eligibility was changed to the same as the year of the award; in effect, this meant that books published in 1970 were not considered for the Booker in either year. The Booker Prize Foundation announced in January 2010 the creation of a special award called the "Lost Man Booker Prize", with the winner chosen from a long list of 22 novels published in 1970.[3]

Sir Michael Caine, Chief Executive of Booker private limited company from 1975 and later Chairman until his retirement in 1993 wrote a detailed inside story about the formation of the Booker Company. He says, "I was always keen that we should not have unknown people as judges. My greatest anxiety was about the balance of the judges—gender, age, practitioner or critic, Left or Right—and asked that this balance should, when necessary, outweigh the choice of even a highly qualified individual. To widen perspectives, we have included non-UK citizens among the judges. I was always clear that we could never hope for an ideal combination each year, but felt that the selection of judges should achieve a proper balance over a number of years. In the end, the Management Committee always decided relatively easily whom we should invite. We tended not to resort to majority voting. Rather one committee member's blackball was sufficient to discard a prospect. As Chairman, my view was often decisive between two wholly acceptable suggestions."[4]

Many times it was discussed that Booker Prize may be replicated in other countries like US. But previously the idea was rejected due to the fact that the "sheer size was too great and correspondingly expensive". In the words of Sir Michael Caine, "In the US, it would have been difficult with five judges to have satisfied the multiplicity of regional, cultural or ethnic interests." Surprisingly, the replication of The Booker Prize finally took place in 1992, when The Booker Russian Novel Prize was launched with substantial help from the British Council and in particular from John Crowfoot, now secretary of the Russian Management Committee.[5]

There are some more terms related with the name Booker. The judges have the responsibility for compiling a long list which consists of twelve to thirteen books. This is known as "The Man Booker Dozen". The judges then create a shortlist of six books that they feel are exceptional and it is the shortlist nominees that are submitted for the prize. At least one judge must fully support a nominee for it to make it to the shortlist. Each author that makes the shortlist will receive 2,500 pounds in addition to a hard bound copy of their book.

The Man Booker International Prize

A separate prize, for which any living author in the world may qualify, the Man Booker International Prize, was inaugurated in 2005 and is awarded biennially. A Russian version of the Booker Prize was created in 1992 called the Booker-Open Russia Literary Prize, also known as the Russian Booker Prize. In 2007, Man Group Plc and the Hong Kong Literary Festival Ltd. established the Man Asian Literary Prize, which seeks entries from Asian writers for works that are yet to be published in English. The Man Booker International Prize recognizes one writer for his or her specific achievement in fiction. Alice Munro was announced as the winner of the third Man Booker International Prize, on 27 May 2009. Worth £60,000 to the winner, the prize is awarded every two years to a living author who has published fiction either originally in English or whose work is generally available in translation in the English language.

The winner is chosen solely at the discretion of the judging panel; there are no submissions from publishers. Nigerian writer Chinua Achebe won the 2007 prize and Albanian writer Ismail Kadare won the inaugural prize in 2005 and went on to gain worldwide recognition for his work. In addition, there is a separate prize for translation and, if applicable, the winner can choose a translator of his or her work into English to receive a prize of £15,000.

The Man Booker International Prize echos and reinforces the annual Man Booker Prize for Fiction. The Man Booker International Prize is significantly different from the annual Man Booker Prize for Fiction in that it highlights one writer's overall contribution to fiction on the world stage. In seeking out literary excellence the judges consider a writer's body of work rather than a single novel.

Booker of Booker Prize Winners

In 1993, the Booker of Bookers Prize was awarded to Salman Rushdie for *Midnight's Children* (the 1981 winner), as the best novel to win the award in the first 25 years of its existence. A similar prize known as the Best of the Booker was awarded in 2008 to celebrate the 40th anniversary of the prize—this was also won by *Midnight's Children.*

India has been consistently producing award-winning authors or inspiring other writers to base their works on Indian colours, themes and identity. Writers from India or Indian writers living in some foreign land often dominate the shortlist of authors competing for the Booker prize. The sale of books shortlisted for Booker sells like hot cakes in India and abroad among Indians. It seems that Indian readers in English have more time and, perhaps, inclination to read books than their counterparts in the UK and other countries. An unprecedented seven authors, including three from India and writers from Pakistan, South Korea, Japan and China, were in the competitions for the 2011 Man Asian Literary Prize after judges expanded the shortlist from its usual five. BBC correspondent Razia Iqbal, who heads the judging panel, said "The shortlist had been expanded to accommodate the current strength of Asian contemporary fiction and 'the imaginative power of the stories now being written about rapidly changing life' in the region."

The seven shortlisted books include Rahul Bhattacharya's *The Sly Company of People Who Care.* Set in Guyana, it chronicles a man's decision to give up his job and travel to escape his humdrum life. Bhattacharya, an Indian cricket journalist, said his shortlisting was a welcome surprise akin to finding money in the street. "I am trying to block the idea from my mind that such a prize exists, leave alone thinking whether I will win it", he told AFP in New Delhi. "Just being nominated is a huge bonus." Another shortlisted work is "Rebirth" by Indian doctor and author Jahnavi Barua, about a young woman faced with an uncertain marriage and portraying the bond between a mother and her unborn child. Amitav Ghosh's historical epic "River of Smoke", the second volume of a planned trilogy, charts the storm-tossed journey of a convict ship from Calcutta into China's crowded harbours.

We all know that within no time the authors selected for long list and shortlist, become the stars for the reading public. 'Thanks to the Booker effect, they are now selling much better.' The Man Booker Prize 2011 was awarded to Julian Barnes on 18 October for his novel *but even before that* all six shortlisted works have been experiencing the biggest bump in sales the Booker prize has seen. The latest data from Nielsen Books can clearly demonstrate this Booker effect. 'In the week following the prize ceremony, Barnes' novel sold 14,534 copies, almost twice as many as AD Miller's Snowdrops (7,684), which has been this year's Booker success story so far. In the week before the win (to 15 October), *The Sense of an Ending* sold only 2,535 copies. The shortlisted books have all benefited from their Booker approval. Weekly sales of all five runners up increased considerably in the days following Barnes' win, while sales of the other seven long listed novels tailed off. No doubt other writers in the shortlist get disappointed but this story has got a better positive side. The consolation is that Booker expands the sales of every novel shortlisted.' Novelists become stars. Bookstores get flooded with their titles. Now onwards whatever they write becomes saleable. Noted writer and Booker nominee for three times, Anita Desai said in an interview: "Literary scene changed absolutely with *Midnight's Children* in 1981. Publishers realized that one could write in an Indian version of English and do it with great vitality. Rushdie's success and voice encouraged a whole generation of younger writers and set them free. Then, from the late 1980s, with more publishers coming in, writers had an outlet. The huge commercial success of Arundhati Roy was another inspiring moment—that you could make this much money, that thought was dazzling, it was almost like getting a contract from Bollywood. You could actually have a life of fame and celebrity by writing a book!"[6]

While Shashi Deshpande raises a very pertinent question about the acceptability of Booker in India. "The Booker is a prize awarded by the British literary establishment according to its value system; yet the book that receives it becomes, in our country, the most important book of its time. The question is: why do we have to wholeheartedly accept their valuation and dismiss the response of readers in this country? Even Salman Rushdie, that most international of writers, says that the readers you write for are the people you are writing about. But the Booker—undoubtedly an important literary prize—has become so important to us that while we ignore the prizes given in our country, discussions about the Booker long list, and then about the shortlist go on for months. This makes it hard to accept the argument that winning the Booker is an act of subversion."[7]

This debate cannot be completed without mentioning the comment of Booker winner Kiran Desai when she was asked about winning the prize, that senior Desai failed to get. "Awards are such a lottery" said Desai laughing "as she recalled the four-hour event full of nervous publishers", in London that culminated with her name being called out. "You see behind the scenes and you become conscious of how much awards are down to luck. It depends on which books are put forward by the publishers and if a major author has a book out then the publishers are obliged to put those ones forward. Desai admits she herself has 'been on the road for almost two years now' in a global effort to promote the book from India to Poland to Canada."[8]

But at the same time the fact cannot be denied that Booker places on shortlisted authors a great strain by inviting them to a dinner where winner is to be announced. Out of all, four or five of them have to hide their disappointment as they know that their reactions are being covered by the television. It is a half-an-hour programme with author interviews and a panel of critics—media interest remains intense. Kiran Desai narrates her experience about her Booker. She narrates how one day in mid-September, she went looking for herself. The Man Booker Prize shortlist had just been announced, and her second novel, *The Inheritance of Loss,* was among the final six, along with works by Kate Grenville, M.J. Hyland, Hisham Matar, Edward St Aubyn, and Sarah Waters—none of which she had read.

Desai left her apartment in Brooklyn and headed to the largest bookshop she knew. Kiran Desai tells Laura Barton "I went in search of the books shortlisted for Booker to the big Barnes and Noble. And none of the books were there, including my own," she says with a prickle of surprise. When asked where in her heart she would like to be celebrating her success, she does not hesitate and accepts boldly: "I would like to be in India because they care for the Booker so much. Sometimes it means something in America and sometimes it doesn't. It would have been a lot of fun to be in Delhi, with lots of family and all the generations."[9]

Such popularity is good for the writers but is it the only correct criterion to judge the real worth of a novel? Sir Michael Caine told another story related with Booker. He said, "I remember another time when a shareholder protested that 'novels are for entertainment and uplift and should have a happy ending', and added that 'Booker should give a prize for novels of the civilised way of life'. How, I wondered, would Charles Dickens, Joseph Conrad or Graham Greene have fared, if this were the criterion? However, even Jock Campbell, in his later years, expressed the wish that the modern literary novel had 'better story-lines'."[10]

If we talk about its inside story, it has got one more very important aspect, which is generally hidden. It is seen that almost every known publisher is ready to expand his business in India. The two global biggies who are not yet publishing in India are Simon & Schuster (part of the Viacom group) and Little Brown Time Warner Books (now part of Hachette Book Group). Hachette is planning to set up shop in India and Simon & Schuster expects to be publishing in India within the next five years.

Hachette U.K. deputy CEO Peter Roche said that they are looking at opening in India. 'We're meeting everyone and I'm going over in November. We're the only group with no presence there—we sell in but we've got no one on the ground.' Hachette needs to have a presence. Picador India began brilliantly, and still has authors of the caliber of Amit Chaudhuri and Allan Sealy on its list. Tapping into the desi market was one of the key reasons why major international publishing houses strengthened their Indian divisions. Harper Collins started its functions in India in 2003—at a time when the market was ripe for change. Lipika Bhushan, Marketing and Sales head at Harper Collins, says, "Until last year, we had about 75 IWE titles. We've already seen a jump of 38 titles this year till April, taking the tally to 108. I think the favorable attitude of the Indian readers has led to the change. More and more people are globe-trotting, but the more successful books in recent times are those set in India."[11]

She and many others like her truly feel that readers are gravitating towards Indian Writing in English because they can relate to it. Another important reason for fiction writers getting visibility is the authors themselves getting savvy and aggressive in their promotional strategies. Now authors don't. Limit themselves to a secluded place in Hills or elsewhere for writing the book. Today's authors conduct book launches in various cities, interact with their readers, talk about their works and keep their agents to promote the cause. All this helps them to 'connect' with people and results in more copies being sold. The fastest selling winner was Roddy Doyle's Paddy Clarke Ha Ha Ha (1993), which sold 27,000 copies in hardback within half an hour of bookshops opening the day after the announcement.

Now let us ponder over the issue of its marketability. How easy is it for an author to move out with his editor'? In the West, according to literary agent David Godwin, author-editor loyalty invariably wins over contractual obligations. He should know: remember how he wriggled Arundhati Roy out from her contract with Harper Collins India when Pankaj Mishra quit? "If they want to keep their authors, they must keep the editors who got them the authors in the first place", is his take on the issue.

Tara Press is part of India Research Press, known for working in close conjunction with authors and editors. The emphasis on design, layout and editing shifts wildly; some books are almost-perfect, others riddled with errors. The question is how many novels have they published?

Random House India has just a scant handful of books touts credit—Manju Kapur's *Home,* Abha Dawesar's *That Summer in Paris*—but it seems to have its own respectable place in India.

We confront many questions like why all of a sudden, the marketing possibilities of Indian fiction in English changed after *Midnight's Children*? How many books does an author have to sell before it is classified as bestseller in India? Why are Indian authors suddenly in demand? Have readers started noticing them because there is a proliferation of these authors in the bookshops in India? I believe there are many more questions to ponder along with factors that have tapped into the collective potential of Indian authors—especially those who write in English. The biggest question is what role is being played by the publishing industry in the publication, distribution, marketing and taking them to the awards like Booker, etc.? So how and when did this change come about and what does this mean for a genre and the publishing industry that is seeing a healthy 10 per cent growth even in times of a global meltdown?

It is every publisher's nightmare—passing up a Booker prize winner—and every year publishers big or small try their level best to produce an award winning novel. The war between publishers force them to reject good titles as well. Yann Martel's *Life of Pi,* Booker winner, was turned down by at least five London publishing houses. The same thing happened with J.K. Rowling and Beatrix Potter before him, who similarly did the rounds of the reject piles, it took the small Edinburgh publisher Canongate and its visionary editor Jamie Byng to see the potential of Martel's magical tale. The organiser of the Man Booker Prize said that major book publishers have missed out award because they are "no longer taking risks" in working with new authors. Ion Trewin, literary director of the Booker Prize Foundation, said financial worries had meant many larger publishers were "going for the tried and the trusted" and missing out on some of the country's best new writing talent. "All the real invention—the new talent—is being published by new publishers who are prepared to take those risks and they are being rewarded by having four or five books on the shortlist this year."

A bonus here is that both the winner and the shortlisted authors gain worldwide attention, which incidentally translates into an increase in book sales. For instance, the prize winning *Disgrace* marked an increase in sales by a whopping thousand per cent plus in an incredibly short time.

The Indian author Arundhati Roy's first novel *The God of Small Things* (1997) sold well over a million copies. In 1998, when the list was announced bookshops reported a dramatic increase in the sale of all books in the list, and the trend continued even after the results were announced on October 27, 1998. I sum up this debate with the words of award winning novelist Shashi Deshpande, who expressed a different view regarding the Booker Prize. In the essay *Debating Spaces* she writes as a response to Vijay Nair's article in the *Literary Review*, 'While one can understand Nair's enthusiasm for the three books in question, it is difficult to know why he thinks all readers should share his enthusiasm. As a writer and reader one should know that responses to literature are always subjective. And even the fact that a book wins a prize—however prestigious it may be—cannot automatically make all readers think it wonderful. One also hopes that a reader's response to literature does not factor in patriotism and that a book cannot become more appealing merely because it has been written by an Indian. Judges themselves sometimes admit that the book chosen was not their first choice. Readers can be, and are, more open about their opinion and in recent years, even being on the shortlist has not done much for the sales of some novels. As for the prize-winning books becoming classics, this is something only time can tell. And time has consigned many of the prize-winning books to oblivion."[12]

REFERENCES

1. www.themanbookerprize.com/perspective/articles/1014.
2. "Booker Prize: rules", bookerprize.com. Retrieved 3 September 2009.
3. *Ibid.*

4. www.themanbookerprize.com/perspective/articles/1014.
5. The Booker Prize Story: Tracing the Origins of the Prestigious Prize. *The New Statesman* 9 October 2008. Retrieved 3 September 2009.
6. Anita Desai, The Desai's iSahitya.com
7. 'Shashi Deshpande/Debating Spaces', *Literary Review.* (courtesy: *The Hindu*, Feb. 1, 2010)
8. Kiran Desai on the Booker, www.google.com/AbeBooks.com
9. Laura Barton. Interview with Kiran Desai. *The Guardian*, Thursday, 12 October 2006.
10. "Booker Prize: rules", bookerprize.com. Retrieved 3 September 2009.
11. www.google.com. The summing up. India on the 'write' path. 30 May 2009.
12. 'Shashi Deshpande/Debating Spaces', *Literary Review.* (courtesy: *The Hindu*, Feb. 1, 2010)

6

Reconstruction of "Suppressed Histories" in India: *A Wounded Civilization*: V.S. Naipaul's Search for an Indian Identity

P.C. Pradhan

I

It is necessary to contextualize our discussion by referring to some key ideas in relation to the ideas of a nation-state in the Indian context. Though the nation-state aims at providing the opportunities of equality and liberty, it seems difficult to keep itself aloof from the colonial system. Benedict Anderson is quite right when he views that postcolonial nation-states have been modeled on colonial patterns because the native intelligentsia of the colonies were trained into European values and adept in Western culture and the "models of nationalism nation-ness, and nation-state produced elsewhere in the course of the nineteenth century" (1991: 116) although formation of nation-states is based on anti-colonial struggles. This problematic has also been discussed by Foucault in "The Ethic of Care for the Self as a Practice of Freedom":

> When a colonized people tries to free itself of its colonizer, that is truly a practice of liberation, in the strict sense of the word. But as we also know this

> practice of liberation does not define the practices of liberty which will then be necessary for this people, this society and those individuals to define themselves receivable and acceptable forms of their existence or of a political society. (Bernauer and Rasmussen, 1988: 13-14)

In this context, Partha Chatterjee's arguments are however more appropriate with regards to the formation of Indian Nation. He argues that nationalism in the non-European context was "historically fused with the colonial question" (1986: 18). The anti-colonial struggles of these nations assert the national identities in the context of colonial exploitation. The intellectuals in the non-European World were fully aware of the Enlightenment idea of rationality and progress as well as autonomous identity of a national culture. It is however difficult to revitalize the shaky economic structure of a colonized nation like India where intellectual tradition is deeply rooted in religions and moral ideologies. Chatterjee therefore questions the function of ideologies of a nation set in contradictions:

> What significance do these elements of modernity acquire when looked in the context, of the evolving colonial economy of massive deindustrialization and destitution...of the crushing of peasant resistance, of the growing gulf...between a modernized, western educated, urban elite and the rest of the nation. (1986: 23)

Chatterjee thinks that the nation may depend partially on the Western ideas in the matters related to politics, science and economics to lead itself in the path of modernization. He however regards nationalism as a cultural sentiment fused with emotional attachment to a politically organized entity. He therefore pleads for a judicious combination of the material and spiritual worlds:

> Nationalism launches its most powerful, creative, and historically significant project: to fashion a "modern" national culture that is nevertheless not western. If the nation is an imagined community, then this is where it is brought into being. In this, its true and essential domain,

> the nation is already sovereign, even when the state is in the hands of the colonial power. (1993: 6-7)

Studies on the freedom struggle show that the native resistances on the basis of groups and regions were vital in India and other colonized nations. These subaltern struggles are quite different from the national movements in the Western culture. They were rather based on regional needs and interests. Ranjit Guha therefore argues that it is necessary to understand the difference between the anti-colonialist imaginations of the 'nation' by the bourgeoisie nationalist and peasant nationalist. In this context, Chandra Chatterjee thus argues: "Questions of identity and selfhood are central to any discursive formation of a nation. The individual in the postcolonial situation is consciously looking for a bounded, linear and ideological concept wherein he can safely place his idea of nationhood" (2000: 12).

In contemporary India, an Indian Identity is rather pluralistic. The multiple images of the nation and the national self are sometimes complex as well as contradictory. In the context of multiple languages, races, ideologies, cultures, castes and religions, sometimes the concept of the nation-state of Western model does not fit into India. It is therefore necessary to bring out a compromise among the various group identities in regard to national integration. Stuart Murray's views here may be considered:

> The desire for a bounded, linear and empirical version of selfhood that is so strong in many postcolonial societies finds in nationalism a set of useful ideological tools, yet the consequences of these ideological moves may actually produce multiple and often contradictory images of the national self. (Murray, 1997: 8)

Anti-colonial nationalism poses a duality because it has to decide whether it should encourage the richness of cultural diversity in the geographical boundary of a nation or it has to create a political discourse with an authoritarian stand to be imposed by the nation-state. It is perhaps correct for the nation-state to "use historically inherited cultural religious tradition to legitimize its version of nationalism and mark its difference from colonial rule" (Chatterjee, 2000: 14). During anti-colonial struggles in the colonial countries, the people should organize themselves on the level of a national culture with certain agenda of socio-cultural progress. That is therefore the views of Fanon in *The Wretched of Earth* should be considered here:

> A national culture is the whole body of efforts made by a people in the sphere of thought to describe, justify and praise the action through which that people has created itself and keeps itself in existence. A national culture in underdeveloped countries should therefore take place at the very heart of the struggle for freedom which these countries are carrying on. (1967: 190)

To Aurobindo, 'nation-building' is an issue of deep-rooted conviction that should not be done in a mechanical way: "But a nation cannot be made,—it is an organism which grows under the stress of a principle of life within. We speak indeed of nation-building and of the makers of a nation, but these are very convenient metaphors" [(1907) 1972: 309]. The common bond of a people is evident when there is some serious threat to the nation. A nation is therefore an expression of its people which may be marked well: Aurobindo furthers the argument in right perspective:

> A nation is indeed the outward expression of a community of sentiment, whether it be the sentiment of a common blood or the sentiment of a common religion or the sentiment of a common interest or any or all of these sentiments combined. Once this sentiment grows strong enough to develop into a will towards unity and to conquer obstacles and make full use of favoring circumstances, the development of the nation becomes inevitable. [(1907) 1967: 309]

He emphasized "the organized strength of the nation, gathering to a powerful central authority and guided by the principle of self-development" ("The Doctrine of Passive Resistance", Introduction, *op. cit.* Vol. 1, [1907] 1972: 95). He also viewed that the power of the people should have to be invested in a strong political ideology. Aurobindo's concepts of organized strength of nationalism and the self-development of the individual were idealistic. These were based on a united moral basis which could not be questioned in those days. He viewed that political freedom was an essential component of spiritual strength. This idea of Swaraj or 'self-rule' was based on uniting all disparate political arguments under one, i.e. "Nationhood". He however believed in the democratic principles of fraternity by which there would not be any tendency among the individuals to dominate or subjugate others. He also advocated for "A League of Nations—an association of friends and allies which would be a world-state." As a result, the marginalized people of Asia and Africa could be protected through such a world-state.

Like Aurobindo Gandhi's idea of Nationalism is also rooted in moral and ethical principles. To liberate India, Gandhi believed that the people of India must shun violence and should be organized as true Indians. They must be "Swadeshi" to have the 'Swaraj', i.e. 'self-rule' by the method of Satyagraha, sticking to the principles of truth and non-violence. Gandhi expresses his political manifesto in *Hind Swaraj* where he writes that every Indian must impose self-rule on himself before Home-rule is achieved. Gandhi's conclusions in *Hind Swaraj* reveal that Gandhi emphasizes moral rigidity which does not give any scope for democratic pluralism. Morality, according to Gandhi, should be cultivated within the framework of "idea of Dharma" which is rather violated because of the modern civilization. He therefore abhors the material pursuits for an individual:

> There is yet time to escape it, but everyday makes it more and more difficult.... My first complaint is that India is becoming irreligious. Here I am not thinking for the Hindu, the Mohammedan, or the Zoroastrian religion, but of that religion which underlies all religions. We are turning away from God.... We should remain passive about worldly pursuits...[and] set a limit to our worldly ambition, our religious ambitions should be illimitable. (*Hind Swaraj*, 42-43)

Gandhian thinking was more rigid for maintaining moral principles. Sometimes it seemed impossible on the part of the common people to practice it. Again the leaders, who continued the struggle, preferred the use of power and domination in practice rather than Gandhian theories of ethics and morality. Nehru went to the past to understand the idea of nation. He also traveled to most of the places to understand the people so as to find out a means of organizing them. Chandra Chatterjee's remarks about Nehru's perception of the Indian Nation during colonial rule are worth-mentioning here:

> The political flavor of this anti-colonial rhetoric sought to bind on enormous social and religious diversity under a pre-conceived state umbrella. Nationalism had to seek the sanction of antiquity to be accepted by the enslaved masses. Nehru's critique of ancient Indo-Aryan society not only brought history into contemporary focus, it also began to establish the principles which the modern Indian Nation would set itself. (2002: 39)

In visualizing the Upanishadic societies, Nehru aspires for a political objective of social unity:

> It is obvious that the ideas of the authors of the Upanishads...were confined to a small body of the elect who were capable of understanding them. They were entirely beyond the comprehension of the vast mass of the people. A creative minority is always small in numbers, but if it is in tune with the majority...a stable and progressive culture results. Without that creative minority a civilization must inevitably decay. But it may also decay if the bond between a creative minority and the majority is broken and there is a loss of social unity in society as a whole.... (*The Discovery of India*, 70)

However, Nehru does not approve of "the intense individualism of the Indo-Aryans" (*DI*, 71) fully because "individualism" led men away from society. To him caste-system was also responsible for that. Moreover, the tolerant inclusion of every belief and superstition harmed the society to a great extent. He therefore pleaded for heroic "self-sacrifice" of the individuals for the sake of building the nation. Nehru wanted to awaken this "amazing spirit of man" (*DI*, 16) among the enslaved people to "recharge the battery of India's spirit and awaken her from her long slumber" (*DI*, 37). Chatterjee thinks that "this national spirit also included making people politically aware of their subjection. It was supposed to help them to see their position as timid and subservient and this burden of subjection was to unite them in their fight for freedom" (2000: 41). To Nehru, nationalism is thus "a group memory of past achievements, traditions and experience", which has relevance in the present in the form of national memories. He wanted the foundation of a nation—a state that could be linked to national tradition. "Nehru's ideas have a strong political structure. The constructive role of history is restricted to its ability to identify its commonness with the present and to emphasize the adaptability of its ideas to changing situations. Both past and present are then to be seen as dominated by the idea of national progress" (Chatterjee, 2000: 43).

Gandhi and Nehru made efforts to force a unity among people. They aimed at social equality on the basis of ethical values. They desired that the national strength can be achieved by bringing all the cultural diversities together by the force of morality and religion. The ideology of unity later on was transformed to a totalitarian and monopolising effect. Aurobindo had however been very careful not to emphasize a pluralistic society in his worldview. To him a nation could be evolved when the smaller living units developed closer links, and he did not want an erasure of cultural differences. He therefore wanted a unification through a spiritual religion of humanity rather than mechanical unification imposed by the state. For Aurobindo the ideal of unity should be combined with the fact of liberty. Nehru viewed that the individual should give up his ego by self-sacrifice and this sacrifice is 'nationalistic'. He is more practical than Gandhi because of his less emphasis on moral stringencies. He tried to arouse popular sentiments of truth, faith and honor within the framework of a political movement. In their own ways, these luminaries have searched for alternative, relevant ideological and realistic structures to build up the nation from the debris of the colonial empire: "The anti-imperialism of Aurobindo, Gandhi and Nehru was the site where a strong affirmation of morality was the hallmark of political ideology. They emphasized this to be a particular characteristic of Indian patriotism which was inspired by more than geographical barriers" (Chatterjee, 2000: 46).

In *Illegitimacy of Nationalism*, Ashis Nandy writes about the ideas of Nationalism of Aurobindo, Gandhi and Tagore: "They saw themselves belonging to a civilization that refused to view politics only as a secularized arena of human initiative. While associating the country with maternity and sacredness, they...imposed a responsibility on the individual to maintain that sacredness" (85). Frantz Fanon believes that such a force is capable of cutting the barrier of class distinctions and uniting the peasants and landowners, the workers and capitalists, and revitalizing a decadent, colonial society. He argues: "This people that has lost its birth right, will now proceed in an atmosphere of solemnity to cleanse and purify the face of the nation as it appears in various localities" (*The Wretched of Earth*, 105). The chief goal of nationalism is not merely to achieve the political freedom; it should also focus on the moral well-being of the common people and their self-discipline. The fight for freedom should go along with validation of a national culture which was developing simultaneously. The problem lies here because neither "the masses" nor "national culture" are monolithic, static units. The efficiency of the nation-state banks upon its strong political, social and religious mechanism. That does not mean it will be ruthless and crush the liberty of the people for the sake of an ideal unity for the existence of a nation. Within the framework of the nation, the pluralistic existence of people's cultures must be understood in the proper perspective. In the Indian context, the pluralistic existence of people needs to be understood properly. That is because it is a country of diverse cultures and peoples. In order to grant dignity and liberty to the individuals, the nation-state may have to be liberal and overcome its totalitarian standing. In the context of the Indian situation, Chatterjee's arguments are befitting:

> Populations live between the constructed official "nation" and the very opposition they had tried to contest against. Liberation is still a fight for political Justice and the affirmation of individual dignity.... Before the doors of liberty, then, nation and nationalism fall apart, the nation-state has to overcome its totalitarian outlook and nationalism has to find a way to reimagine its diversities within the sentiment of unity. (2000: 47-48)

II

Naipaul's excessive engagement with India again and again is due to his subconscious concern for this country. That is why in the foreword to the book *India: A Wounded Civilization* he writes: "India is for me a difficult country. It's not my home and cannot be my home; and yet I cannot reject it or be indifferent to it; I cannot travel only for the sights. I am at once too close and too far" (*IWC*, X). Hundred years had already passed by the time of his first journey to India in 1962 since his ancestors migrated to Trinidad. He has therefore washed himself clean of many Indian religious attitudes for which India seems to be "strange" to him. He further elaborates his stand on his inquiry about India:

> An inquiry about India—even an inquiry about the Emergency—has quickly to go beyond the political. It has to be an inquiry about the civilization itself, as it is. And though in India I am a stranger, the starting point of this inquiry...has been myself. Because in myself, like the split-second images of infancy which some of us carry, there survive, from the family rituals that lasted into my childhood, phantasmal memories of old India which for me outline a whole vanished world. (*IWC*, XI)

An analysis of India's history shows that it has an old civilization which has been constantly invaded. That is so because it has been "ill-equipped to cope with the outside world; no country was so easily raided and plundered, and learned so little from its disasters" (*IWC*, IX). Naipaul thinks that even in the late 20th century India is deeply "rooted in its own civilization" (*IWC*, X):

> ...it takes time to understand that its independence has meant more than the going away of the British; that the India to which independence came was a land of far older defeat; that the purely Indian past died a long time ago. And already with the Emergency it is necessary to fight against the chilling sense of a new Indian dissolution. (*IWC*, X)

Naipaul's visit to India during Emergency rule of Indira Gandhi was meant for observing the functioning of the Indian systems and prospectus of this old civilization. He believes that the further decay during Emergency might help in revitalizing this old civilization for strengthening the country to a better future:

> The stability of Gandhian India was an illusion; and India will not be stable again for a long time. But in the present uncertainty and emptiness there is the possibility of a true new beginning, of the emergence in India of mind, after the long spiritual night. (*IWC*, 161)

In the past, India was constantly subjected to "intellectual depletion" due to frequent invasions: "In the history books, in the accounts of wars and conquests and plunder, the intellectual depletion passes unnoticed, the lesser intellectual life of a country whose contributions to civilization were made in the remote past" (*IWC*, 8). In the periods of apparent revival, "India had not only been making itself archaic again, intellectually smaller, always vulnerable" (*IWC*, 8). Naipaul comments on the contradictory nature of Indian nationalism based on political awakening and religion: "But of independent India, with its five-year plans its industrialization, its practice of democracy, has invested in change. There always was a contradiction between the archaism of the national pride and promise of the new; the contradiction has at last cracked the civilization open" (*IWC*, 8). The archaism of India could neither move the country forward nor resolve its crises: "Her borrowed institutions have worked like borrowed institutions;

but archaic India can provide no substitutes for press, parliament and courts. The crisis of India is not only political or economic. The larger crisis is of a wounded old civilization that has at last become aware of its inadequacies and is without the intellectual means to move ahead" (*IWC*, 8). As back as in 1961, Narayan's remark about India, "India will go on", indicates that he believes in the continuity of India in spite of its multiple problems. Naipaul cannot reconcile with Narayan for such a view about India. He therefore writes:

> To get down to Narayan's world, to perceive the order and continuity he saw in the dereliction and smallness of India, to enter into his ironic acceptance and relish his comedy, was to ignore too much of what could be seen, to shed too much of myself: my sense of history, and even the simplest ideas of human possibility. I did not lose my admiration for Narayan; but I felt that his comedy and irony were not quite what they appeared to be, were part of a Hindu response to the world, a response I could no longer share. (*IWC*, 11-12)

Referring to Narayan's novel of 1949 titled *Sampath* Naipaul understands that the individuals are indifferent to the problems of India. They do not think that their responsibility is to face the difficulties and make efforts for a better India. They think India can take care of herself:

> ...India is eternal and forever revives, there comes not a fear of further defeat and destruction but an indifference to it. India will somehow look after itself; the individual is freed of all responsibility. (*IWC*, 15)

In India, "responsibility" and "past" hung together. He refers to Indira Gandhi's speech published in *The Indian Express* in this context: "Mrs. Gandhi said no social welfare program could succeed unless the basic attitudes of mind change.... 'we must live in this age' Mrs. Gandhi said, adding that this did not mean that 'we must sweep away' all our past—while people must know of the past, they must move towards the future, she added" (*IWC*, 16-17). His reading of Narayan's move is also a reading of "a fable, a classic exposition of the Hindu equilibrium, surviving, the shock of an alien culture, an alien literary form, an alien language, and making harmless even those new concepts it appeared to welcome. Identity became an aspect of *karma*, self-love was bolstered by an ideal of non-violence" (*IWC*, 17).

Though Naipaul is critical of Indian Philosophy, he is often puzzled to decide to which aspect he would embrace. Let us consider the following passage from this book:

> But to those who embraced its philosophy of distress India offered an enduring security, its equilibrium, that vision of a world finely balanced that had come to the hero of *Mr. Sampath*, that arrangement made by the gods: only India, with its great past, its civilization, its philosophy and its almost holy poverty, offered this truth. So, to Indians, India could detach itself from the rest of the world. The world could be divided into India and non-India. And India, for as its surface terrors could be proclaimed, without disingenuousness as quality, as perfect. (*IWC*, 23)

To the people of India, it provided great security and stability. The outside world is changing fast. India however does not change much, it is rather fixed and stable for which the foreign married girl of Delhi, whom Naipaul met, came to India whenever she felt void, isolated: "In the midst of world change India, even during this Emergency, was unchanging: to return to India was to return to a Knowledge of the world's order, everything fixed, sanctified, everyone secure" (*IWC*, 26). The apparently stability of the Hindu world is destabilized the moment it comes in contact of the outside world, a non-Hindu idea of human possibility. This Hindu world is therefore fragile and subject to shattering at any moment. The ultimate Hindu retreat is a retreat to chaos. It is also a retreat from "civilization and creativity, from rebirth and growth to magic and incantation, retrogression to an almost African night, the enduring primitivism of a place like the Congo, where, even after the slave-trading Arabs and the Belgians, the past is yearned for as *le bon vieux temps de nos ancetres*. It is the death of a civilization, the final corruption of Hinduism" (*IWC*, 33).

During the clean-up programme of Emergency the raids were like terrors. Since this was based on a political crisis, it did not frame any moral principle for the society. Even it did promise "a better regulated future". It only reinforced the high Hindu ideal of self-realization which may even take the form of worldly corruption. After a thousand years of defeat and withdrawal the Hindu society had broken down:

> The Emergency, whatever its immediate political promptings, only made formal a state of breakdown that had existed for some time; it needed more than a political resolution. In 1975, the constitution was suspended; but already in 1974, India had appeared to stall, with civil disobedience campaigns, strikes, and student disturbances. The political issues were real, but they obscured the bigger crisis. The corruption of which the opposition spoke and indiscipline of which the rulers spoke were both aspects of a moral chaos, and this could be traced back to the beginning, to independence. (*IWC*, 35)

The Hindu society enabled by Gandhi during freedom struggle had started disintegrating with the rebirth and growth that came along with independence. In a harsh tone, Naipaul therefore makes his own judgment of the post-independence Indian society:

> With independence and growth, chaos and loss of faith, India was awakening to its distress and the cruelties that had always lain below its apparent stability, its capacity simply for going on. Not everyone now was content simply to have his being. The old equilibrium had gone, and at the moment all was chaos. But out of this chaos, out of the crumbling of the old Hindu system, and the spirit of rejection, India was learning new ways of seeing and feeling. (*IWC*, 38)

Referring to Tendulkar's play, Naipaul understands that his India has changed: "The world has opened out, and men have become more various and, individualistic; the will rages." Sensibility has been modified. India is less mysterious: "Tendulkar's discoveries are like those that might be made elsewhere" (*IWC*, 39). Hinduism in its degradation has not helped much. It has rather brought a lot of negative aspects to the Indian society:

> Hinduism hasn't been good enough for the millions. It has exposed us to a thousand years of defeat and stagnation. It has given men no idea of a control with other men, no idea of the state. It has enslaved one quarter of the population and always left the whole fragmented and vulnerable. Its philosophy of withdrawal has diminished men intellectually and not equipped them to respond to challenges; it has stifled growth. So that again and again in India history has repeated itself: vulnerability, defeat, withdrawal. And there are not four hundred millions now, but something nearer seven hundred. (*IWC*, 41)

Due to decay, the Indian civilization lost its vitality. During the Emergency, the intellectual deficiencies of archaic civilization are well-marked: "India stalled, unable to see its way ahead, to absorb and render creative the changes it has at last generated" (*IWC*, 41). Naipaul keenly observes that the awakening of the marginals in the society has put the middle-class people to rethink about their future. These marginalized people can no more be neglected: "Their illegal hutments in which they live are knocked down; but they rise again, a daily tide wrack on the margin of cities and beside the railway lines and the industrial highways" (*IWC*, 43). Naipaul further notes: "...it was this great uncertainty, this sense of elemental movement from below, and an almost superstitious dread of this land of impressive, unfinished ruins, that made professional man say in Delhi: 'It's terrible to see your life's work turning to ashes'. And his wife said: 'For the middle classes for people who live like us, it's all over. We have a sense of doom'" (*IWC*, 44).

Naipaul understands that the people in the lower rank are awakening in India. The big cities like Bombay are flooded with the rural people who go there in search of work and live in the slums. They live a very miserable life in the dirty slums. There are provisions of latrine. Every open space is a latrine in India. The division of labor in India is quite disturbing. Only the sweepers are to remove the excrement, people have wrong notions of cleanliness: "It was unclean to clean; it was unclean even to notice. It was the business of the sweepers to remove excrement, and until the sweepers came, people were content to live in the midst of their own excrement" (*IWC*, 57).

Indians do not look for an objective Indian identity. An Indian identity is to belong to India, an established country with an established past. Naipaul's encounter with the journalist in Bombay reveals that an economist journalist who believes in the development and change believes that an "Indian identity was not something developing or changing but something fixed, an idealization of his own background, the past he felt he had just lost. Identity was related to a set of beliefs and rituals, a knowledge of the gods, a code, an entire civilization. The loss of the past meant the loss of that civilization, the loss of a fundamental idea of India, and the loss therefore to a nationalist-minded man, of a motive for action" (*IWC*, 60-61). This is however a part of the feeling of purposelessness of many Indians to speak about. It was also a middle-class burden to have an idea of India after a long period of subjection. However, in the slums and squatter settlements in Chawls, the real Indian Identity is quite obvious. These poor people who have migrated from the villages strive for their basic needs of life: food, shelter, water, a latrine. It was a great discovery of identity. Of the "unaccommodated men making a claim on their land for the first time, and out of chaos evolving their own philosophy of community and self-help. For them the past was dead; they had left it behind in the villages" (*IWC*, 61). These unacknowledged, unknown people actually represent India. Their needs are basic and India needs to address them rather than boasting on its glorious past. These emigrants from the villages have been suffering from the tyrant leaders, Sarpanches and Zamindars. Naipaul writes the agonies of these marginalized village people who are oppressed by the tyranny:

> All the way from Poona—except in certain defense areas—it was dotted with sodden little clusters of African-like huts: the encampments people in flight from

> the villages, people who had been squeezed out and had nowhere else to go, except here, near the highway, close to the towns, exchanging nullity: people fleeing not only from landlessness but also from tyranny, the rule in a thousand villages of men like the Patel and the Sarpanch. (*IWC*, 77)

In the wake of Naxalite movement to save the poor and oppressed in the villages, many university students joined the battle to fight for justice knowing little about the problems of the country. It was just a rage, an excitement to sacrifice their lives, to stain their hands in violence and blood for the oppressed. That is why Naipaul makes the following satirical comments:

> India remains so little known to Indians. People just don't have the information. History and social inquiry, and the habits of analysis that go with these disciplines, are too far outside the Indian tradition. Naxalism was an intellectual tragedy, a tragedy of idealism, ignorance, and mimicry: middle-class India after the Gandhian upheaval, incapable of generating ideas and institutions of its own, needing constantly in the modern world to be inducted into the art, science, and ideas of other civilization, not always understanding the consequences, and this time borrowing something deadly. Somebody else's idea of revolution. (*IWC*, 82)

Though Naxalite movement failed in India, it however alarmed everybody. The poor people are no more to be taken for granted. Millions of the people living in the margin both in cities and villages are on the move with a new claim on the land. Naipaul finds that the Indians have a defective vision because they are mostly guided by obsessions rather than observations and ideas. Referring to U.R. Anantmurti's book *Sanskar*, Naipaul comments: "Knowingly or unknowingly, Anantmurti has portrayed a barbaric civilization where the books, the laws, are buttressed by magic, and where a too elaborate social organization is unquickened by intellect or creativity or ideas of moral responsibility" (*IWC*, 97). The Acharya of *Sanskar*, imprisoned in his dead civilization, can only define himself within it. Like Gandhi he has no chance of coming into contact with an outside world. Gandhi had to work out his faith in alien societies:

> Gandhi, maturing in alien societies, defensively withdrawing into the self, sinking into his hard-won convictions and vows, becoming more obstinate with age, and always seemingly headed for lunacy, is constantly rescued and redefined by external events, the goading of other civilizations: the terror and strangeness of England, the need to pass the law examinations, the racial pressures of South Africa, British authoritarianism in India. (*IWC*, 98)

Naipaul analyses that the Acharya's self-absorption at the time of crises is rather sterile, without any chance of bringing him any new idea whereas new ideas were peering to Gandhi at critical juncture. That is so because the Acharya remains an individual limited to his own perceptions. But India is to change, must come in contact with the outside world. In a changing society, according to Sudhir Kakar, the underdeveloped ego of the individual is a "dangerous luxury". The perceptions can be individual rather than a social function: "caste and clan and security and faith and shallow perception all go together; one cannot be altered or developed without the rest" (*IWC*, 99). The individual therefore gets lost, gets "drowned in the immensity of the unknown world" (*IWC*, 99).

The individual obsessions in India sometimes merge with the political movements of protest. Shiv Sena movement in Bombay and Dravidian movement in the South are brilliant examples. Jan Sangh is another such party. With the Emergency many such parties have been banned and the leaders imprisoned:

> In India, where the problems are beyond comprehension, the goals have to be vague. The removal of poverty, the establishment of justice: these, however often stated now, are like abstractions. People's obsessions are more immediate. (*IWC*, 103)

Naipaul attacks the Indians for their intellectual confusion. Theoretically, they go on professing how to eradicate poverty, but they have failed to do so because they have no sharp vision how to deal with it practically. Naipaul is therefore critical of the Indian concerns to eradicate poverty:

> In their attempt to go beyond the old sentimental abstractions about the poverty of India and to come to terms with the poor, Indians have to reach outside their civilization, and they are at the mercy then of every kind of imported idea. The intellectual confusion is greater now than in the days of the British, when the worlds seemed to stand still, the issues were simpler, and it was enough for India to assert its Indianness. The poor were background then. Now they press hard, and have to be taken into account. (*IWC*, 105)

To cope with the problems of India, the leaders seek to exercise all the disciplines and skills borrowed from European civilization. Naipaul feels that "European methods of historical inquiry, arising out of one kind of civilization, with its own developing ideas of the human condition, cannot be applied to Indian civilization; they miss too much" (*IWC*, 116). The idea of *dharma* in India accommodates bonded-labor as it could accommodate widow-burning. The laws in India must serve *dharma*: "Yet *dharma*, as expressed in Indian social system, is so shot through which injustice and cruelty, based on such a limited view of man" (*IWC*, 119). Law therefore avoids any collision with *dharma*: "Yet it is this *dharma* the law must grapple with if the law is to have a 'dynamic role'. That is the difficulty: to cope with the new pressures, India has in some ways to undermine itself, to lose its old security" (*IWC*, 121). The borrowed institutions are to function as an integral part of Indian institutions by way of synthesis. As a conquered people the Indians have been dependent on other civilizations:

> To survive in subjection, they have preserved their sanctuary of the instinctive, uncreative life, converting that into a religious ideal: at a more worldly level, they have depended on others for the ideas and intuitions that make a country work. The Emergency—coming so soon after independence—dramatizes India's creative incapacity, its intellectual depletion, its defenselessness,

> the inadequacies of every Indian's idea of India. (*IWC*, 121)

Naipaul is not appreciative of Gandhi's approach to India and its problems though he acknowledges his great contribution: 'Archaic emotions' 'nostalgic memories'. When these were awakened by Gandhi, India became free. But the India created in this way had to stall. Gandhi took India out of one kind of *Kal Yug*, one kind of Black Age; his success inevitably pushed it back in another (*IWC*, 139). Gandhi's followers diluted everything he strived hard to emulate: Gandhi swept through India, but he has left it without an ideology. He awakened the holy land; his mahatmahood returned it to archaism. He made his worshipper vain (*IWC*, 146). In the context of Bhave, Naipaul argues that he is a decadent Gandhian and does not know much about the Indian civilization: Bhave, in the vanity of his spiritual perfection is more than a decadent Gandhian. His religion is a kind of barbarism; it would return men to the bush. It is the religion of poverty and dust (*IWC*, 149). Naipaul further exposes that Bhave's ideals are not based on Gandhi's vision:

> Bhave, even if he understood Gandhi's stress on the need for social reform, was incapable of understanding Hindu India; he was too much part of it. The perfect disciple, obeying without always knowing why, he invariably distorted his master's message. (*IWC*, 152)

With his simplicity and distortions Bhave only offered Gandhianism as a kind of magic and he himself offered as a magician. He was unable to understand Gandhi's complex vision. Naipaul therefore comments: "It seems to be always there in India: magic, the past, the death of the intellect, spirituality annulling the civilization out of which it issues, India swallowing its own tail" (*IWC*, 153). During Emergency, India was however left alone "with the blankness of its decayed civilization" (*IWC*, 154). The borrowed inherited democratic institutions were dismantled. There were no foreign rulers to establish a new order. These borrowed institutions that gave India freedom remained alien and "separated from the internal organization of the country, its beliefs and antique restrictions" (*IWC*, 154). With independence, India grew with industrialization and five-year plans. However, India was unable to cope with the new problems: The population grew; the landless fled from the tyranny of the villages; the towns choked; the restlessness created by the beginnings of economic development (*IWC*, 154). The triumph of democracy therefore brought the destruction of India. Politics and press could not save it. Press served the objectives of political anarchy: "India will at the end be face to face with its own emptiness, the inadequacy of an old civilization which is cherished because it is all men have but which no longer answers their needs" (*IWC*, 155). India has come to this mess because it has no ideology. India and Gandhi as well have failed together: "Its people have no idea of the state, and none of the attitudes that go with such an idea no historical notion of the past no identity beyond the tenuous ecumenism of Hindu beliefs, and, in spite of the racial excesses of the British period, not even the beginnings of a racial sense" (*IWC*, 154). Centuries of conquests have reduced the Indian civilization to such nullity, struggle for survival. The idea of *dharma* in India is responsible for India's decline according to Naipaul. He believes that "Indian poverty is more dehumanizing than any machine; and more than in any machine civilization, men in India are units, locked up in the straightest obedience by their idea of their dharma" (*IWC*, 157). Naipaul's severe indictment of India in the following needs to be reflected upon:

> So India ever absorbs the new into its old self, using new tools in old ways, purging itself of unnecessary mind, maintaining its equilibrium. The poverty of the land is reflected in the poverty of the mind; it would be calamitous if it were otherwise.
>
> The civilization of conquest was also the civilization of defeat; it enabled men, obeying an elastic dharma, to dwindle with their land. Gandhi awakened India; but the India he awakened was only the India of defeat, the holy land he needed after South Africa. (*IWC*, 159)

Naipaul understands that Gandhi has awakened the emotions of people by which India could become free. However, the

Gandhian fantasies—his fantasies of spirituality, Ram raj, a return to the villages, simplicity and so on—cannot help India to deal with its multiple socio-economic crises and problems. Naipaul therefore thinks that India must not look to the past for its glory and spiritual revival. It must look to the past for enquiry and analysis. He therefore writes: "The past can now be possessed only by inquiry and scholarship, by intellectual rather than spiritual discipline. The past has to be seen to be dead; or the past will kill" (*IWC*, 161).

Naipaul therefore thinks that India must act according to its needs rather than bank upon past spirituality and Gandhianism. The India of 1975 was not the India of 1930 when Gandhi performed a symbolic act of picking up a handful of salt from the shore at Dandi. He firmly expresses his views: "The needs of 1975 were more worldly and difficult. India wasn't to be cleansed again; it was (as Mrs. Gandhi intuited) to be cleaned up and got going; it was to be seen to be offering worldly opportunities. The very fierceness of the Emergency answered the public mood, assuaged old frustrations" (*IWC*, 128): Naipaul's *India: A Wounded Civilization* is his interpretation of India based on his rational analysis of Indian situations. Despite his explorations of truth about India, it cannot be argued that he was writing the only truth about India. It was only one of the interpretations about India. We will also examine how he analyses India in *India: A Million Mutinies Now*. The vastness of India and its diversity have often baffled the Western travelers to this country. Though Naipaul normally considers himself to be a westerner, he is however a doubly diasporic writer because his ancestors migrated to Trinidad from a village (Dubes) near Gorakhpur and he himself lived in England after his completion of studies there. Though his first Indian experience was rather bitter, he could not remain indifferent to India for which he writes: "I cannot travel only for the sights. I am at once too close and too far" (*IWC*, 8-9). His travel impressions during 1975-76 were recorded as socio-political/ethnographic analyses in the travelogue *India: A Wounded Civilization* (1977). Naipaul resents the Indian attitude to begging when he writes that the

Hindus consider it a "religious theatre, a demonstration of the workings of *Karma*, a reminder of one's duty to oneself and one's future lives" (*IWC*, 58). His hatred of beggars is more conspicuous in his utterances: "...the beggars have become a nuisance and a disgrace. By becoming too numerous they have lost their place in the Hindu system and have no claim on any one" (*IWC*, 58). Naipaul's judgment on Hinduism by seeing the ruins of Vijayanagar seems to be harsh: "Hinduism...had already reached a dead end, and in some ways had decayed, as popular Hinduism so easily decays, into barbarism" (*IWC*, 16). Although there has been much development in the region of Vijayanagar, the peasantry do not understand the substantial changes that take place because of the intellectual depletion. Naipaul therefore writes: "The crisis of India is not only political or economic. The larger crisis is of a wounded old civilization that has at last become aware of its inadequacies and is without the intellectual means to move ahead" (*IWC*, 18). Naipaul's anguish is well marked when he writes that for a thousand years India had always retreated before its conquerors and when it was about to revive it had always been moving itself archaic, intellectually smaller and vulnerable. Such a stand has been further elaborated by the writer focusing on a number of problems that have crumbled the foundation of Indian civilization. Poverty, slums, lack of facilities, illiteracy, exploitation, child labor, bonded labor, want of planning and leadership, over-population, corruption and lack of direction have shaken India. Naipaul feels that the Indians have no intellectual initiative to cope with such problems. The Indian intellectuals like Narayan, to Naipaul's disapproval, argue that "India will go on" in spite of all these problems.

Naipaul is not happy to note that Indians have a habit of ecstatic contemplation of the past and nostalgic reiteration of Gandhi. He also indicts the Indians for self-indulgence and self-pity rather than trying to solve the grievances and problems. The "mythology of the past", which has often a significant bearing on the "culture of the present", does not help much to lessen the problems. That is why Naipaul argues: "The intellectual confusion is greater now than in the days of the British, when the world seemed to stand still, the issues were simpler and it was enough for India to assert its Indianness. The poor were background then. Now they press hard, and have to be taken into account" (*IWC*, 118). Naipaul attacks the Indian concept if *dharma* a significantly cohesive force to the people, as it does not help to remove bonded labor, widow-burning and other social atrocities. The law even does not interfere in the Indian concept of *dharma*. He feels that the *dharma* in Indian Social System is replete with "injustice and cruelty based on such a limited view of man" (*IWC*, 132). Being disturbed by this issue, he refers to Indira Gandhi's remarks published in *The Times of India* on 5 October 1975. Indira argued that "the Indian legal system should assist for liberation of human spirit and human institutions should strive for removing the obsolete customs. To her, it should function within the purview of the Indian ancient view that "society should uphold *dharma* so that *dharma* sustains society" (*IWC*, 132). Naipaul therefore rejects the Indian idea of synthesis also. He writes:

> Indians say that their gift is for synthesis. It might be said, rather that for too long, as a conquered people, they have been intellectually parasitic on other civilizations. To survive in abjection they have preserved their sanctuary of the instinctive, uncreative life, converting that into a religious ideal; at a more worldly level. They have depended on others for the ideas and institutions that make a country work. (*IWC*, 134)

Naipaul observes that the Indian political leaders have no progressive vision because of their obsession with such on archaic, outdated cultural tradition. He indicts the cultural primitivism of such leaders as Gandhi, Bhave, Indira, Jai Prakash Narayan, and Morarji Desai who have failed utterly to pull the Indian civilization out of the move of stagnation and decay. They could not regenerate the Indian strength and vitality. Naipaul believes that Gandhi was able to draw all India together in a new kind of politics during 1919-30 because of his 'racial sense', which is not an Indian quality.

This "racial sense" was qualified by such religious sense of Gandhi that he had exhibited in South Africa for which he viewed that "no man was an island and that the disunity of the high was bound up with the dignity of the low" (*IWC*, 154). This attitude helped him to remain away from the divisive politics of religion, caste and region. However, such perspective changed later when he was elevated to a holy man in the emergence of his "Mahatmahood". This emergence did not serve his Indian cause. In the post-independence India, Naipaul thinks that religious ecstasy reduces Gandhianism to Mahatmahood as a result of which "racial sense", the individual sense of dignity is removed from the Indian scene. That is why Naipaul remarks: "...Gandhi awakened the holy land, his Mahatmahood returned it to archaism, he made his worshippers vain" (*IWC*, 159). His disciple, Vinoba Bhave, though regarded as a saint for his emphasis on the development of inner life, failed to bring any substantial creative change in the lives of the Indians. Naipaul criticizes him severely: "He is not particularly an intelligent man and, as perfect disciple of the Mahatma, not original; his political views came close to nonsense" (*IWC*, 107). To Naipaul's understanding Gandhi was unable to remove the inhuman social evils because his archaic ways were not visionary: "Bihar, where Bhave did much of his walking, remains—in matters of land and untouchability—among the most backward and crushed of the Indian states" (*IWC*, 165). Naipaul's sincere indictment to Mr. Morarji Desai has been due to his pompous exhibitionist methods which are the "old Indian attitudes of defeat, the idea of withdrawal, a turning away from the world, a sinking back into the past" (*IWC*, 141). Naipaul, thus, dismisses the Indian leaders who have merely spiritual fantasies without any coherent ideologies with a consistent vision:

> India is old, and India continues. But all the disciplines and skills that India now seeks to exercise are borrowed. Even the ideas Indians have of the achievement of their civilization are essentially the ideas given to them by European scholars in the nineteenth century. India by

> itself could not have rediscovered or assessed its past. Its past was too much with it, was still being lived out in the ritual, the laws, the magic—the complex instinctive life that muffles response and buries even the idea of inquiry. (*IWC*, 129)

Naipaul interprets the concept of *dharma* in the end of this travelogue. He views that the concept of *dharma* must be understood in the perspective of action rather than *contemplation*. He refers to such writers as Balzac and Proust in this context. If Naipaul believes that *action* should be the basis of *dharma*, then Indian concept of *dharma* is also based on action, which is the key guiding principle of the *Gita*. Naipaul often indulges in European standards and "points of view" to judge India, to portray the Indian image. That is why he sometimes fails to understand the Indian philosophy, culture and viewpoint. In their proper perspective, this does not however mean that *India: A Wounded Civilization* should be dismissed outright. What is significant about this travelogue is that it makes us understand our strengths and weaknesses, our achievements and failures. It also significantly argues that civilizations can thrive only on constant renewals and revitalization of the national energies and attitudes to avoid stagnation and decay.

During the second visit, Naipaul was also haunted by the duality of his consciousness: his childhood memories and his encounter with the "strangeness of India". Remembering the "old unchanging India", he is pained to observe the various invasions on it: the Muslim conquests, the British trade and the imposition of Emergency in 1975. Naipaul therefore writes in grief about the invasions made by the Central Asian tribes:

> The invasions are in all the school books. But I don't think people understand that every invasion, every war, every campaign, was accommodated by slaughter, a slaughter always of the most talented people in the country. So these wars, apart from every thing else, led to tremendous intellectual depletion of the country. ("A Million Mutinies" in *India Today International* August 18, 1997: 20)

Naipaul rejects the romantic notion of India regarding the Muslim attacks. He does not agree on the point that India always absorbed her conquerors. He rather feels that India has been esteemed low because of the invasion. That is why he argues that post-independent India must start afresh with "the memory of loss as the basis of nationhood" (Chatterjee, 177). He therefore destabilizes the Indian notion of "wholeness" by questioning the socio-ethical issues. In this context, he supports his enquiries about India by referring to popular novels, newspaper headlines, journalistic writings, school buses and travel companions. His aim is to reconstruct the Indian consciousness about the past, by way of deconstructing the socio-cultural and political history of India. In this context, Chatterjee's remarks are quite pertinent:

> His method is to catch prevalent culture and study some of its roots, such as the relevance of past history or the ionization of Gandhian philosophy. Most of his observations have the value of an outsider viewpoint, they are not meant to be deep philosophical reasoning—they are intended to cause a thoughtful ripple on modern Indian day-to-day existence. (2000: 177)

Naipaul's observations on a temple and Hindu kingdom of Vijaynagar in the South persuade him to comment on India's inability to face the challenges of the present world. The "archaic India" (*IWC*, 18) has not yet been changed to understand the meaning of freedom of press and proper functioning of parliament and court. Naipaul is confused to understand why the Hindus go on chanting the mantras 50 million times while reinstalling the deity in the temple. He also feels that it is meaningless to remember the glories of the past of the Vijaynagar Kingdom. To him, the need of the hour is to focus on the improvement of the people who are starving in the slums of India. Because of his too much obsession with European values and standards, Naipaul is perhaps unable to understand the meaning the starving people find in rituals of religion. During the thirty years of independence (1947-76), though Indian politicians have not been able to tackle all the problems following the democratic model of governance, yet many changes are taking place in course of time. It is rather disheartening that the country is groaning under the pressure of corruption and nepotism, tyrannical governance of emergency. There are also some good efforts to develop the country. Naipaul's confusion is thus quite obvious when he makes the following remarks on India of 1976:

> Since independence much money had been spent on the region. A dam has been built across the Tungabhadra River. There is an extensive irrigation scheme which incorporates the irrigation canals of the old kingdom.... A Vijaynagar steel plant is being planned; and a university is being built, to train men of the region for jobs in that steel plant and the subsidiary industries that are expected to come up, the emphasis is on training men of the region, local men. (*IWC*, 17)

Naipaul's perception of India of 1976 has been mostly guided by the condition of Vijaynagar which seems to be myopic because India is not one; there are many 'Indias' in different parts of the country. As a migrant with a European-centric mindset, Naipaul has not been able to understand the complexities of the Indian nation, "each having its own history and particular ways of negotiating with the present" (Chatterjee, 179). Naipaul unknowingly diagnoses his own "myopic vision" when he says that "passions alone cannot give validity to ethics for ethical views also rise from the culture of the place in which they are held" (Chatterjee, 179). Naipaul understands that the Indian nation is aware of her intellectual and creative depletion, but then people think that there is no escape from it. Naipaul is enraged and says that this is the antiquity of Indian attitude which has no relevance in the present context. Naipaul is therefore raged to note the stagnating attitude of the Indians to move forward for progress through a consistent ideology. He refers to the Indian villages in Bihar and Rajasthan. To him Bihar's poverty is due to the continuous ravages by famine, flood, earthquakes and political squabbles. Naipaul is disheartened to note the exploitation of child labor and strong caste discriminations. Referring to Rajasthan, Naipaul points out how the poor peasants and their children work as laborers in the estate of the prince of Bundi-Kotah region because they still retain a misplaced notion that his subjects still consider him to be their ruler. Naipaul is not happy with the situation because people have not yet changed their mindset due to the fact that they are under the pressure of food and survival.

WORKS CITED

Anderson, Benedict. *Imagined Communities: Reflections on the Origin and Spread of Nationalisms*. London and New York: Verso, 1991.

Bhat, Yashoda. *V.S. Naipaul: An Introduction*. New Delhi: B.R. Publication, 2000.

Chatterjee, Chandra. *Surviving Colonialism: A Study of R.K. Narayan, Anita Desai, V.S. Naipaul*. New Delhi: Radha Publications, 2000.

Chatterjee, P. *Nationalist Thought and the Colonial World: A Derivative Discourse?*. London: Zed Books, 1986.

——. *The Nation and Its Fragments: Colonial and Postcolonial Histories*. Princeton, NI: Princeton University Press, 1993.

Davies, Carole Boyce. *Black Women, Writing and Identity*. London and New York: Routledge, 1994.

Eagletan, Terry. *Exile and Émigrés*. London: Chatto and Windus, 1970.

Fanon, Frantz. *The Wretched of the Earth*, trans. Constance Farrington. 3rd edition Harmondsworth: Penguin, 1967.

Foucault, Michel. "The Ethic of Care for the Self as a Practice of Freedom" in *The Final Foucault*, eds. James Bernauer and David Rasmussen. Cambridge: MIT Press, 1988: 13-14. (1907).

Gandhi, M.K. *Hind Swaraj*. Ed. A.J. Parel. Cambridge: CUP, 1947.

Ghosh, Aurobindo. *Bande Matram* (1907). Rpt. In *Sri Aurobindo Birth Centenary Library*. Vol. 1, Pondicherry. Sri Aurobindo Ashram, 1972.

Joshi, B. Chandra. *V.S. Naipaul: The Voice of Exile*. New Delhi: Sterling Publishers, 1994.

King, Bruce, *V.S. Naipaul*. Houndmills, Basingstoke, Hampshire and London: Macmillan, 1993.

Lamming, George. *The Pleasure of Exile.* London: Michael Joseph, 1960.

Memmi, A. *The Colonizer and the Colonized.* Boston, MA: Beacon Press, 1967.

Murray, Stuart. "Introduction" in S. Murray, *Not on Any Map: Essays on Postcoloniality and Cultural Nationalism.* Exter: University of Exter Press, 1997.

Mustafa, Fauzia. *V.S. Naipaul.* New York: Cambridge University Press, 1995.

Naipaul, V.S. *Half a Life.* Picador, 2002.

——. *Magic Seeds.* Picador, 2004.

——. *An Area of Darkness.* New Delhi: Penguin, 1968.

——. *Finding the Centre.* London: Penguin, 1985.

——. *India: A Million Mutinies Now.* London: Vintage, 1998.

——. *India: A Wounded Civilization.* London: Picador, 2002.

Nandy, Ashish. *Illegitimacy of Nationalism.* Delhi: OUP.

——. *The Intimate Enemy.* Delhi: OUP, 1983.

Nehru, J.L. *The Discovery of India.* Calcutta: The Signet Press, 1946.

Panwar, Purabi, ed. *V.S. Naipaul: Anthology of Recent Criticism.* Delhi: Pencraft International, 2007.

Ray, Mohit K. ed. *V.S. Naipaul: Critical Essays.* Vol. III. New Delhi: Atlantic Publishers, 2005.

Said, Edward. 1946. *Culture and Imperialism.* London: Chatto and Windus, 1993.

Singh, M.J. *The Poetics of Alienation and Identity: V.S. Naipaul and George Lamming.* Delhi: Ajanta Books International, 1988.

Tagore, R.N. *Nationalism.* 1917. rpt. Madras: Macmillan, 1976.

Abbreviations

IWC: *India: A Wounded Civilization*

DI: *The Discovery of India*

7

An Area of Darkness: A Post-Colonial Overview

Neeraj Kumar

Naipaul occupies a coveted place among the most celebrated 20th century writers in interrogating post-imperial realities. He is the seventh Indian with Indian roots to be awarded the Nobel Prize. Born in Trinidad of Indian parentage, educated in Port of Spain and Oxford University, Naipaul has to his credit more than fourteen works of fiction and ten works of non-fiction. He has made and maintained his own myth of a writer, who was a displaced person having no country, no side and no community of his own. He projects himself as an individual, a figure who has achieved a brahmanical "ideal of non-attachment, a non-believer and a man without a home". Irving Howe has called him 'the world's writer' since he has mapped cultural spaces in his speculative journey around the globe. His writings express the ambivalence of the exile, a feature of his own experience as an east Indian in the West Indies, a West Indian in England and a nomadic intellectual in a postcolonial world who writes about people with varying cultures. The highlights of his works are the carefully controlled tension of longing for an essential identity, a remembering, a putting together of the dismembered past to make sense of the trauma of present. In Naipaul's works this sense of fragmentation, the sense of deep and unshakable loss, of being the perpetual outsider comes across powerfully. He is to a very high degree a cosmopolitan writer, a fact that he himself considers to stem from his lack of roots, he often feels that his roots lay in India. But he feels alienated from India.

Naipaul started his literary career in 1957 with *The Mystic Masseur* and continues the craft of writing till the present day. His masterpiece *An Area of Darkness* (1964) is a travelogue describing his journey to the home of his ancestors, revealing his deep antipathy for the immensity and chaos of the country, the sloth and simplicity of its citizens, the strange hold of tradition, the display of religiosity, the corruption of its rulers. The India then which was the background to his childhood was an area of imagination. But when he visited India and saw its condition full of squalor, dirt and poverty, he was shocked. He was amazed to see that the golden memories and history of India changed into a real area of darkness. This phase of retrospection questions his self and illusion and reality cause a conflict in him. He travels widely in India—arrives at Bombay, then travels as far north as Kashmir, east to Calcutta and south to Madras taking a pilgrimage of to a holy cave in the Himalayas and a stay on the Dal lake. He describes the places, people and incidents and manages to carry the meaning which lies behind them.

A relentless explorer of the traumas of postcolonial change with a moralist's outrage, Naipaul in all his writings focuses on individuals attempting to escape Fate, for fate belongs to a world of magic, myth and ritual where the past exists, but not history, a world which provides a sense of wholeness and belonging but curbs freedom. All this and more urged him to denounce India as an area of darkness and in turn provoked the Indians to see it as the darkness of his sad soul. His acquaintance with India was only through what he had heard about it from his parents in Trinidad who used to work in the British Caribbean sugarcane plantations. His ancestors were Brahmins of eastern Uttar Pradesh who left India as indentured labourers. Since his childhood he had romanticized India and on his visit to the country he sought to realize the romanticized image of the land of his forefathers. He writes with a touch of feeling:

> And India had in a special way been the background of my childhood. It was the country from which my grandfather came, a country never physically described and therefore never real, a country out in the void, beyond the dot of Trinidad, and from it our journey had been final. (27)

In the very first chapter "A Resting Place for the Imagination" he expresses his views regarding the Muslims. He thinks that they are somewhat more different than others. They are not to be trusted. He further adds that in their cap and grey beard, lay every sort of threat. Naipaul is also critical of the ritual in which people give food to animals in plates that they themselves use. He talks about the caste system prevalent in India. In Trinidad, caste had no meaning in day-to-day life: in India it implied a brutal division of labour. He had a sense of the ridiculous regarding religious ritual. He took no pleasure in religious ceremonies. He refused to go through the *janaywa* or thread ceremony of the newborn. Though growing up in an orthodox family, he remained totally ignorant of Hinduism. Though Naipaul never favoured tradition, he was shocked when he heard that in Bombay the people used candles and electric bulbs for the Diwali festival and not the rustic clay lamps, of immemorial design which in Trinidad people still used. Naipaul also expressed his views on Indian films and Indian religion:

> Indian films were both tedious and disquieting; they delighted in decay, agony and death; a funeral dirge or a blind man's lament could become a hit. (41)

In the chapter "Degrees", Naipaul sketches the various characters of Indians such as some inhabitants who are discriminated due to their menial jobs; some Indians are degraded by those who returned from abroad after completing their education; some are low in status due to the hierarchical system in bureaucracy; then there are expatriates who have not separated their origin and Indianness like Naipaul himself either in the form of superiority of their caste or due to their aristocracy. According to Naipaul, this is the Indian withdrawal and denial from the state of being a complete Indian.

Naipaul also talks about poverty which is an inexhaustible source of tears, an exercise of the purest sensibility. He quotes Premchand who writes:

> They became so poor that year that even beggars left their door empty-handed. (44)

When Naipaul had visited Bombay he saw Indian villages: the narrow, broken lanes with green slime in the gutters, the choked back-to-back mud houses, the jumble of filth and food and animals and people, the baby in the dust, swollen bellied, black with flies, but wearing its good luck amulet. He had seen the starved child defecating at the roadside while the mangy dog waited to eat the excrement. The city of Bombay revealed itself in the broad, choked and endless main road of suburbs, a chaos of shops, tall tenements, decaying balconies, electric wires and advertisements, an ampler breast and hip, a more fruitful womb.

Paradoxically, his vision of self and the evolution of self is universalized; his problematic identity is valorized by calling such Indians Anglo-Indians who represent the multi-cultural ethnicity or trans-cultural content. He writes satirically:

> No people are as capable to mimicry as the Indians. This is mimicry not of England, a real country, but of the fairy tale land of Anglo-India; of Clubs and sahibs; flatterers and bearers. (57)

Ironically, the national identity of an average Indian has not been formed fully and he continues to be a part of neo-colonialism because Naipaul feels:

> The outer and inner worlds do not have the physical separateness which they had for us in Trinidad.... It is the special mimicry of an old country.... The mimicry changes, the inner world remains constant; this is the secret of survival. (56)

In the chapter "The Colonial", Naipaul refers to the habit of giving alms to the beggar which is the automatic act of charity and reverence to God, like the offering of a candle or a spin of the prayer-wheel. He also talks about the habit of uncleanliness. The large areas of the large slopes of the Dal lake are used as latrines by Indian tourists. He quite ironically observes that for the people of Goa, as for those of imperial 'Rome' defecating is a social activity; they squat close to one another. Indians defecate everywhere. According to him, sanitation was linked to caste, caste to callousness, inefficiency and a hopelessly divided country division to weakness, weakness to foreign rule.

Naipaul comments on the businessman, too. He says that the function of the businessman is to make money. The tailor also stiches the trousers with a false hem. He makes a little extra money by saving on material. Naipaul further adds that every morning he pauses at the door of his shop, bows and touches the dust of the threshold to his forehead. This is how he guards his luck; his enterprise is a contract between God and himself alone. In a way, the duty of the public woman resembles the duty of the businessman. After acceptance she pleases him; when he is infatuated with her she sucks him dry of his wealth and at last abandons him. He also refers to a poet, Kadir whom he had met in Kashmir. His shirt opened at the neck was dirty; there was a hole at the top of his pullover. He was small and sensitive. He drank too much and that was the proof of his talent. In India poets and musicians are required to live the part; it is necessary to be sad and alcoholic. Indians are willing to eat only what they have always eaten; and staples vary from province to province.

Naipaul also visited the ruins and the fort of the Pandavas. He recalled the gaiety of the excursion party, the giving of small coins to the begging children, the food, etc. The Pandavas were the heroes of *The Mahabharata*, one of the two Hindu epics which are universally known and have something of the sanctity of holy books; the *Gita* is embedded in the *Mahabharata*. He also opines that luxury, with Indians and especially Hindus, always seems contrived and strenuous. No people are so little interested in interiors. This lack of interest appears to be historical.

Naipaul's self which had once related itself to the India of his imagination feels a sense of desolation when he confronts the real India. But soon his nativism and traditional consciousness overwhelm him when he had an encounter with the Brahmin tourist family in Kashmir:

> The encounter had done more than dislodge a childhood memory. It awakened a superseded memory. (141)

Indeed, in the chapter "Pilgrimage" the mysterious authenticity of the Lingam at Amarnath cave strengthens the narrator's beliefs who justifies the religious consciousness of Hinduism and the elemental rituals which are symbols of the essential India. Naipaul in search of his holistic nativity travels to Amarnath cave and faces the hardships of cold weather, rough journey and difficult terrain but when he reaches his destined Sheshnag temple, his self is overwhelmed with ecstasy and brightness at the sight. He says:

> They had seen the god; they were exuberant and aggressive. They were unwilling to give way. They shouted, Jai Shiv Shankar. (165-66)

He further writes:

> The god existed: the faces and cries of the returning pilgrims carried this reassurance. I wished I was of their spirit. I wished that something of their joy awaited me at the end. (167)

His experience while on pilgrimage and during all his time in Kashmir and among the Himalayas was so special, joyful that all those things about India became a part of his fantasy and enlivened his recreations of his experiences. In the chapter "Fantasy and Ruins", Naipaul re-examines and explores the mosaic of identity of Indianness which India had tried to sustain in the pre-colonial, colonial and postcolonial periods. He says:

> It is a history whose only lesson is that life goes on. There is only a series of beginnings, no final creations.... To the Indian surrounded by ruins, this is a sufficient explanation of creation and decay. (202-03)

And,

> Shiva, God of the Phallus, performing the dance of life and the dance of death. What a concept he is, how entirely of India! The ruins were inhabited. (204)

The word 'rain' is a recurring motif, which symbolically suggests that it washed away all memories of destruction and interruption that happened in the history of India. Naipaul's conscious journey of self-experiences emotional, passionate moments when he visits his native ancestral village of the Dubes in the eastern Uttar Pradesh. It was difficult for him to link his essence to Indianness but when he found villagers emotional and intimate and they narrated to him the history of his family, he was thrilled and this unlikely adventure changed his concept of time. When he attempted to write all that, isolated memories were released and the next morning he chanced to hear a song from a shop across the road, that held him mystically and compelled him to recreate all that he had experienced.

N.C. Chaudhuri's expatriation on the contrary, seems to be essentially patriotic. Although his migration to England, his open condemnation of contemporary India, his admiration for the erstwhile British Raj indicate his renunciation of India, a deep study of his writings reflect that he is disillusioned by life in England as well and is ambivalent towards his country of adoption, too. What makes his treatment different from Naipaul is that he is deeply concerned about what happens in India and he seems to be anxious to bring about a new order in which there would be rational thinking, discipline and high moral standards resulting in a happy and contented life.

He analyses the different aspects of different societies—their men and morals, ethnic and race relations caste and class.... And in this process, he sometimes assumes the role of a social moralist and preacher; at other times he is essentially a social critic bitterly criticizing these societies for their lapses. C. Paul Verghese has rightly observed:

> Non conformist in his approach and erudite in his manner he has something new and extremely controversial to say on the past and present of India. (10)

At present everyman seems to live in a state of tension. The result is complete loss of harmony in social life. Everywhere there is crowd and carelessness, acrimony and hatred that are the concomittants of deep-rooted personal jealousy and egotism. A sense of alienation and isolation is the most remarkable feature of the character of post-Independence period. Culturally, there is complete loss of moral values as Eliot finds in *Gerontion* and *The Wasteland*. Chaudhuri's fierce frankness, original intelligence and brilliant expressive powers make him a fascinating figure. To quote Iyengar:

> Nirad Chaudhuri remains the Grand Solitary, the master of a prose style that has often a fascinating spidery quality, a writer and a thinker and a Universal Mamus who stands apart from the muddy mainstream. (601)

Indeed, Chaudhuri, like Shaw compels our attention by saying the unusual and doing the unexpected like Orwell, he discusses the social and cultural problems involved in Imperialism; like Henry James he reveals an intense love and unusual understanding of the subtle ties of European culture and like Swift, he makes a vitriolic attack on the entire social fabric of a people, its men and its morals. However, his ideas are controversial, singularly personal and original, characterized by self-opinionatedness and at times anti-Indian and anti-Hindu, but there is the force of clearcut logic and commonsense at the back of all these that makes much of his pungent criticism tolerable. And herein lies the difference between him and V.S. Naipaul.

Thus, Naipaul's unidentified, negated dark floor of his self got a direction into the beauty, into the love of India which so long had been dormant in the area of imagination. His self was freed from polarized framework of Trinidad, England on one side and India on the other side. Just as in Eliot's *Journey of the Magi*, the Magi after having encountered Christ's nativity had their birth in the sense that their soul was spiritually enlightened, Naipaul after his visit to India finds himself in dilemma and tries to express his authorial voice and perspective in terms of his journey of his being enlightened through the area of darkness which was once in his childhood memories. Naipaul in *An Area of Darkness* finds himself frustrated and disappointed in all his attempts to recover and restore the lost original home akin to the sense of not belonging anywhere. That is why, he again and again tries to understand and discover the reality of India for himself. Naipaul's imagination and impression combined with sharp, critical perceptions of the social and moral concerns of the Trinidadian Hindus give us completely dry yet detached humane pictures of abiding human comedy.

Naipaul's work is of utmost relevance in a world in which we are all in exiles. He had explored with great sensitivity the predicament of the exile—the pain of the homelessness and loss of roots. His ruthless adherence to his dark vision, his refusal to pretend to an optimism, he cannot feel, gives a compelling, persuasive power to his depressing fictional world. Naipaul also uses his art to rebuild the lost home in fictional terms. To express this it needed total awareness, clear-eyed assessment of his position as a writer. His pain, anguish and perception at his own displacement and rootlessness are central to his creative talent. And it is visible in almost all his novels in general and in *An Area of Darkness* in particular.

WORKS CITED

Iyengar, K.R.S. *Indian Writing in English*. New Delhi: Sterling Publishers Pvt. Ltd., 1985.

Naipaul, V.S. *An Area of Darkness*. London: Penguin, 1977.

Verghese, C. Paul. *Nirad C. Chaudhuri*. New Delhi: Arnold Heinemann, 1973.

8

Blurring Distinctions Between 'High' and 'Low': Bollywood and Rushdie's *Midnight's Children*

Manisha Mathur

Salman Rushdie's biography is a part of postmodern history today. The circumstances of his displacement and the resultant cultural hybridity of his work are features shared by all other diasporic writers of the world, but when in 1989, his life became the site for a clash of forces between orthodox Islam and liberal humanist worldviews, Rushdie became the focal point of a major public debate. He was transformed into a symbolic persona and for the next few years everybody regardless of whether they had read his books or not felt compelled to take positions on what came to be known as the Rushdie phenomenon.

Rushdie's novel *Midnight's Children* which was awarded the Man Booker Prize in 1981 is replete with eclecticism. The novel demonstrates how epic, fable, national events, family saga, films and popular songs can be utilized in one comprehensive sweep that is historic, cosmic and mythic at the same time. Bollywood has a strong presence in Rushdie's work as he presents the cinematic influence on Indian culture in a joyous manner through the novel. The Bombay film industry is a major influence on the lives of Indian people and is the most pervasive source of popular culture in India. Bombay cinema is widely considered to be a microcosm of the social, political, economic and cultural life of

India. Vijay Mishra is of the opinion that despite its melodramatic design and its detachment from the 'real' Bombay cinema represents the multicultural and multiethnic identity of India.

The presence of films is wide-ranging in Rushdie's imagination. While novels like *Haroun* and *The Sea of Stories* are largely influenced by fantasy films of Satyajit Ray like *Goopy Gyne* and *Bagha Byne*, there are explicit references to Bollywood stars in *Satanic Verses* as well. In *Midnight's Children*, films make their presence felt because it is a novel steeped in the spirit of Bombay and thus cannot escape the city's biggest cultural influence. In *Imaginary Homelands* the author describes the origins of *Midnight's Children* in the film diction of the 1950s. "I wanted to restore the past to myself, not in the faded greys of old family album snapshots, but in whole Cinemascope, glorious Technicolour" (*Imaginary Homelands*, 10). Rushdie has fully incorporated Bollywood in his novel by making use of formulaic devices from Hindi films like exchange of babies at birth, something that happens to his protagonist Saleem Sinai when the nurse Mary Pereira changes nametags at the hospital and the poor baby gets the life of privilege and the rich baby the life of poverty. Amnesia and sudden return of memory is a device commonly used in Hindi films and Rushdie's protagonist loses his memory after being hit on the head by a silver spittoon, regaining it several years later. By incorporating Bollywood in his novel, the writer blurs the distinction between 'high' and 'low' art thereby making *Midnight's Children* a typical postmodern novel. The influence of cinema is apparent in Rushdie's observation that "film has made people more sophisticated about accepting what might once have been thought to be very strange techniques...the whole experience of montage technique, split screens, dissolves and so on have become a film language which translates quite easily into fiction and gives you extra vocabulary that traditionally has not been a part of the vocabulary of literature" (qtd. in Qazi, 10).

To begin with, Rushdie uses the vocabulary and technique of cinema to allow Saleem to piece together the fragments of his life, thereby achieving a cinematographic effect within a prose narrative. Deepa Chordiya is of the view that the writer employs cinematic technique from the beginning. For example as Adam

Aziz is praying for the last time, the lines of his prayer are interspersed with memories of his years in Germany creating a montage which effectively "illustrates the conflict between two main interpellations of Aziz's subjectivity" (Chordiya, 108). The language of Saleem's narrative is highly visual and paragraphs read as filmic images with repeated use of words like 'watch' and 'see' highlighting the cinematic quality of Rushdie's narration. Saleem repeatedly interjects directorial comments into the narrative "we cut to a long shot" (*MC*, 30), "no close up is necessary" (*MC*, 33).

The manifestations of Bollywood in *Midnight's Children* are often playful and mocking with Rushdie using parody and pastiche to depict certain situations once again displaying strains of postmodernism. However, despite the mocking tone he seems to revel in the loudness, vitality and popularity of Hindi films in India. Vijay Mishra is of the view that Rushdie reads Indian urban culture through the eyes of his beloved Bombay and its dominant art form, Bollywood cinema. The stock formula of 'masala' films of the 1970s is parodied in many places. For instance, Rushdie uses the plot of the popular film *Amar Akbar Anthony* to comment on the multiple lineage of his protagonists identity, India's identity and an Indian's identity. Meenakshi Mukherjee points out that the hybridity and co-existent diversity of India is portrayed through the different mothers that Saleem has. Thus, Vanita is the biological mother, Amina the adoptive one and Mary the nurturing mother. The women happen to be Hindu, Muslim and Christian. Saleem Sinai's fathers too are varied—Methwold the Factor represents the colonizer, Wee Willie Winkie is the entertainer, Ahmed Sinai the businessman, Uncle Hanif the film-maker and Picture Singh the snake charmer. The film *Amar Akbar Anthony* too is a story of three brothers separated by circumstances and brought up by parents from different faiths. Chordiya is of the opinion that Bombay cinema can be considered to reflect India literally, metaphorically and allegorically and Saleem Sinai makes a similar claim for himself in *Midnight's Children*.

Dreams sequences were fairly common in films of yesteryears as dreams were used to shed light on the psychical process of the character. In *Midnight's Children*, Naseem Aziz is able to enter the dreams of her daughter and Saleem's mother too dreams before his birth. The novel is replete with references to dreams as Dr. Narlikar dreams of tetrapods, Ahmed Sinai dreams up his ancestors and the final dream is Saleem's dream like plunge into Hell with Picture Singh. Mukherjee points out that films come in handy in difficult moments of narration, an instance being when Saleem watches his mother meeting her first husband and describes their propinquity by pretending that he is watching a love scene in a Hindi film. The introversion of the 1950s and 60s films where the physical contact between the hero and the heroine had to be demonstrated implicitly is parodied when Amina and Nadir kiss the same glass in the Pioneer Café. In *Imaginary Homelands*, Rushdie describes this as "kisses brutalized by prudish scissors which chopped out the moments of actual contact" (*Imaginary Homelands*, 37).

Saleem relies heavily on flashbacks and flash forwards to unify the fragments of his narrative. The protagonist's story takes us back by thirty-two years as he narrates his story to a patient Padma. The narrator compares the passage of time to movie trailers. The passage of time is indicated through the flying pages of a calendar a formula often used in old Hindi films: "I permit myself to insert a Bombay-talkie style close up. A calendar ruffled by breeze its pages flying off in rapid succession" (*MC*, 414). Further, the construction of Naseem Aziz is made through a camera technique familiar in Bombay cinema. The camera focuses on the heroine's body not at once but part by part. The popular 1960s film *Mere Mehboob* depicts the gradual discovery of the heroine by the hero their first contact being on a university campus with the heroine behind a veil. In *Midnight's Children*, Adam Aziz views Naseem bit by bit through a perforated sheet until he sees her fully for the first time when the First World War ends.

The realism versus fantasy debate that is germane to all of Rushdie's novels is also addressed through the issue of films. Saleem's Uncle Hanif toys with the idea of making a realistic, 'high art' film in the tradition of the 70s New Wave cinema of Mrinal Sen and Shyam Benegal. Hanif's first film *Lovers in*

Kashmir was a typical Bollywood style movie. However, after his fabulist beginnings Hanif had remembered that he was his father's son and dedicated himself against everything which smacked of the unreal. He now desired to make a film capturing the comprehensive reality of a pickle factory and the process of 'chutnification'. He would use details like the pickling process and trade union issues to make his film hard hitting and real. Hanif is strictly against fantasy "the temple of illusions". Saleem notes that his uncle was "fond of railing against princes and demons, gods and heroes, against the entire iconography of Bombay films" (*MC*, 279). However, Uncle Hanif (despite his wife's proteststations that he inserts the regular Bollywood song and dance routine in his film) fails miserably in his attempt to make a realistic film and reality in fact kills him. Saleem believes that Hanif died due to spurning the 'low' melodramatic, cheap thrill style of Bombay cinema.

Rushdie as is evident from *Imaginary Homelands* appears to be quite impressed by films of Satyajit Ray who is associated with art cinema and especially films like *Pather Panchali* and the *Apu Triology*. In *Satanic Verses*, however, parallel cinema is rubbished as 'art house crap' and in Moor's *Last Sigh* films like *Boot Polish* and *Do Bigha Zameen* are derided. Mujeebuddin Syed believes that the ending of *Midnight's Children* is more like 'art' or 'serious' cinema as opposed to popular or mainstream cinema. Syed mentions two films in particular Benegal's *Ankur* and Ray's *Shatranj Ke Khiladi*. In *Ankur*, the last scene shows a young boy throwing a stone at the landlord's house which suggests a revolt against the system of oppression. Moreover, the seed planted by the landlord in the maidservant's womb suggests that every oppressive system sows its own seeds of destruction. In Ray's *Shatranj Ke Khiladi* the last shot shows the nawabs engaged in a game of chess as the British army approaches the city of Lucknow. The only one to display a patriotic feeling in this scene is a young boy. Syed comments "Rushdie seems to offer a subaltern solution to India's numerous problems by concluding the novel with its focus on the boy and the future." Saleem is tempted to fill in the jar of the future too; "One empty jar how to end?" but resists doing so and though he writes his own future he does not touch the jar "but the future cannot be preserved in a jar; one jar must remain empty" (qtd. in Mukherjee, 163). Despite the influence of highbrow cinema however, in *Midnight's Children* the influence of Bollywood melodrama is more than apparent even though it is parodied in many places.

Bollywood movies until recently were considered as 'low' art and the conventions of Bombay cinema were ridiculed and dismissed by Indian and Western critics as lacking in realism, and 'filmi' was looked upon as cheap and trashy. Although Rushdie too has been quite dismissive of Bollywood, Hindi films nevertheless figure prominently in his narrative. Deepa Chordiya makes an interesting comment when she says that the hybridization that is seen in Hindi films, which make an attempt to incorporate a seemingly infinite number of disparate influences and unify them into a single whole, is a quality that is seen in Rushdie's work as well. Further, the fragmentary structure of Bombay cinema mirrors and elucidates the likewise fragmentary nature of everyday reality in *Midnight's Children.*

WORKS CITED

Chordiya, Deepa P. *Taking on the Tone of a Bombay Talkie: The Function of Bombay Cinema in Rushdie's Midnight's Children.* www. synergiesprairiesxa

Mishra, Vijay. *Bollywood Cinema: Temples of Desire.* London: Routledge, 2002.

Moumin, Manzoor Quazi. *The Blurred Boundaries between Film and Fiction in Salman Rushdie's Midnight's Children, The Satanic Verses and Other Selected Works.* Ann Arbor: Bell and Howell Information and Learning, 1999.

Mukherjee, Meenakshi (ed.). *Rushdie's Midnight's Children: A Book of Readings.* Delhi: Pencraft International, 2003.

Rushdie, Salman. *Imaginary Homelands.* London: Granata Books, 1991.

——. *Midnight's Children.* New York: Penguin, 1980.

9

Roy's *The God of Small Things*: A Search for Female Identity

R.N. Rai

Arundhati Roy, a powerful contemporary Indian English writer, is a vehement critic of neo-imperialism and the leading figure of anti-globalization/alter-globalization movement. Her well-known novel *The God of Small Things* won Booker Prize in 1997 and received half a million pounds in advance from Harper Collins. She remained on the top of the *New York Times* and *London Times* best-seller list for a long time. Gillian Beer, Professor of English at Cambridge and the Chairperson of the Judging Panel, had observed that the Judges had been deeply 'engrossed" by the novel's extraordinary linguistic inventiveness. In the opinion of *New York Times Book Review*, Roy's narrative is "so morally strenuous and so imaginatively supple that the reader remains enthralled all the way through".

Arundhati Roy's popular novel *The God of Small Things* successfully draws our attention to the miserable plight of women and centres round the character of Ammu who lives in a village named Ayemenem located near Kottayam in Kerala. Roy brilliantly presents the endless sufferings and exploitations of three generations of women—the protagonist Ammu, her mother Mammachi, her daughter Rahel and highlights the weaknesses of the discriminatory Patriarchal social order. Let us first discuss the sufferings of Ammu's mother Mammachi who was married to a person 16 years older than her. Though Ammu's father, Mr. Pappachi was a senior entomologist in Delhi, he was governed by the cruel norms of Patriarchal society. Ammu's mother was almost regularly beaten by her father on one pretext or the other. Though Mr. Pappachi had created the impression of a "sophisticated, generous, moral man" on the public platform; as he used to donate money to orphanages and leprosy clinics, he very often "turned into a monstrous, suspicious bully, with a streak of vicious cunning" in his relationship with wife and children. Consequently, they were often "beaten, humiliated and then made to suffer the envy of friends and relations for having such a wonderful husband and father" (180). That was not the end of Mammachi's suffering. Mammachi had to endure many cold winter nights in Delhi hiding in the mehandi hedge around her house because her husband had beaten her and driven her out of the house. When he was not satisfied with so much, "he tore down curtains, kicked furniture and smashed a table lamp" (181). Ammu's father was so arrogant and dominating that her mother's first lessons on the violin were abruptly discontinued when her teacher made the mistake of admiring her mother as "exceptionally talented and in his opinion potentially concert class" (50) in front of her father. Ammu's father could not digest this kind of admiration of his wife.

Pappachi's cruelty continued even after his retirement. One day when Ammu's brother, Chacko returned from Oxford for a summer vacation, he found Pappachi beating Mammachi in the study room. Chacko could not tolerate it, strode into the room, caught Pappachi's vase-hand and twisted it around his back. Rebuking his father he firmly stated: "I never want this happen again" (48). His father never beat his mother again but inflicted greater torture on her: "He never touched Mammachi again. But he never spoke to her either as long as he lived" (48). Only the mode of oppression changed. Physical torture was replaced by mental torture but the torture continued till Ammu's father survived in the world. Ammu gradually developed the habit of living with "this cold, calculating cruelty. She developed a lofty sense of injustice and the mulish, reckless streak that develops in Someone Small who has been bullied all their lives by Someone Big" (181-82).

Arundhati Roy also gives a vivid account of the endless suffering of Ammu. Ammu's father retired in the year Ammu completed her school education. After retirement, Ammu's father decided that his son Chacko would persue his higher study at Delhi University and then move to Oxford as Rhodes Scholar, but the daughter Ammu would go back to the village in order to assist her mother in her household affairs. Was it not a case of gender discrimination and gender injustice? After two years Ammu completed the age of 18. The only thing Ammu's parents were worried about was the marriage of Ammu by hook or by crook. They had sufficient money for the higher education of their son but no money for the marriage of their daughter. Hence, no proposal of marriage came from anyone. Nobody was worried about Ammu. Her eighteenth birthday came and went unnoticed. Ammu grew desperate. Her suffering is vividly presented by Arundhati Roy in the following manner: "All day she dreamed of escaping from Ayemenem and the clutches of her ill tempered father and bitter, long suffering mother" (38-39).

Ammu thought of several little wretched plans of her escape from her village. One day she got an opportunity to spend the summer with a distant aunt at Calcutta where she had an opportunity to meet her future husband who was a small but well-built and pleasant looking man working as an Assistant Manager of a tea estate in Assam. She accepted his proposal of marriage not because she had fallen in love with him but because she thought that "anyone at all would be better than returning to Ayemenem" (39). Recalling her Calcutta wedding Ammu realized that the feverish glitter in her husbands eyes "had not been love, or even excitement at the prospect of carnal bliss, but approximately eight large pegs of whisky. Straight. Neat" (39).

When Ammu moved to Assam with her husband, she soon realized that her husband was not just a 'heavy drinker' but a "full blown alcoholic with all of an alcoholic's deviousness and tragic charm" (40). When Amu was giving birth to her twins—

Estha (son) and Rahel (daughter) in Shillong hospital, her husband was lying drunk on a hard bench in the corridor of the hospital. He became so alcoholic in due course of time that he stopped going to his office and kept on lying in his bed. Eventually, his English manager, Mr. Hollick summoned him to his bungalow and asked him to resign. When Ammu's husband started weeping, Mr. Hollick made an alternative proposal—he would not insist on his resignation and would make an arrangement for his treatment also, provided 'his extremely attractive wife' is sent to his banglow to be 'looked after' during this period. Everybody in the locality knew that Mr. Hollick had bequathered a number of ragged, light skinned children on the estate.

When Ammu did not favourably respond to this proposal, her husband grew uncomfortable and suddenly "he lunged at her, grabbed her hair, punched her and then passed out from the effort" (42). This infuriated Ammu and for the first time in her life she lost her patience and turned violent. She picked up the heaviest book from the shelf and "hit him with it as hard as she could. On his head. His legs. His back and shoulders" (42). Domestic violence against Ammu became a daily routine. It gradually included her children also. Repelled by this kind of suffocating situation Ammu finally decided to leave her husband and return to her parents 'unwelcomed'. She returned to "everything she had fled from only a few years ago. Except that now she had two young children. And no more dreams" (42). Ammu, however, had no option but to stay and reconcile with the present humiliating situation. She was much worried about the future of her children who seemed to her "like a pair of small bewildered frogs engrossed in each other's company, lolloping arm in arm down a highway full of hurtling traffic" (43). When she looked at herself in her wedding photographs, she felt as if she was a foolish jewelled bride who had "permitted herself to be so painstakingly decorated before being led to the gallows" (44).

Now the question that arises in our mind is: who is responsible for this pathetic state of Ammu—Ammu herself or her parents or the socio-cultural set-up of her family life?

If Ammu was not given proper education and sufficient opportunity to choose her husband, how can she be held responsible for this miserable plight? Through this novel, Arundhati Roy raises the question—What is the constitutional status of a woman who is economically dependent on others? Where do her rights and privileges lie—with the parents or the husband or with none? The cultural construct, as stated by Simone de Beauvoir in *The Second Sex*, is mainly responsible for this kind of gender discrimination. Unless and until we radically modify our socio-cultural norms, we cannot be able to fulfill even the legitimate demands of gender equality. Through the character of Ammu, Arundhati Roy tries to highlight the woman's right to her body. Her act of marrying a Bengali fellow out of the Syrian Christian community and her denial to appease Mr. Hollick even if it resulted in leaving her husband forever, are said to be a quite assertion of her right over her body.

Ammu's bua, Baby Kochamma subscribed wholeheartedly to the traditional view of woman. She resented Ammu as she found her "quarelling with a fate...of the wretched Manless woman" (45). In her opinion, a divorced daughter had no position anywhere at all and so far as the fate of the divorced daughter from an intercommunity love marriage is concerned, she was not willing to say anything but preferred to "remain quiveringly silent" on the subject. She firmly believed that nobody would like to marry the issues of an intercommunity marriage and hence the future of Ammu's children is quite bleak or uncertain. Baby Kochamma regarded Estha and Rahel to be known better than "Domed, fatherhood waifs": "Worse still, they were half-Hindu Hybrids whom no self-respecting Syrian Christian would ever marry" (45). Ammu's children have no legal or moral right to live in the house of maternal grandfather. Though Ammu did as much work in the factory as Chacko did, Ammu had no legal claim to the property. Ammu was aware of this 'wonderful' male chauvinist society which did not provide any *locus standi* to Ammu. Once when Ammu asked her brother what he had done for her children, Chacko immediately put the counter-question: "Are they my responsibility"? He further added that in fact Ammu, Estha and Rahel were milestones around his neck.

Through the character of Ammu and her children, Arundhati Roy puts forward a perplexing question to the so-called custodians of our society: Who is supposed to shoulder the responsibility of Ammu and her children if Ammu is not allowed to stand on her own feet? Why are Ammu's mother and other family members interested only in getting rid of them? The possible answer seems to be that Ammu is not economically independent and hence she is a burden to each member of the family. In this suffocating situation, Ammu finds herself quite helpless and demoralized.

One day in the afternoon while Ammu was dreaming, she "travelled upwards through a dream in which a cheerful man with one arm held her close by the light of an oil lamp" (215). She was wondering and trying to know "who was he, the one-armed man? Who could he have been? The God of Loss? The God of Small Things? The God of Goose Bumps and Sudden Smiles?" (217). She sensed that a pact had been forged between her Dream and the World. Though she was not willing to know what each day held in store for her, she gradually started realizing that her children were feeling attached to Velutha and she was also feeling inclined towards him. Velutha was working as an accomplished carpenter in the factory of Chacko. He belonged to the community of the Untouchables known as Paravan caste which was in Mammachi's time, not allowed to walk on public roads. Though Velutha and Ammu knew each other for a long time, they attentively looked at each other and for the first time realized that both of them have sufficient to offer each other. All of a sudden they felt so much attached to each other that their traditional bonds disappeared. Arundhati Roy has powerfully presented the climax of their intimate moments and highlighted Ammu's active participation in the Sexual Act:

> Clouded eyes held clouded eyes in a steady gaze and a luminous woman opened herself to a luminous man. She was as wide and deep as a river in spate. He sailed on

> her waters, she could feel him moving deeper and deeper into her. Frantic. Frenzied. (336-37)

Waves of youth started pouring into her heart. She felt as if the journey of her life is just like the 'lost traveller' or 'inexperienced lover' who has no awareness of her destination. She was worried to think how the ideas of developing physical relationship with Velutha came to her mind? It may lead to the terrible and fatal consequences. Standing on the verge of youth she could not control her passions and finally yielded herself to Velutha. What was wrong with Ammu if she had discovered love for her children and safety for her future through her relationship with Velutha? For the next thirteen nights, they went on sticking to their physical needs and thought of their brighter and happier dreams. Velutha was perhaps not aware of the fact that the path he was treading will lead to his disastrous end.

Velutha's father, Velleya Paapen saw Velutha and Ammu in objectionable situation and immediately reported the matter to Ammu's mother: "They had made the unthinkable and the impossible really happen" (256). There was terrible commotion in the family and the surroundings. Velutha's father was weeping, grovelling and offering to "kill his son. To tear him limb from limb" (256) and Ammu's mother was spitting into the rain and asking how could she stand the smell of Velutha, a Paravana? Mammachi's tolerance of 'Man's Needs' as far as her son's relationship with many women was concerned, became the fuel for her unmanageable fury at her daughter's relationship with Velutha. She burst out and said:

> She had defiled generations of breeding and brought the family to its knees. For generations to come, forever now, people would point at them at weddings and funerals. At baptisms and birthday parties. They'd nudge and whisper. It was all finished now. (258)

They were now planning to take revenge against Velutha. Baby Kochamma turned to Mammachi and said: "He must go. Tonight. Before it goes any further. Before we are completely ruined" (257).

Both the old ladies—Mammachi and Baby Kochamma—planned everything very carefully. They locked Ammu in her bedroom and lodged a false F.I.R. against Velutha in the Kottayam police station pointing out that they had to dismiss a Paravana factory worker, Mr. Velutha because "a few days ago he had tried to...force himself on her niece...a divorcee with two children" (259). Baby Kochamma misinterpreted their relationship just to "contain the scandal and salvage the family reputation in Inspector Thomas Mathew's eyes" (259). They also managed to win the support of Comrade Pillai who did not question the false allegation against Velutha, though Velutha was also a member of the Communist Party. Velutha was arrested by the police and was so much tortured in the Police Station that he could not survive and even his dead body was removed from there. When Ammu went to the Police Station to inquire about Velutha, she was humiliated by the Inspector and ultimately turned out of the Police Station. Police Inspector stared at Ammu's breast and told that Kottayam Police didn't take statement from Vesyas or their illegimate children.

Arundhati Roy is trying to draw our attention to an important issue of gender inequality. Why is it so that society considers Chacko's illegimate relationship with many women as 'man's needs' but Ammu's physical relationship with Velutha only as highly detrimental to the healthy growth of society? Why is society so indifferent to the physical needs of a woman? Ammu is just 30 and a neglected divorcee. Should she completely forget about her physical needs and worldly aspirations? Simone de Beauvoir has rightly pointed out that the sole reason behind this is the cultural construct which determines the status of woman in society. Man is free to do whatever he likes but no freedom is granted to a woman. If man determines the cultural code of conduct for woman, why cannot woman determine the cultural code of conduct for man? If something is prohibited for a woman, how can it be desirable for a man? Is it not a glaring issue of gender discrimination? Ammu was ill-treated by her father, betrayed by her husband, insulted by Police and rendered destitute by her brother. Everyone was supporting patriarchal ideology which asserted that Ammu should have no right anywhere—as a daughter, wife, citizen or sister.

The suffering of Ammu does not come to an end with the death of Velutha. She is still moving towards a more serious tragic end. When Ammu returned from the Police Station insulted and humiliated, the family members asked her to 'pack her bags and leave'. Even at this point gender discrimination was made. Ammu's son Estha was sent to his old Bengali father for proper education and he gladly accepted the responsibility also, but nobody in the entire family was willing to accept the responsibility of Ammu's daughter, Rahel. In the post-Independence India, though sufficient progress has been made in the direction of women education, the discrimination against women is still very common in the villages and the backward classes of society.

Ammu was trying her best to get some job so that she could earn her livelihood but prolonged suffering had made her the patient of asthama. When she last came to the village to meet her daughter, she was seen very sad, sick and perturbed. She had lost her job also. When she was going back in search of a new job, her mother told her that it would be better if she seldom comes to the village to meet her daughter. Ammu was so shocked with the reaction of her mother that she did not even say good bye to her. After a few days, she was found dead in a lonely room in Bharata Lodge. Arundhati Roy has presented a very pathetic picture of her death:

> She died alone. With a noisy ceiling fan for company and no Estha to lie at the back of her and talk to her. She was thirty-one. Not old, not young, but a viable, die-able age. (161)

The church refused to bury her for several reasons. Hence, her brother Chacko hired a van to transport the body to the electric crematorium where "nobody except beggars, derelicts and the police custody dead were cremated" (162). When Ammu's turn came, even her son, Estha was not present. There were no tears in any one's eyes.

Let us now discuss the fate of the third generation—Ammu's daughter, Rahel who drifted from school to school after the death of Ammu. Chacko and Mammachi provided the care (food, cloth, fees), but withdrew the concern from Rahel. She 'grew up without a brief' and there was none to worry about her. She spent eight years in college without finishing her five years undergraduate course for taking her degree. Rahel could not learn much either from college or from family or from society because no one was bothered about her at all except Ammu who was no more in this world. She married an American Mr. Larry McCaslin. She drifted into marriage like a passenger who drifts towards an unoccupied chair in an airport lounge. She was soon divorced and came back to India. She had no option but to lead a miserable life in the village.

Baby Kochamma often used to feel that Ammu and Rahel were the worst transgressors. They all broke the rules and crossed into the forbidden territory. They all tampered with the laws and hence suffered immensely. However Ammu, while going back from the village for the last time in search of a new job for her survival, was asking herself—what was in fact her crime which resulted in this kind of prolonged suffering? Was it a crime that she refused to lead a suffocating life under the dominance of her 'full blown alcoholic' husband? Was it a crime that she refused to spend nights with the manager, Mr. Hollick on the insistence of her drunkard husband? Or was it a crime that she decided to establish relationship with Velutha for the happiness of her children and the safety of her future? Why is the patriarchal society so indifferent to the agony and suffering of woman? What was the 'sin' of Ammu? Was it a sin that she was born a woman or that she had married a person of Hindu Community? What was the fatal consequence coming out of it? Did it not lead to the wastage of two lives—that of Estha and Rahel, the loss of 'two children's childhoods'? It turned out to be a lesson of history for 'future offenders'. Will the society ever think over these issues seriously and try to find out a healthy solution to them? Arundhati Roy has successfully drawn our attention to these fundamental issues related to the emancipation of women in our Indian society.

The God of Small Things may apty be regarded as a protest novel. Roy herself admits that there is in her book a 'cold', 'deep-set' unforgiving anger which is born out of her own 'Naxal sensibility' against the age-old rotten systems and social hypocrisies, all sorts of boundaries—boundaries between Ammu and Velutha, Estha and Rahel, parents and children, touchables and untouchables, life and death have been transgressed upon.

Ammu and Velutha transgress the limits of caste system and pay heavily for it. Velutha suffers the fatal consequences of his transgression through the brutal mutilation of his untouchable and subaltern body which is completely swept away and erased from the record of hegemomic history. In this connection Rahel's observation that Velutha's body leaves "no footprint in sand, no ripples in water, no image in mirrors" is quite relevant and speaks much about the darker aspects of caste ridden social system.

Whereas the transgression of Ammu and Velutha destabilizes the socio-cultural norms, the transgression of Estha and Rahel breaks the age-old taboo of incest prohibition. Since they have been emotionally destroyed and alienated by their social milieu, they try to create their own world in which they may share their hideous grief, their desires and anxieties:

> Only that they shared that might was not happiness, but hideous grief. Only that once again they broke Love Laws. That day down who should be loved and how much. (311)

Estha and Rahel transgress the sacred law of human relationship; their relationship may be regarded as a return to the primitive or natural state of human existence when Love Laws had not been formulated by the human society.

Arundhati Roy thinks of human history as an aweful burden. Its laws are so cruel and inhuman that anyone who tries to defy it, has to pay very heavily for its defiance. The aspirations of the small things of human history—women, children and untouchables have been deliberately ignored and ruthlessly suppressed for their instinctive urges. Velutha dies in police custody and Ammu in a lonely hotel; they are abandoned both by God and History. The novel delves deep into the intricacies of human nature; it narrates the brutality we are capable of. Estha was forced to act as an accomplice in the brutal elimination of Velutha who consequently withdrew from the world and stopped talking altogether. He harboured his guilt as an uneasy octopus and remained perturbed since then.

Arundhati Roy has thrown sufficient light on the contemporary issues of hybridization and degeneration of human culture. Chacko feels that his Syrian Christian family will not be able to retain its distinct identity. Inter-caste, inter-community and inter-racial marriages have trapped them outside their own history and made them unable to retrace their steps. There was no escape to them from the cultural ravages and hence they lost their identity and sense of belongingness:

> We belong nowhere. We sail unanchored on troubled seas. We may never be allowed ashore. Our sorrows will never be sad enough, our joys never happy enough. Our dreams never big enough, our lives never important enough to matter. (53)

Roy wants to remind us that indiscriminate and unassimilated cultural borrowings may disfigure our cultural identity and lead us nowhere. In this context, it is pertinent to recall what Franz Fanon has said on this issue. Fanon has rightly stated that the colonizing culture "is not satisfied merely with holding a people in its grip and emptying the native's brain of all form and content", but also "turns the past of the oppressed people and distorts, disfigures and destroys it" (169).

Roy is not only concerned with the emancipation of women but the protection of environment also. If we keep eco-feminist approach in mind, we better appreciate her serious concern with the both. She compares the miserable plight of the people of Narmada valley with the fatal ending of Velutha in the novel. How can their dignified survival be ensured? In her book *The Greater Common Good* (1999) she expresses her confidence that the present century will be "the century of the

Small, and perhaps right now, the very minute, there's a small god up in heaven readying herself for us" (5).

WORKS CITED

Beauvoir, Simone de. *The Second Sex*, trans. Parshley, H.M. Harmondsworth: Penguin, 1974.

Fanon, Frantz. *The Wretched of the Earth*. Harmondsworth: Penguin, 1990.

Roy, Arundhati. *The God of Small Things*. New Delhi: India Ink Publishing Company, 1997.

——. *The Greater Common Good*. Bombay: India Book Distributors, 1999.

10

Sensuousness in *The God of Small Things*

Chhaya Jain

Arundhati Roy's debut performance *The God of Small Things* is a popular novel. It has sold about nine million copies the world over and has been translated into more than twenty-nine languages. Arundhati Roy is the first Indian citizen to win Britain's most prestigious award, the Booker Prize—an amount of twenty thousand pounds sterling, a big prize for a big thing. The most coveted Booker Prize provided her an internal status of celebs and the position of a millionaire. In fact, she has stunned the literary world by winning the prize for the novel, *The God of Small Things*. To be more precise, she took the Indian literary world by storm. This has happened at the age of thirty-seven. Khushwant Singh admits very frankly, "Money wise she has surpassed everybody." Kamala Das says, "She is lucky. We are not." This kind of popularity stimulates us to examine this novel thoroughly. One of my scholars has chosen to investigate her writings in the light of the social injustice. This has prompted me to go through the novel, albeit in a cursory fashion. This is, how I could pen few lines to present before you on the sensuousness in *The God of Small Things*.

This 331-paged novel in twenty-one chapters with engrossing sub-titles is remarkable for its quality of innocence and originality. It is a playful book, full of poetry and wisdom. A serious reading of the novel fills us with ecstasy and we agree with Dr. S.K. Paul to regard it as an out and out modern prose-epic, ever written anywhere in the world. Roy's novel surpasses those of many novelists of the past and the present in portraying scores of characters and narrating incidents very tenderly, craftily and in a highly poetical manner. It is a beautiful love story in which all forms of love have been dealt with touchingly. The canvas of the novel is so big that we can say that it is not a book about India, rather it is a book about humanity—human nature, human virtues, love, vices, attainments and dissociated sensibility. The novel deals with life and living and questions some of the key-issues confronting a society poised between tradition and modernity.

Set in Kerala in 1960s, *The God of Small Things* is about two children—Estha and Rahel, the two-egg dizygotic twins and two adults—Ammu and Velutha and the shocking consequences of a pivotal event in their young lives, the accidental death by drowning of visiting English cousin. In magical and poetic language, the novel paints a vivid picture of life in a small rural Indian town, the thoughts and tender feelings of two small children and the complexity and hypocrisy of the adults in their world. It is also a poignant lesson in the destructive power of the caste system and moral and political bigotry in general. In *The God of Small Things*, Roy's 'Big God' is the capitalistic 'Americans' and the 'Small God' is the 'Government of India'. In other words, big gods are the privileged ones who never look at the East but towards the West and the 'small gods' are the underprivileged who flourish under dollars which they value more than rupees.

Professionally, Roy is a learned architect but she has a heart of a born poet like Kamala Das and Sir Aurobindo. The main faculties of human personality—the 'body' the 'mind' and the 'heart'—have blended in harmony in her personality and this harmonious blending has provided a rhythm to her activities as a writer. *The God of Small Things* deals with an ordinary story about ordinary people leading ordinary lives deprived of social-justice, but her expression throughout is that of non-stop newsreels with sensational music produced by the words, phrases and epithets she has used.

It is a fascinating experience to focus on the text's play with the imagery which is pre-eminently sensuous. Her fiction vibrates with deep sensuousness. Unquestionably, she may be called a novelist of senses (i) because in her writings, the sensuous appeal is most intense and all-pervading, (ii) because her emotions are immediately exited by her senses, and (iii) because her presentation is full of sensuous imagery. Her sensuousness is not confined to the eye and ear but embraces all the five senses and their delights. Just as the beauties of nature appeal to her eye and sweet sound to her ear, so does sweet odour and delicious taste and soft touch appeal to her other senses. All her senses are keen and respond quickly to the outer world and her sensitive soul vibrates to every kind of sense impression.

I am convinced that Arundhati Roy's novel is not only rich in line, style, colour, light and shade, and sound but it is also rich in image of the physical sensations of taste, touch, smell, sight, temperature and pressure. Her novel is also rich in the image of the organic sensations such as hunger, thirst and sex—thus, her imagery is both sensuous and comprehensive. Her novel abounds in sensuous imagery. The text opens describing Ayemenem in the month of May and moves to early June referring to the monsoon rains in Kerala. The opening lines in "Paradise Pickles and Preserves" have a rich sensuous appeal:

> May in Ayemenem is a hot, brooding month. The days are long and humid. The river shrinks and black crows gorge on bright mangoes in still, dust green trees. Red bananas ripen. Jackfruits burst. Dissolute blue bottles hum vacuously in the fruity air. Then they stun themselves against clear window panes and die, fatly baffled in the sun. (1)

Even more sensuous are the details of the defecating exercise. "Children hung their bottoms over the edge and defecated directly onto the squelchy, sucking mud of the exposed river bed" (125). Baby Kochamma's way of defecation is narrated as:

> Baby Kochamma balanced like a big bird over a public pot.... Fat knees...dimpled.... Head thrust forward. Silly smile. Bosom swinging low.... When the gurgling bubbling sound came, she listencd with her eyes. A yellow brook burbled through a mountain pass. (95)

Roy is not unaware of the modern technology and the impact it has on human minds. Talking of cable T.V. network, her description becomes more sensuous:

> On weekdays she (Baby Kochamma) watched *The Bold* and *The Beautiful* and *Santa Barbara*, where brittle blondes with lipstick and hairstyles rigid with spray seduced androids and defended their sexual empires. (27)

Further she adds:

> Kochu Maria, the cook, still wore the thick gold earings that had disfigured her earlobes for ever. She enjoyed the *WWF Wrestling Mania* shows, where Hulk Hogan and Mr. Perfect, whose necks were wider than their heads, wore spangled Lycra leggings and beat each other up brutally. (28)

Roy always selects the objects of her description and imagery with a keen eye on their sensuous appeal. For the novelist, Velutha is first and foremost a human being and has natural weaknesses of man. The lovers surrender to the call of their mind:

> Biology designed the dance. Terror timed it. Dictated the rhythm with which their bodies answered each other. As though they knew already that for each tremor of pleasure they would pay with an equal measure of pain. (335)

The intensity of sensuousness reaches its peak:

> If he touched her, he couldn't talk to her, if he loved her he couldn't leave, if he spoke he could not listen, if he fought he couldn't win. (330)

Our senses of sight and sound are also gratified when she describes "Behind them the river pulsed through the darkness, shimmering like wild silk. Yellow bamboo wept" (335). We get reminded of Keats' sensuousness in the following lines:

> The scurrying, hurrying boat world was already gone.
> The white termites on their way to work
> The white ladybirds on their way home
> The white beetles burrowing away from the light.
> The white grasshoppers with whitewood violins.
> The sad white music
> All gone. (336)

In "The River in the Boat" we have a series of pictures which please our senses. The lemon squash, the grape-crush, thick fresh jam, banana-jam, pine-apple—are a kind of feast which we enjoy as we go through the book. Even more sensuous is the picture of Kalyani being watched by Chacko when she returns with a stainless-steel glass of filter coffee;

> She was a lush, beautiful woman with golden brown skin and huge eyes. Her long frizzy hair was damp and hung loose down her back, plaited only at the very end. (270)

The sensuousness is the principal charm of her novel. Sometimes the sensuousness deteriorates into sensuality. In other words, she often shows a tendency to dwell too much upon the charm of the masculine body and refers to his moustache, shoulder, abdominal muscles, arms, etc. She also describes the charms of the feminine body and refers to the lips, cheeks, breast and a little more than is necessary. The bed-room scene descriptions are presented so vividly and artistically that they regenerate the hope for physical warmth which is life's genuine passion. Lovers' blending of mind and heart lead to a point where nothing would separate "Sex from Love. Or Needs from Feelings" (328). *The God of Small Things* has it all in its kitty—the echoes, the calls and the cries of the Earth. We feel like moving through beautiful landscapes, seascapes and cloudscapes of sensory imagery. The readers remain enthralled all the way through. The novel ends with a "Tomorrow", perhaps indicating that there is no end for the emotions and passions of the human heart.

There is no doubt about Roy's brilliant power of entering into the life of external objects which accounts for so much intensity and vividness of her imagery. Her sensuousness—the sense for taste, sight, odour, sound and touch surpasses Keats' and Shobha De's tactful use of allusive remarks in the writings. Her clever use of body language and physical journey is an orgy of scintillating words—'gurgling-bubbling', 'viable-die-able age', 'fan-whirring', 'peanut-crunching', 'knolls and dells', etc. She creates a deep and dense web of actualities and eventualities related to the behaviour and language of the 'body'. At one end of the spectrum, it broadens into sensuality and at the other end, it becomes aerial and ethereal. Thus, it leaves the reader in a dilemma to choose between the earth and God. With the coming of the closure of the novel *The God of Small Things* I would cry in ecstasy and like to call it a sensuous 'picture gallery'.

WORK CITED

Roy, Arundhati. *The God of Small Things* (New Delhi: Penguin Books India, 2002).

11

Theme of Human Nature in the Novel of Arundhati Roy *The God of Small Things*

Bhupendra Pratap Singh Chauhan

If Salman Rushdie revolutionized the image of South Asian fiction with *Midnight's Children*, it was truly popularized by Arundhati Roy in 1997, when her first novel, *The God of Small Things* became international sensation. Arundhati Roy has stunned the literary world by winning Bookeı Prize for the novel *The God of Small Things*, which can be described as a "wondrous creation for first novel". Praise has been heaped upon the book from several quarters, and for several aspects of brilliance in the book. The Booker citation calls it a 'moving novel' which tells a story fundamental as well as local.

This paper tries to focus on the various images of Human nature that emerges from the novel.

> Any thing is possible in Human Nature—Love, Madness, Hope, Infinite joy.[1]

Roy's exploration of the horizon of Human Nature collides and intersects with the steady progression of relentless, inevitable fate and her chapter refrain thematically in a well-developed sequence, involving from the simple philosophy, "thing can change in a day" to elaboration "any thing can happen to any one so it's best to be prepared".

In Shakespeare's famous comedy *Merchant of Venice*, he said about love "But love is blind, and lovers cannot see, the pretty follies that themselves commit." It occurs in the novel when Ammu enters into an illicit relationship with Velutha. A liaison between a high caste Syrian Christian woman and an untouchable Paravan is unthinkable, even detested by the society overcome by him, she ventures to love him by night while her children love him by day. Rahel and Estha in this way become the "twin midwives of Ammu's dream".

"They all crossed into forbidden territory. They all tempered with the law that lay down who should be loved and how much?"

Ammu had entered into wedlock to escape from her ill-tempered father and embittered mother when her husband proposed to her, she did not pretend to be in love with him; instead she just considered the pros and cons of the situation and consented. She actually never loved her husband and he himself turned out to be one who could not have been loved by women like Ammu. She always deserved a much better love than her indolent, irresponsible alcoholic man. The luminous woman in Ammu yearned to love and to be loved. So when she saw the right man she did not wince.

Velutha, while playing with Rahel catches Ammu watching them with a tinge of envy. He also notices things that had not done before.

> Simple Things, for instance, he saw that Rahel's mother was woman. That she had deep dimples when she smiled...that her shoulders shone but her eyes were some where else.... He saw too that he was not the only given of gifts. That she had gifts to give him too.[2]

They knew that they had no future, so they instinctively struck to "Small Things" while "Big Things lurk unsaid inside". Doomed as their love was from the beginning, they lost their lives due to it, one after the other Baby Kochamma loses her heart to emerald eyed, handsome young father Mulligan. For a year she tried hard to seduce him, but all efforts were futile. The priest though enthralled by the feeling that he awoke in an attractive girl, never did anything else and returned to his seminary after a year. Baby Kochamma with her aching and bruised heart became a Roman Catholic and entered a convent in Madras in hope to find her lost love.

> She pictured them together in dark sepulchral rooms with heavy velvet drops; discussing Theology.... That was...all she ever dared to hope for just to be near him.... To love him just by looking at him.[3]

But his prayers went unanswered; she detested convent life so his father brought her back to Ayemenem where she lived her wretched, mean, lonely, man-less life. Every night she unfailingly wrote 'I love you, I love you in her diary; years after years. She however kept in touch with father Mulligan through letters. She was utterly dejected when father Mulligan became a Hindu and sent her a photograph of him in saffron robes addressing white sari-clad widow Hindu women. She continued making identical entries in her diary even alter father Mulligan passed away as for her, his death did not alter anything in her life. Dead or alive, he was not available to her in any condition.

Other episode of love is love of Chacko. His love at Oxford is love with a simple English woman Margaret who felt 'life a blithe genie released from her lamp' with a magic her eyes, in his company. As for Chacko.

> He loved the fact the Margaret Kochamma didn't cling to him. That she was uncertain about her feelings for him.... He as grateful to her for not wanting to look after him. For not offering to tide his room.... He grew to depend on Margaret Kochamma for not depending on him. He adored her of not adoring him.[4]

A year after their ill time marriage Margaret Kochamma was pregnant and found in Joe, a biologist what Chacko was not, 'Steady, solvent thin.' She asked for divorce and Chacko left London to return to Ayemenem a broken man.

Human nature carries within its endless boundaries, wisps of madness consequent of in these high passions, that break the limits and escape now and then. Ammu learnt from Mammachi the steak of madness ran in their family.

In Chacko's opinion occurrence of frequent insanity among Syrian Christians was direct result of the practice of inbreeding. Ammu worried on all these accounts, bordering on the edge of sanity and madness as she was forced to withhold the passions she felt for Velutha.

> Would future generations say, "There was Ammu—Ammu Ipe, married a Bengali went quite mad died young. In a cheap lodge somewhere."[5]

Her mercurial moods swings made people a bit wary of her. They left alone thinking a woman who is already damned and has little to lose could very well be dangerous. So they let her be. She talked to on one and sat listening to the songs from her transistor, smoked endless cigarettes and had midnight swims.

Pappachi's behaviour too, borders on insanity. He acted as a psychic, a maniac who took delight in tormenting and bullying those who were dependent on him. His disdaining attitude towards his family, beatings and viciously cunning action were far from being normal. The day Chacko prevents him from beating Mammachi he crushed his favourite rocking chair to pieces. The ways he shreds Ammu's gumboots, also point the same thing.

> When the last strip of rubbed had ripped to the floor, her father looked at her with cold, flat eyes, and rocked and rocked and rocked.[6]

Chacko, too lives with his 'invisible companion' and 'insanely friendly smile' that so endears him to Margaret Kochamma. He often speaks in his 'Reading Aloud Voice'.

> He didn't care whether anyone was listening to him or not. And if they were, he didn't care whether or not they understood what he was saying. Ammu called them his Oxford moods.[7]

Esthappen, too is considered quite mad by other people, except Rahel, when he starts doing household chores instead of going to college, when he stops talking altogether and walks incessantly on roads.

Rahel's waywardness and lack of ambition make people drift away from her. In New York, she draws comfort sitting by a mad woman in the train.

> Memory was that woman on the brain. Insane in the way she sifted through dark things in a closet and emerged with the most unlikely ones,—a fleeting look of feeling.[8]

Kuttappen, Velutha's paralyzed elder brother is so dejected lying all day in one corner of his hut, that he is ready to trade in his sanity in return for legs,

> Insanity hovered close at hard, like an eager waiter at an expensive restaurant (lighting cigarettes, 'refilling glasses). Kuttappen thought with envy of mad men who could walk. He had no doubts about the equity of the deal; his sanity, for serviceable legs.[9]

Another aspect of human nature, Roy chooses to bring to focus the inherent cruelty in human nature through her tragic tale. The conflict in the book in largely initiated by this barbarous cruelty in man.

Pappachi's cruelty is cold, cunning and calculative, designed to ferment and humiliate his family. He had in him the sadness of an insufficiently renowned entomologist who wanted to hurl insults at the world around him, wanting others to suffer with him. Similar is the case with Baby Kochamma, his heart felt hopes of love are thwarted and smashed so she in turn, feared and despised the intimacy of twins, and tries to destroy Ammu.

The twins are introduced to this motivation in human nature when they watch the policeman destroying Velutha without caprice and without anger.

> The sober, steady brutality, the economy of it all.... History's henchmen. Impelled by feelings that were primal yet paradoxically wholly impersonal feelings of contempt born of inchoate, unacknowledged fear civilization's fear to nature, men's fear of women, power's fear of powerlessness, man's subliminal urge to destroy what he could neither subdue nor defy...what

> Esthappen and Rahel witnessed that morning...was a clinical demonstration of human nature's pursuit of ascendancy. Structure order complete monopoly.... They were not arresting a man they were exorcizing fear.... They were merely inoculating a community against outbreak.[10]

The God of Small Things is a tragedy of battered hopes and crushed desires. Baby Kochamma's thwarted dreams of love, ferment her heart into vinegar, she in turn, tries to do the same to Ammu. Comrade Pillai's high hopes of entering prominent political circles make him betray Velutha sending him to his own annihilation. Chacko's hopes of regaining his lost family is brutally damaged turning him into a monster, breaking bedroom doors throwing Ammu to her, road of death. Inspector Thomas hopes of making headlines in the newspapers praising police efficiency make him act impulsively. Pappachi's hopes of fame, for his discovery of a new species of live peacefully and won't let other live, too Estha and Rahel are 'twin midwives of Ammu's dream', leaving space for Velutha to walk in, instead of their father. Their hopes of a happy complete family are shattered as they watch 'History in live performance' and learn about 'the ways of breaking man'.

Like D.H. Lawrence's revolutionary work *Lady Chatterley's Lover*, Roy has voiced sexual sentiments of many people. In the depiction of the illicit love-affair between Ammu and Velutha, Roy touches the most boundaries of sensual, intense breath taking, aching goose, bumpy surrender to the desires of flesh. She zooms in closely to capture individual moments and sketch a highly detailed world which springs to life. Here is a lust and very sensuous environment, with an anthropomorphized backdrop and pacing to match real life.

> Biology designed the dance. Terror timed it. Dictated the rhythm with their bodies answered each other as though they knew already that for each tremor of pleasure of pain. As though they knew that how far they would be measured against how far they would be taken. So they held back tormented each other.... It only raised the

> stakes. It only cost them more. Because it smoothed the wrinkles, the fumble and rush of unfamiliar love and roused them to fever pitch.[11]

There is also a fairly disgusting bit of child abuse, Estha's revolting experience with the Orangedrink Lemondrink man at the Abhilash Talkies.

> His hand closed tighter over Estha's light and sweaty, And faster still.
>
> Fast faster fest
>
> Never let it rest
>
> Until the fast is faster
>
> And the faster's fest.[12]

There are indirect references to homosexuality, when she tells us the story of Kari Saipu, the English man who had "gone native". He shot himself through the head when one of his young lover boy was ripped apart from him.

Mr. Hollick is presented as a lusty tea estate manager who has bequeathed the estate with several light skinned ragged children born of the tea-pickers whom he fancied. His fascination for Ammu accelerates the process of Ammu's divorce from her husband.

Chacko is a Marxist with "feudal libido", "a case of a spoiled prince ling playing comrade! Comrade! An Oxford avatar of the old Zamindar mentality."

There is also the little noticed love-making of the twins, in the sequal, 23 years on. The incest scene is rendered quite unthinkingly.

> There is very little that anyone could say to be clarified what happened next. Nothing that (in Mammachi's book) would separate sex from love of needs from feelings...only that they held each other close, long after it was over. Only that what they shared that night was not happiness but hideous grief.[13]

Thus, Arundhati Roy succeeds to depict the various images of human nature throughout her novel, *The God of Small Things*, all sections of the novel devoted to reflections of secret passion and frustration, fears and forbodings, dream and reality.

NOTES

1. Arundhathi Roy, *The God of Small Things* (New Delhi: India Ink Pvt. Ltd., 1997), 118.
2. *Ibid.*, 176.
3. *Ibid.*, 24.
4. *Ibid.*, 246.
5. *Ibid.*, 223.
6. *Ibid.*, 181.
7. *Ibid.*, 54.
8. *Ibid.*, 72.
9. *Ibid.*, 207.
10. *Ibid.*, 308-09.
11. *Ibid.*, 335.
12. *Ibid.*, 104.
13. *Ibid.*, 328.

12

Segregational Trait and Social Exclusion in *The God of Small Things*

R.P. Pradhan

Arundhati Roy's novel *The God of Small Things* reveals an ongoing conflict between the 'God of big things' and the 'God of small things'. The novelist expresses it through the symbols of 'laltain' and 'mombatti'. The former refers to the rich who are well fed and well protected. The latter points to the poor and the downtrodden who are great sufferers. Pappachi, Baby Kochamma, Mammachi, Chacko, Comrade Pillai and the inspector Thomas Mathew represent the higher section of society while Ammu, Velutha, Rahel and Estha are associated with the lower and the depressed class.

The conflict is caused by social stratification in which a section of society is segregated for being untouchable. The conflict goes on between the conventional and the non-conventional, between the individual and the society. The conventional follow primitive ways of life and insist on preserving the old order. The non-conventional like Velutha are rebellious and want to break orthodoxical norms of society. The novelist seems to arouse the sympathy of the reader for the persons like Ammu and Velutha who bear all sorts of social tyranny and tortures and in the end pay the penalty of their lives.

Ammu is the victim of male chauvinism and social discrimination. She is regarded as a weaker sex and hence inferior to man in all respects. Her alcoholic husband reduces her to the level of a toy and urges her to go to his boss Mr. Hollick for gratifying his sexual lust so that his job might be secure. Ammu cannot bear such humiliation and hits her husband in a mad frenzy and leaves the place with her two kids. She is deserted by her husband and she comes back to her Ayemenem House. She is given stepmotherly treatment in her own home. Her father does not believe "that an English, any Englishman, would covet another man's wife".[1] Baby Kochamma also disliked the twins, "for she considered them doomed, fatherless waifs. Worse still, they were Half-Hindu Hybrids whom no self-respecting Syrian Christian would ever marry" (45). She thought that they were living on sufferance in the Ayemenem house which was their maternal grandmother's house "Where they really had no right to be" (45). Baby Kochamma resented Ammu and held the view that "a married daughter had no position in her parents' home" (45). Again, a divorced daughter, according to Baby Kochamma, had no position anywhere at all.

The attitude of Chacko towards his sister Ammu was also hostile. He asserted his authority in the family and disregarded his sister thinking that she had no claim to the property of the family. He said to her, "What's yours is mine and what's mine is also mine" (47). Chacko had also been estranged from his wife but he was enjoying all the legacy of the family. He claimed to be the legal inheritor of the wealth of the family. When he flirted with low women, he was encouraged by Pappachi in the name of man's needs but Ammu was condemned when she sought love with an untouchable. Such love was cursed as forbidden class-caste love.

Ammu's tragedy reaches its climax when she indulges in love affairs with Velutha. He was a Paravans or an untouchable. Pappachi like other persons would not allow Paravans into the house. "They were not allowed to touch anything that Touchables touched" (73). Mammachi told Estha and Rahel that "She could remember a time, in her girlhood, when Paravans were expected to crawl backwards with a broom, sweeping away their footprints so that Brahmins or Syrian Christians would not defile themselves by accidentally stepping into a Paravan's footprint" (74). One day Velutha's father saw Ammu and his son together in a compromising position. He informed Baby Kochamma about it. Ammu was locked up in a room and was beaten up mercilessly. Her distant relations came to see her and expressed their sympathy but Ammu knew it full well that they were mocking at her. The novelist shows how Baby Kochamma thought that Ammu "had defiled generations of breeding and brought the family to its knees. For generations to come, for ever now, people would point at them at weddings and funerals. At baptisms and birthday parties. They'd nudge and whisper. It was all finished now" (258).

When Ammu went to see Velutha and make a statement at the police station, she was badly insulted by the inspector Thomas Mathew. He told her that it was a little too late for all this. He further stared at Ammu's breasts and spoke, "The police knew all they needed to know and that the Kottayam Police did not take statements from veshyas or their illegitimate children" (8). Again, "he tapped her breasts with his baton. Gently. Tap, tap. As though he was choosing mangoes from a basket" (8). Ammu left the place with her children. She started crying. It was the first time the children had seen their mother cry. "She was not sobbing. Her face was set like stone but the tears welled up in her eyes and ran down her rigid cheeks. It made the twins sick with fear" (8).

The end of this unfortunate woman was all the more tragic. She woke up at night "to escape from a familiar, recurrent dream in which policemen approached her with snicking scissors, wanting to hack off her hair. They did that in Kottayam to prostitutes whom they'd caught in the bazaar-branded them so that everybody would know them for what they were. Veshyas" (161). Ammu had noticed such scenes in the market where women appeared with vacant eyes and forcibly shaved heads. It was in the apprehension of such nightmare that she breathed her last all alone with no Estha to lie at the back of her and talk to her. She was thirty-one, she was found dead in the morning by a sweeper who came to clean the room in the Bharat Lodge in Allepey where she had gone for a job.

The story of Velutha's life is no less tragic. He has been called "the God of loss" by the writer. He has been elevated to the state of a tragic hero. He is loved dearly by Rahel, Estha and Ammu. He is a master carpenter and a talented craftsman. He suffers because of his being an untouchable. He is deemed to be a trespasser into a touchable woman's world. His love with Ammu is regarded as something sinful and illicit. Due to his relationship with Ammu he is socially discarded and physically tortured. He is victim of social ostracism. He is forced into remaining silent.

'Velutha' in Malyalam means 'Whiteness' that stands for purity. Velutha is pure in his heart but his complexion is black and he comes of a low birth. With the result he suffers social inferiority and is socially segregated. Velutha is a rebel, he has joined the communist movement in Kerala. He takes part in the activities of the communist parties. However, his 'touchable' fellow workers in the factory make discrimination and neglect him. Velutha has worked day and night for Comrade Pillai. He goes to him for help but Pillai refuses to help him. The Police administration is very cruel to him. Comrade Pillai goes to the Police Station and totally denies the role of Velutha as his party worker. He does it in order to please the touchables. If he had used his political power, Velutha would have been saved. Inspector Thomas Mathew helps Baby Kochamma to fabricate a case against Velutha in the alleged abduction of the two children and in the death of Sophie. Velutha is falsely charged for the death of Sophie which is caused by drowning in the river. He becomes a victim to the brutality of 'touchable' policemen. He is innocent but he is beaten to the verge of death by the merciless policemen who bear resentment against him for keeping illicit relationship with Ammu. Velutha dies in the police custody. His death is described by the novelist in a pathetic manner:

> Blood spilled from his skull like a secret. His face was swollen and his head looked like a pumpkin, too large and heavy for the slender stem it grew from. A pumpkin with a monstrous upside-down smile. Police boots stepped back from the rim of a pool of urine spreading from him, the bright, bare electric bulb reflected in it. (320)

The portrayal of Velutha in the novel shows how the untouchables are believed to be worse than animals. On the other hand, Ammu is not an untouchable yet she is humiliated by her father, betrayed by her husband, ill-treated by Baby Kochamma, rendered destitute by her brother and insulted and crushed by the police.

Ammu's daughter Rahel and the son Estha are also included in the "small things" of the novel and hence they are equal sufferers with a little difference. Rahel is deserted by the father and is separated from the mother who dies young. She is neglected by her maternal uncle, grandmother and grandaunt. She bears her sufferings in a courageous manner. Their ill-treatment has made her independent resulting in a "release of the spirit". Rahel was only seven when her mother died. She carried in her mind the sufferings of her mother who had been ill-treated by her husband and also by men and women in her home. She was often haunted by the sad memory and it left its ugly impact on her married-life. Her husband was exasperated because he could not comprehend the meaning of the strange look of Rahel from time to time. The novelist describes the mental state of Rahel with particular reference to her husband:

> He was exasperated because he did not know what that look meant. He put it somewhere between indifference and despair. He did not know that in some places, like the country that Rahel came from, various kinds of despair competed for primacy. (19)

Their marriage was soon broken. After divorce Rahel worked at an Indian restaurant as waitress in New York. Later on she came back to Ayemenem House where she was an unwanted figure as before.

Estha is also a forlorn and desolate character. He suffers more than his sister. It is because he is submissive and not assertive like her. His childhood is also unhappy. He is a neglected figure like his mother and sister at the Ayemenem House. At the funeral of Sophie Mol all the three, the mother and the twins are made to stand separately. They are socially segregated and isolated. Estha and Rahel come to know through their grandaunt that they have a mixed parentage both on the religious and the ethnic grounds. Their father was Hindu and their mother was a Syrian Christian, again their father was a Bengali and mother was a Keralite. Besides, they are children of a divorced woman who has no right of property in her parental home. Baby Kochamma disliked them. The maternal uncle Chacko tells the children that Ammu has no right in his family. On another occasion Chacko tells Ammu that the children are not his responsibilities. The maidservant Kochu Maria also reminds Estha of his position in the house. She said to him that she would complain to Mammachi:

> Tell your mother to take you to your father's house. There you can break as many beds as you like. These are not your beds. This is not your house. (83)

Estha was taken to the Kottayam police station by Baby Kochamma and was persuaded to identify Velutha as the man responsible for kidnapping and murder. The accusation was false and ill-founded yet Estha had to concede to the proposal of Baby Kochamma because he thought that this was the only way to save his mother. Baby Kochamma said to him, "Do you want to save Ammu or shall we send her to jail?" (318). Estha suffers such type of humiliation. He has to make a statement against the man whom he loves as a father. Estha's torture is more mental than physical.

Estha was returned to his father much against his wishes. Anyhow he finished his school education without participating in group activities. His college education was retarded and he found himself engaged in a domestic work like sweeping, cooking and shopping. He led an isolated life and remained confined to his solitary life. By and by he stopped talking. He was returned to Ayemenem after twenty-three years by his father. He lost his speech. The loss of speech is attributed to his ill-treatment by Baby Kochamma, Kochu Maria, inspector Mathew and the soft drink man. He did not protest against his tormentors and so he could not open his mouth. Besides, his sense of shame and sin born out of the evil treatment of his mother is also responsible for his going into silence:

> That such an innocent child was subjected to the worst cruelty of the adults and his childhood was destroyed and his life ruined for no fault of his own, constitutes a major tragedy in the novel. Such wanton destruction of childhood is staggering to our imagination and pathetic to our heart.[2]

The novelist shows the plight of twins how they are scolded, abused and separated on the basis of class, caste and religion and such discrimination affects their growth and career. Roy further paints the miserable condition of wamen and seems to rid the society of discrimination based on caste and gender. She is the powerful voice for "small things".

NOTES

1. Arundhati Roy, *The God of Small Things*, New Delhi, IndiaInk Publishing Co. Pvt. Ltd., 1997, 42. (All citations from this novel refer to this text.)
2. Amitabh Roy, *The God of Small Things: A Novel of Social Commitment*, New Delhi, Atlantic Publishers and Distributors, 2005, 95-96.

13

Reverberations of the Diasporic: Kiran Desai's *The Inheritance of Loss*

Reena Mitra

Indian English literature, and particularly Indian English fiction, reflects plausibly and credibly, the new social, political and cultural challenges that have come to the fore in the recent past. The frontrunners of this relatively new bulk of fiction are mostly writers of the Indian diaspora who, being exposed to significant modern literary movements in the West, are able to provide a revitalized and fresh orientation to their works. Salman Rushdie's novels are a remarkable illustration of the works of the clan of diasporic writers of Indian origin who rivet our attention to new insights into the Indian social predicament by virtue of the content and mode of depiction in their narratives. For Rushdie, facts themselves have been of little interest as they have been repeatedly doled out to us by several novelists as well as historians. What is significant is how he has fantasized his depiction of historical reality. The proficient commingling of the magical with the real has lent Rushdie's representative work, *Midnight's Children*, a dimension that makes it characteristically the author's own for he has his typical way of brewing an inimitable blend of art and life. Kiran Desai, another such writer with the Man Booker Prize bagged for her novel, *The Inheritance of Loss* (2006), is now fervently and tenaciously being claimed as an Indian English writer of fiction. The fact that both her novels, *Hullabaloo in the Guava Orchard* and *The Inheritance of Loss* deal primarily with life in India validates her inclusion in the league of Indian English writers of fiction. Rushdie himself presents her as "welcome proof that India's encounter with the English language, far from proving abortive, continues to give birth to new children, endowed with lavish gifts".[1]

Most expatriate writers of the second generation of Indians abroad have an imprecise and nebulous comprehension of life as lived in contemporary India and are inclined to depict not the actual but what Salman Rushdie calls "imaginary homelands". What they portray most confidently is what they have seen from close quarters, i.e. the lives of Indian immigrants primarily in Great Britain and the United States of America. Kiran Desai, unlike this majority of writers living abroad delineates both life in India in the recent past and the life of Indian Americans, settled in the United States with a verisimilitude and a sureness of touch that is rare. In her endeavour to rewrite specific chunks of history and to reconstruct new narratives which underline the interactions of family, society and nation, she tries to bring alive the past as experiential reality. This past, whether conjured up in the context of a migrant who has moved from his own original place of residence to another locale in the same country or of one who has entered an altogether different country imposes on one the feelings of alienation and estrangement which ultimately lead to a sense of displacement and rootlessness and a consciousness of a loss of identity and of a sense of belonging. In *The Empire Writes Back*, Bill Ashcroft, Griffith and Tiffin, taking immigration itself to be an aspect of postcolonialism, say that "a major feature of post-colonial literature is the concern with placement and displacement".[2] Diasporic fiction, thus, is a study in homelessness in which the state of being an alien in the very society in which one lives has a deleterious effect and pulverizes one's sense of identity.

Kiran Desai's *The Inheritance of Loss* (2006), a work far more tenable in its presentation than her maiden work, *Hullabaloo in the Guava Orchard* (1998), analyzes with confident insight the distressful and torturous experiences of the non-Nepalese in Darjeeling, Kalimpong and other neighbouring areas in the hills, all of whom were unsparingly subjected to persecution and discriminated against by the Gorkha National Liberation Front that was persistent in its demand for Gorkhaland. The novel, also, at a parallel front, depicts the victimization of the Indians and nationals of other Third World countries in the capacity of expatriates trying hard to realize themselves and be assimilated by their country of adoption.

Victor Ramraj in his essay "Diasporas and Multiculturalism"[3] discriminates between immigrant writing which is more inclined towards contemporary experience in the host society and diasporic works which are liable to be more preoccupied with the idea of the forsaken or imagined homeland. In *The Inheritance of Loss*, Kiran Desai has skilfully blended immigrant and diasporic writing for on the one hand she depicts the problems confronted by immigrants like Biju in the United States and on the other, she delineates the heart-rending pangs of being away from one's homeland and being disfavoured for having permanently settled in a geographical area one does not belong to. Disaffection and embitterment are inherent aspects of the migrant situation in which the individual's identity is torn between the old and the new worlds of experience.

Kiran Desai, an established member of the Indian diaspora in the United States of America makes the best of the prevalent multiculturalism in her country of adoption by reliving in *The Inheritance of Loss* a significant chunk in the history of India when inordinate insurgency born of the Nepalese Movement during the 1980s perpetrated heinous crimes on the pretext that the community was being persecuted and tormented in Bengal. The Nepalese demanded statehood, a homeland in and around Darjeeling and Kalimpong. The GNLF men assaulted affluent Bengalis and people from other states who they believed had encroached upon their land. One such victim was the Gujarati judge, Jemubhai Patel, who had chosen to settle in Kalimpong after retirement. Born in pre-Independence colonial India,

Jemubhai had gone to England for advanced studies after which he had returned to India to serve under the British Government. He lived alone in his old bungalow, Cho Oyu in Kalimpong. His only companion here was his cook, who still, like his master, laboured largely under the impact of the colonial rule, and who, after he had lost five mango trees to his brother in a court case, left his village in Uttar Pradesh to work for Jemubhai, who is still his employer. The only person who joined Jemubhai later in Cho Oyu was his granddaughter, Sai, who arrived in Kalimpong after the untimely death of her parents. But there was no end to her misery either, for Gyan, the young Nepalese Mathematics tutor who she had fallen in love with, could not remain fully committed to her when he had to choose between her and his allegiance to his native place, Kalimpong.

The other aspect of the immigrant experience in the book is that of Biju, the only son of the cook who had migrated to the United States in the hope of a "better life". The cook, enamoured of the prospect of a "legal employment in the U.S.A." had manipulated some counterfeit recommendations for his son which had finally helped Biju in being selected at the interview. Overjoyed at this success, the cook started bracketing himself with Mrs. Sen whose daughter was also in America. Ironically, however, he was totally unaware of the pressing circumstances under which his son worked in the U.S. to survive there.

Mrs. Sen considered herself fortunate in having a daughter working in America and never failed to take a dig at her neighbour, Lola, whose daughter worked in England as a BBC newsreader. The cook, however, seemed the most contented of the lot at his son's apparent success for he could never comprehend the fact that though his son and many others like him had acquired a tourist visa to go to America, they were treated as illegal immigrants after the expiry of the visa and were under stress from all sides. They could neither live respectively as immigrants nor return to their country to be jeered at. Each one including Biju, embroiled in this typical predicament had no standing of his own and strove to avoid being discovered as an illegal immigrant who had stayed on longer than permitted by law. Biju very soon realized that people from the Third World countries were engaged in a losing battle for existence. The severity of the cold in the country added to his woes.

Alienation, estrangement, humiliation and bone-chilling frost, all contributed to the sense of utter loneliness Biju experienced in America. He soon realized with desperation the essential gulf that existed between the legal and the illegal immigrants and knew that unless his immigration was given a legal sanction, he would be unable to go back home to his native land and would continue to be exploited by restaurant owners like Harish-Harry. Biju, however, was not alone in his misery abroad for there were many in a similar predicament:

> ...it WAS so hard and YET there were so many here. It was terribly, terribly hard. Millions risked death, were humiliated, hated, lost their families—YET there were so many here.[4]

The novel thus underscores the collapse of the 'American dream' of the poor of the Third World countries like India. These people suffering deprivation are lured by the hope of better prospects abroad but the 'exile'[5] that they thrust upon themselves to attain a better living, ironically compels them to live in disgrace and wretchedness. The following statement of Santwana Haldar corroborates this view:

> Kiran Desai highlights that the process of globalization has its loopholes, that the cartographical binaries have collapsed only for a blessed few. The poor people of the third world countries who dream of a better future and are lured by the affluence of the American society have no place in the world of their dream. They are compelled to suffer in their homeland and the exile they opt for only increases their suffering.[6]

In *The Inheritance of Loss*, then, Kiran Desai perceptively depicts the lives of the entire gamut of Indian immigrants in the U.S.A.—the affluent and the successful as well as the poor and the hunted and has demonstrated effectively the erosion of identity in the lives of woe begone people. The constant tension prevailing in the mind of immigrant between the two socio-cultural environments and between the feelings of rootlessness and nostalgia and the desire to assimilate the new way of life leaves him with a lacerated self trying to piece it together. Bharati Mukherjee unerringly observes that all such immigrants are seen "...surrendering little bits of self every year, clutching the souvenirs of an ever retreating past, you'll never belong anywhere".[7]

NOTES

1. Salman Rushdie, "Introduction", *The Vintage Book of Indian Writing: 1947-1977*, eds. Salman Rushdie and Elizabeth West (London: Vintage, 1997), ix-xxii.
2. Bill Ashcroft, Griffith and Tiffin, *The Empire Writes Back: Theory and Practice in Post-colonial Literature* (London: Routledge, 1989), 8.
3. Victor Ramraj, "Diasporas and Multiculturalism", *An Introduction to Post-colonial Theory*, eds. Childs Peter and Patrick Williams (Europe: Prentice Hall, 1997).
4. Kiran Desai, *The Inheritance of Loss* (London: Penguin, 2006), 189.
5. Edward said in "*Reflections on Exile" and Other Literary and Cultural Essays* (Penguin, 2001) observed that "our age is indeed the age of the refugee, the displaced person, mass immigration (174). Thus 'exile' in the present times is not always banishment. It is often a choice exercised in the hope of better prospects in life.
6. Santwana Haldar, "Exile in Kiran Desai's *The Inheritance of Loss*", *The Atlantic Literary Review*, April-June, 2007, Vol. 8, No. 2: 87.
7. Bharati Mukherjee, "Introduction", *Darkness* (New Delhi: Penguin Books, 1985, rpt. 1990), 2.

14

Losing the Inheritance: An Ecocritical Reading of *The Inheritance of Loss*

Sarvajit Mukherji

Recently, I read *The Inheritance of Loss* again. If a book can be judged by its cover, the familiar oxford blue etched with stylized clouds and delicate white herons seemed to indicate a novel where nature would predominate, seeing that human figures were conspicuous by their absence. Yet the blurbs trumpeted those literary battle cries with which we are all too familiar—postcolonial, dispossessed, exile, immigrant! Where in this fragmented world celebrated so triumphantly by the blurbs was space for that celestial blue, the lightening torn lowering clouds, the fluttering white herons, of the cover? So I decided to read *The Inheritance of Loss* again, but this time as though nature mattered, that eclipsing face of nature that we ignore as we fight to reconstruct the world in linguistic and/or cultural terms.

My paper grows around three pivotal events of the novel—the opening, when the GNLF guerillas invade Cho Oyu, Sai's visit to Bong Busti and the encroachment by the Gorkha settlers on the compound of Mon Ami, Lola and Noni's cottage.

The novel opens with a superb evocation of landscape:

> All day, the colours had been those of dusk, mist moving like a water creature across the great flanks of mountains possessed of ocean shadows and depths. Briefly visible above the vapour, Kanchenjunga was a peak whittled out of ice, gathering the last of the light, a plume of snow blown high by the storms at its summit. (*The Inheritance of Loss*, 1)

The merging of land and sea, of mist and mountain, of day and dusk, of the paradoxically invisible but palpable storm and mist, the fiery light that metamorphoses the icy peak of the Kanchenjunga into a plume of fire, these oppositions so gloriously evoked reveal the simultaneity of nature. It is only in nature that oppositions like the ones above can exist harmoniously. Water and land, sky and earth, fire and ice exist not in hegemonic hierarchies, nor in binary oppositions, but as existence, simultaneous, harmonious.

Cho Oyu, the house that Sai and her grandfather live in has become assimilated into the ridge on which it is built.

> The forest was old and thick at the edge of the lawn; The bamboo thickets rose thirty feet into the gloom. The trees were moss-slung giants, bunioned and Misshapen, tentacled with roots of orchids. (2)

The house has become part of the landscape, moss and ferns grow on the roof, and it is home not only to Justice Desai, Sai and the cook, but to scorpions which nest and breed in the woodpile and a pair of snakes. It is also subject to natural forces of decay—in the dark, when the household sounds are hushed, one can hear the termites gradually sawing down the house into dust. Cho Oyu is thus part of the cycles of nature and not something either opposed or resistant to it. It has overcome the culture/nature binary.

In his masterly introduction to ecocriticsm, Peter Barry divided the outdoor environment into a series of adjoining and overlapping areas, that move gradually from nature to culture. These are:

(i) the wilderness, e.g. deserts, oceans, uninhabited continents.
(ii) the scenic sublime, e.g. forests, lakes, mountains, cliffs, waterfalls.
(iii) the countryside—hills, fields, woods.
(iv) the domestic picturesque—parks, gardens, lanes. (*Beginning Theory*, 242)

"It is clear that we move from pretty well 'pure nature' in the first to what is predominantly culture in the fourth" (242). But Cho Oyu defies these clear categories. The forest and the garden merge and then impinge on and appropriate the house itself. Even though its walls made of local stone are several feet thick, they cannot shut out the mist, the cold and the damp that is part of the environment of Kalimpong. Cocooned within is Sai, a Lucy-like nature's child. But Lucy died on the threshold of adolescence, and the link with nature that Wordsworth celebrated remained presumably unbroken. Sai's world is shattered by the awakening of the sexual instinct, ignited by the presence of Gyan.

Gyan, the handsome, young Nepali tutor is a threat to Sai's world in more ways than one. Initially mesmerized by Sai, and her anglicized, upper middle-class ethos, Gyan soon turns against Sai for these very attributes. She now represents all that the GNLF is fighting against—she is an 'outsider', does not speak Nepali and belongs to the class that succeeded the British in positions of power. Gyan betrays Sai by not only breaking their relationship, but by sending the GNLF boys to loot Cho Oyu of its meager provisions, shored up against repeated *bandhs* and *hartals*, and most importantly the judges guns. But that is not a path I want to follow, for it leads to postcolonial or Marxist analyses of the text, and my destination is ecocriticism. I want to follow Sai, heartbroken by Gyan's desertion and still unaware of his betrayal, to Bong Busti where Gyan lives.

Built on a hillside overlooking the Relli river, Bong Busti lies 'in a poor part of Kalimpong'. Its neighbourhood is characterized by a 'capillary web of paths' connecting huts, shacks and outhouses. The confusion on the ground is repeated by the one above where "crows' nests of electrical wiring [hang] from the corner of the structure". Water is scarce and somehow conducted to the busti by worm like tubes and bamboo cleaved in half. The homes are cramped and wet, the open drain, whose smell permeates the place, empties into a roughly fenced bit of land. But it is the chicken that inhabit this patch that catch Sai's attention, "a grotesque bunch, rape and violence being enacted, hens being hammered and pecked as they screamed and flapped, attempting to escape from the rapist rooster". This is, as Desai pithily sums it up "—modernity proffered in its meanest form, brand new one day, in ruin the next". The people who live here have lost the art of harmoniously coexisting with nature as their ancestors must have surely done. They have purchased into a model of development that has taken away their traditional way of life and replaced it with one where the culture/nature divide is complete. The category that Bong busti occupies is one that Barry did not visualize—it is a category totally devoid of nature. Nature here is represented by the chicken, domesticated and preserved only because of economic benefit. It is only slightly better than Biju's basement existence in Manhattan, where he is driven underground like vermin and always on the run from immigration authorities—a totally urban world, a world from which Nature has been ruthlessly banished.

This seemingly innocuous picture of Bong Busti in fact encapsulates an important problem of ecocritcism. How far is it right to deny any group the benefits of 'development' as they see it just because their movement into so-called modernity and development harms the environment? The residents of Bong Busti are on "the far edge of the middle class—just to the edge, only just, holding on desperately...". They have stripped their surroundings of all natural resources. There is no sign of forest or orchard here, it has all been turned to ashes, fuelling the thick, choking smoke that smothers the place in the evening. Nature and conservation are luxuries that they can least afford. And it is here and in places like this that the backlash to the privileged upper middle class, represented by Sai and her

National Geographic, by Lola and Noni and their peach trees and sweet-peas and Father Booty and his dream of making Kalimpong the Swiss cheese capital of India, is potently brewed.

Lola and Noni, sisters who live in the cottage Mon Ami tending to their vegetable patch, sweet peas and peach trees, recognize the writing on the wall the day Justice Desai's home is ransacked by the GNLF boys. And soon enough, it was their turn as the GNLF cadres invade Mon Ami, taking shelter for the night and leaving in the morning laden with loot. There is worse to follow.

> ...the sisters woke one morning to find that, under the cover of night, a hut had come up like a mushroom on a newly cut gash at the bottom of the Mon Ami vegetable patch. (240)

And still worse.

> The huts had sprung up overnight were being populated. By women, men, children, pigs, goats, dogs, chickens cats and cows. In a year, Lola could forsee, they would no longer be made of mud and bamboo but concrete and tiles. (244)

The fruit trees are cut down and the bamboos. Gradually, Mon Ami comes to occupy the periphery of a bustling busti, stripped of its fruit trees, its vegetable patch and its bamboo. The plot of land that sustained only two individuals, is now required to support a host of people, who may not replenish what they consume. What is the answer to this conundrum? The answer eludes even the heads of states as they sit in conclave in Kyoto or in Cancun. Should those who joined the race for modernity late, be denied those benefits which the developed nations have reaped and continue to reap while the underdeveloped nations shrilly demand their share of the pie?

To whom does the land belong? To those who possess surveyors plans and property documents? To those who covet it and grab it with impunity? Or does it belong only to itself, mirroring the changing seasons, subtly reflecting the time of the day, unchanging and enduring within the flux of time? To whom does the Kanchenjunga belong—that plume of fiery ice that the storms seem to have tossed above the swirling mist with which the novel opens? Who owns those five peaks of the Kanchenjunga, golden with luminous light, with which the novel closes? Such questions need pondering, but what is amply clear is that human activity does have the potential of irreparably damaging the natural world. What price the carving out of another new state, if the mode of 'development' imposed on it would denude it of those forests and pastures, sully the bounding Teesta and strip the glorious Kanchenjunga of its mantle of snow and ice? As the debased urban gradually creeps up and engulfs the threatened natural, these questions need to be asked. *The Inheritance of Loss* poses the question. It is time that we started thinking of an answer.

WORKS CITED

Barry, Peter. *Beginning Theory*. New Delhi: Viva, 2010.

Desai, Kiran. *The Inheritance of Loss*. New Delhi: Viking, 2006.

15

Panna Lal's Tryst with Destiny in *The Inheritance of Loss*

Soumen Mukherjee

Kiran Desai's Booker-winning novel *The Inheritance of Loss*, portrays the suffering of the poor and the powerless by holding up a steadfast mirror to their lives. A careful observer of behaviour, with a fine eye for revealing details, Desai brings her narratives and characters to life. Without making moral judgments about her characters, creating neither positive nor negative individuals, but just ordinary people leading the best lives they can, Desai leads the reader into the inner lives of the helpless people.

The character of the cook, Panna Lal, who works in the household of the judge, is that of a sufferer, who is a typical representative of the economically marginalized class in India. Throughout the novel he is referred to as 'the cook', except once, when his master, the judge calls him by his name. The novelist has very realistically represented him as a type of the cooking class. He has no identity of his own, except by his profession. The cook is the sole domestic—housekeeper, chef, task boy, and servant. Ironic it may sound, but it is a reality, that he succeeds to garner the sympathy from everyone else, but his own master. Although he has spent a lifetime serving the judge, the cook is never able to carve out a niche in the heartless man's heart. The more he has served him with sincerity, loyalty and diligence, the more he has fallen out of the judge's confidence.

The cook stays in the 'out-house' of Cho-Oyu, his master's anglophile bungalow, situated in the lap of the Himalayan mountain of Kalimpong in West Bengal. The so-called 'out-house' is a small tarnished hut made with brick, clay and mud. The bungalow in which the judge, Sai and the cook live together, is considered by the Nepalese boys who invade it to be a place of "intense solitude" (7). The relationship between the cook and his master, the arrogant judge resembles the relationship between the powerful and powerless in India. Though they had shared a number of years together under the same roof and cover, yet there is a total lack of understanding and compassion between the two. Nevertheless, the cook accepts his slavish condition, and all the insults heaped upon him, by his master, as a mere destiny. Actually, in divine culture, it is believed that a person's fate is determined by heaven, and that a person needs to respect heaven and accept his or her own fate. Only if a person does good deeds and accumulates virtue, will he or she be rewarded with a good life.

We get a glimpse of the cook's character, in the very beginning of the novel, when one day, their house is broken into by young men from the Gorkha National Liberation Front, an actual political party that seeks to empower West Bengal's ethnic Nepalese, and once led a separatist uprising. The family's somber habit of reading the National Geographic and eating high tea is interrupted by this sudden invasion. The intruders threaten and humiliate the family and steal the judge's rusty guns and paltry liquor supply. Scared to even face the young boys, the timid cook took shelter under the dining table, in order to save himself, from the wrath of the invaders. He comprehended the hard reality, that as a servant, he had no individuality of his own, and it was useless for him to fight against the armed militants. The bemused boys yanked him out of the alcove and started humiliating him. Age-old slavishness prompted the cook to ask for mercy, which intensified the hesitant boys to take control of the situation and demean both him as well as his master:

> The cook was hiding under the dining table and they dragged him out.
>
> "Ai aaa, ai aaa", he joined his palms together begging them, "please, I'm a poor man, please". He held up his arms and cringed as if from an expected blow.
>
> "He hasn't done anything, leave him," said Sai, hating to see him humiliated, hating even more to see that the only path open to him was to humiliate him further. "Please living only to see my son please don't kill me please I'm a poor man spare me."

His lives had been honed over centuries, passed from through generations for poor people needed certain lines, the script was always the same, and they had no option, but to beg for money. The cook knew instinctively how to cry. These familiar lines allowed tне boys to ease still further into their role, which he had handled to them like a gift. "Who wants to kill you?" they said to the cook. "We're just hungry, that's all. Here your sahib will help you. Go on..." (5-6).

Already deprived of money, the cook got deprived of his wife at a crucial juncture of his life, when his only son Biju was just five. It was mere destiny, that the cook's wife died an unnatural death—leaving away little Biju, under the care of her poor Father. The poor cook's tryst with his destiny, began quite early, than it was actually anticipated; "it was just fate in the way fate has of providing the destitute with a greater quota of accidents for which nobody can be blamed" (14).

However, the judge is insensitive to the mishap as well as the hardships that his cook's life is plagued with. Whenever the poor cook prays for an increase in salary, he is rebuked in harsh words. Gradually, the poor servant gets accustomed to the non-chalant attitude of his master and tolerates every kind of disgrace, in the name of destiny. In fact, he looks after the household work as a devoted wife looks after her domestic chores in typical Indian middle-class families, and the judge's attitude towards the cook is like an imposing father-in-law, completely devoid of any warmth or feeling:

> The cook broke into a loud lament: "Humara kya hoga, hai hai, humara kya hoga", he let his voice fly. "Hai, hai, what will become of us?"
>
> "Shut up", said the judge and thought, these damn servants born brought up to scream. (8)

As a matter of fact, in *The Inheritance of Loss* Desai speaks about the plight of the unorganized domestic workers of India, by portraying the character of the cook. He is treated badly by the judge only because he is an economically marginalized person. So, his devotion to his master goes unnoticed and unrewarded. At par with the general mentality of the rich towards the poor, the self-conceited judge is not ready to understand the cook's poverty and helplessness. His opinion about the poor is like a typical representative of the affluent society:

> Give these people a bit and one could find oneself supporting the whole family forever after, a constantly multiplying family, no doubt, because they might have no food, the husband might be blind and with broken legs, and the woman might be anemic and bent, but they'd still pop out an infant every nine months. If you let such people get an inch, they'd take everything you had. (264)

In India, the poor is generally, looked down upon and referred with contempt for all that they do. In the case of the cook also, there is no exception. All that he gets in lieu of his twenty-four hours of continuous service is the meager salary that he spends on himself and his son Biju. Nonetheless, he performs all kinds of domestic chores including preparing and serving tea and food to his master, polishing of shoes, washing and ironing of clothes, cleaning of utensils, taking care of the dog, etc. In spite of doing all these things earnestly and attentively, he is often abused and even sometimes physically tortured by the judge. In fact, "It was his habit to be a master and the cook to be a servant" (209).

India has gone through different changes through thousands of years, but one thing which has never changed is the belief in spirits and spiritualism. From time incarnate, right from the time of Lord Rama, when it is believed that there was only truth which existed on the Indian soil to this time of modern sciences, the existence of ghosts and demons is still lasting. These are many and varied. Like people the world over, most Indians are highly superstitious, and they believe in the existence of paranormal forces.[1] Many aspects of their life are linked to some superstitious belief and some of these are even mentioned in religious literature. It is very easy to terrorize anyone in India in the name of ghosts and superstitions, especially if they are illiterate or less educated.

The cook in *The Inheritance* is not only poor, but he is also less educated. The people of the cook's ancestral village tell him that his wife's ghost is threatening to take Biju with her. The village priest asks him to sacrifice a chicken to appease the agitated soul. The innocent cook believes in their dictum, as is ready to undergo any adversity for the sake of his only son. It is this ardent desire to see his only son, Biju, successful and comfortable in life, that the cook decides to send him to America, the 'land of plenty'. When he sees an advertisement of conscription for cooks in his 'dream country', he tries his best to take the benefit of this 'golden' opportunity. He arranges several fake recommendations for his son's selection. Along with a medical certificate, he deposits his hard-earned eight thousand rupees as a processing fee and the cost of training camp. His efforts prove futile as the recruiting company proves to be a forged one.

Still, a firm believer of fate, Panna Lal is not dejected and takes a second chance and luckily this time, Biju is successful in going to America. The cook is on the moon, when his son is selected as a waiter in an American restaurant. To whosoever he meets after getting the news of his son's selection he reveals his happiness and boastfully says, "My son works for the Americans" (14). Since he has been humiliated by the judge throughout his life, the cook and his son have greater faith in foreigners than in Indians. In fact, since his master is not a 'white man', the cook is never contended to work under him, but he has his own compulsions:

> The cook had been disappointed to be working for Jemubhai. A severe comedown, he thought, from his father, who had served white men only.

The ICS was becoming Indianized and they did not like it, some of these old servants, but what could you do? He would even had a rival for the position, a man who appeared with tattered recommendations inherited from his father and grandfather to indicate a lineage of honesty and good service (63).

Here, it would be improper for us to believe, that the cook is a brainless person. Since he gets a very meager salary, which has hardly been ever revised by his master, he gets involved in the business of selling "Chhang", a country-made intoxicant, which procure considerable profits in the mountains. Gradually, he becomes successful in this business, and this achievement leads him to venture for more achievements, by expanding and exploring the different facets of his business. However, though Panna Lal was making money, out of his side-business, to turn his dream into reality and to seek the prosperity in his son's life, yet he was not a materialistic person in the strict sense of the term. He was in fact, a family person who believed firmly that "money isn't everything. There was that simple happiness of looking after someone and having someone look after you" (95). Though he does not know the nature of his son's job, nor the name of the organization, for which he was working, yet that does not deter him from making castles in the air for a more secured future:

> But although Biju's letters traced a string of jobs, they said more or less the same thing each time, except for the name of the establishment he was working for. His repetition provided cosiness and the cook's repetition of his son's repetition double-knit the cosiness. "Excellent job", he told his acquaintances, "better even than the last". He imagined sofa, TV, bank account. Eventually Biju would make enough and the cook would retire. He would receive a daughter-in-law to serve him food, crick-crack his toes, grandchildren to swot like flies. (17)

Right from preparing tea for the judge and milk for his pet at 4.30 a.m., his day begins with domestic activities and he works till late in the night. The rigors that he ceaselessly undergoes tell upon his health. Once the sanguine claws of terrorism cut through the world of the hills and the entire peaceful atmosphere turns violent, the cook grows anxious. In this predicament, he loses contact with Biju. The obvious consequence is that he is shaken to his nerves. He feels, and even starts believing that Biju had never existed and that he had only been like a dream:

> The cook did not mention his son...he had none...he'd never had one...it was just his hope writing to him...Biju was nonexistent.... (321)

His realization is one that points toward a true sense of connectedness and communications between individuals, a connectedness which many have been lost, but which Biju's presence in a distant country demonstrates, is not irretrievable. Once, in his psyche, Biju becomes "nonexistent" the entire world breaks down for him. He feels that he has nothing to live for. Being weak by nature, he does not have the mental strength to tide him over the pessimistic thoughts, nor does he possess the mental strength—which is, of course, perverted—to lay hands on himself. He fumbles, "I'd be better dead than alive."

The judge's insensitivity to the helpless cook's pathetic condition fills the heart of his granddaughter Sai as well as that of the readers. May be, it is the sympathy for the cook, which prompts the teenage Sai, to think about the vulnerable person, who is struggling with poverty, all the time:

> They are the poorest family in the village. Their house is still made of mud with a thatch roof. (67)

It really pained Sai's heart to see how little he had: "a few clothes hung over a string, a single razor blade and a sliver of cheap brown soap, a Kulu blanket that had once been hers, a cardboard case with metal clasps that had belonged to the judge and now contained the cook's papers, the recommendations that had helped him procure his job with the judge, Biju's letters, papers from a court case fought in his village all the way in Uttar Pradesh over the matter of five mango trees that he had lost to his brother. And, in the sateen elastic pocket inside the case, there was a broken watch that would cost too much to mend, but was still too precious to throwaway? He might be able to pawn the parts" (13).

When the robbery took place in the household of the judge, a reluctant Panna Lal was sent to the local police station to lodge a complaint. However, after reaching the police station, he was scared enough to narrate the incident of the burglary, in front of the police officials. He was very much sensitive about the hard reality, that he was merely "a powerless man", who is not fit enough to complain to the powerful. It seemed the police officials were also well aware about this class division, and they behaved with the paltry cook accordingly. However, if at all they were worried, it was not because of the unwanted robbery in the peaceful mountain, but to safeguard the interest of the cook's master, who represents the powerful in the society:

> Unfortunately the policemen seemed perturbed and questioned him harshly, while also making their scorn for him clear. As a servant, he was far beneath them, but the robbery of guns from a retired member of the judiciary could not be ignored and they were forced to inform the superintendent. (11)

Nonetheless, the cook has his own ghosts to fight with. He is accused of not looking after the dog, Mutt. The disappearance of judge's pet adds to his plight. The judge holds him responsible for the loss of his pet and threatens to kill him if the dog is not retrieved. He is hounded by this fact, transiting into a state of delirium.

Unable to find the dog despite all the possible efforts, the cook one day drinks heavily and in a state of intoxication requests the judge to punish him for his negligence in looking after the dog. Actually, his muddled brain, which is caused by an overdose of alcohol at Thapa's Canteen and a copious dose of 'chhang' prepared by him, he makes a plan that would release him from the pains of life. He confesses to the judge about his dealings with the poor fellow souls and how due to his fault Mutt is lost. The cook's repeated request to the judge, "Kill me", evinces a passive effort on his part to end his existence. This infuriates the judge to the extent that he beats the cook with his slipper. The judge repeatedly kicks and hits with "all the force of his sagging, puckering flesh" (321). The cook bears all this silently only because he is a servant, without money and so a marginalized entity in the society. He accepts all the tenets of his fate, but at the same time, he is equally horrified by his underprivileged status; "Terrible to be poverty-stricken man, terrible, terrible, terrible..." (34).

The cook's sudden confession of his past crimes is not without a cause. He admits all his faults to his master, in the hope, that his confession, would provoke the judge to such an extent, that he would beat him to death, thereby providing him salvation from this heartless world. This Christian-Hindu way of penance reflects how people from lower class get influenced by the way of elite sensibilities and accept everything and anything in the name of destiny.

Though the cook is beaten black and blue by the judge, yet he was not responsible for the loss of Mutt. The wife and father of the innocent man who was blinded by the police, on the false accusation of stealing in the household of the judge, stole the dog. They had repeatedly requested the judge to help them but, obviously, to no avail. They stole the dog—not in vengeance—but so that they could earn some money, which would hold their body and soul together, by selling it to some fashionable people.

When Biju came to know about the turmoil arising in Kalimpong, he got worried about his father. Somehow he managed some money to make a phone call to him and asked about his welfare. Biju felt a kind of emptiness, as he could not talk to his father in detail. He felt a deep anguish in his heart and a vague yearning hovered in him that "if he continued his life in New York, he might never see his Pitaji". He thereby made a strenuous effort to return and somehow managed a return ticket to India. The cook finally got his son Biju back. The poor chap reached his dear old father in a tattered and mud smeared night-gown, as all his belongings along with his clothes had been snatched away on the way back by the local hooligans. Nevertheless, the weak old eyes of the cook, did not fail to recognize his son and he again accepted the misfortune of his son on the way, as a mere destiny. Despite all hardships, the father was happy enough to get his son back.

The Inheritance of Loss is a narrative of marginalized individuals, where people like the cook, by and large, represent all those less educated powerless men, who work like donkeys all their life, because they accept it as their destiny. The cook's behaviour is apparently puzzling, but the reasons for his, almost suicidal actions lie in his mental praxis. It is actually, Panna Lal's tryst with destiny which prompts him for self-negation and self-abasement.

NOTE

1. Murray, David, *Matter, Magic, and Spirit: Representing Indian and African American Belief*. Pennsylvania: University of Pennsylvania Press, 2007.

16

The White Tiger: A Bakhtinian Reading

Anita Bhela

The work of Russian philosopher and critic Mikhail Bakhtin has acquired increasing importance towards an understanding of the novelists' approach to the novel. Adiga's novel may be seen to lend itself to a Bakhtinian reading by its congruence with his concept of that genre. In his essay "Epic and Novel", Bakhtin cites traits of the novel that distinguish it from other genres, and these characteristics are exemplified by Adiga's text. Among the unique qualities of the novel's form, according to Bakhtin, is a "stylistic three-dimensionality, which is linked with a multi-languaged consciousness realized in the novel" (Bakhtin, "Epic and Novel", 11). The multi-languaged world that the *The White Tiger* represents can be seen on various levels. The most obvious manifestation of polyphonic consciousness in the novel is the presentation of the differing voices of the masters and servants, servants and other servants, masters and their masters—the politicians and these varied voices cumulatively evoke the experience of living in a corrupt and oppressive environment in a way that transcends the narrative of each individual voice.

Adiga's carnivalesque text punctures the grand narratives of the rich upper classes of India. The novel interrogates the normal subject positions created for the poor within socially dominant ideological frames using a Bakhtinian approach to language and narrative. We do not so much see the carnivalesque being enacted in action within the novel, except maybe at the end, but the whole novel is presented in the carnivalesque tradition where a mingling of "the sacred with the profane, the lofty with the low, the great with the insignificant, the wise with the stupid" takes place (Bakhtin, *Problem of Dostoevsky's Poetics*, 123). Carnival's ritual debasement of an exalted thing at the hands of a usually powerless populace is enacted in the treatment of the gods and religion by the narrator Balram. No religion is spared—neither Hinduism nor Islam nor Buddhism nor Christianity. Balram's tone is irreverential towards all. Balram in his letter to the Chinese Premier, Jiabao states that: "[i]t is an ancient and venerated custom of people in [his] country to start a story by praying to a Higher Power" and wonders if he too should start off "by kissing some god's arse" (Adiga, *The White Tiger*, 8). He says:

> *Which* god's arse, though? There are so many choices.
>
> See, the Muslims have one god.
>
> The Christians have three gods.
>
> And we Hindus have 36,000,000 gods.
>
> Making a grand total of 36,000,004 divine arses for me to choose from. (8)

Later in the novel referring to the world-famous Bodh Gaya, where Buddha gained enlightenment and which is situated only a few miles from his home district he says, "I wonder if the Buddha walked through Laxmangarh—some people say he did. My own feeling is that he ran through it—as fast as he could—and got to the other side—and never looked back!" (18), for Laxmangarh is an area of Darkness where filth and ugliness are predominant. He speaks with the same irreverence towards Christianity, though in symbolic terms. At the end of the novel, *Balram* "has eaten and digested his master and become him" and this can be seen as "a parodic subversion of the Eucharist. (You partake of the body and blood of Christ and become Christ or at least a Christian.)" (Lexmipappan). Hanuman, the glorious ideal of service to the masters: "a shining example of how to serve your master with absolute fidelity, love and devotion" (19), worshipped by millions and the favorite God of those in the Darkness, is seen as another ruse to keep the poor oppressed and deprived. Balram always wonders why he always rushes to press Mr. Ashok's feet, the moment he sees them even though he isn't asked to. Why must he "go close to his feet, touch them and press them and make them feel good—why? he says in anguish" (193). And then the answer dawns on him that it was because the desire to be a servant had been bred into him "hammered into [his] skull, nail after nail, and poured into [his] blood, the way sewage and industrial poison are poured into Mother Ganga" (193). The novel stresses the need to rethink the glorified images of sacredness through the mirror of the present.

The sacredness associated with rivers is also questioned. The sacred and revered river Ganges at Haridwar, "daughter of the Vedas, river of illumination, protector of us all, breaker of the chain of birth and rebirth" is in reality shown to be the black river of death (15). "Everywhere this river flows, that area is the Darkness" as her "banks are full of rich, dark, sticky mud whose grip traps everything that is planted in it, suffocating and choking and stunting it" (14-15) and a dip in this holy Ganga, only fills the mouth with "faeces, straw, soggy parts of human bodies, buffalo carrion, and seven different kinds of industrial acids" (15). The Ganga at Benares is no better than the Ganga at Haridwar; it is so full of mounds of filth that his mother's corpse refuses to enter its muddy waters. Describing his mother's elaborate funeral on the banks of the river Ganga at Benaras he says:

> Underneath the platform with the piled-up fire logs, there was a giant oozing mound of black mud where the river washed into the shore. The mound was littered with ribbons of jasmine, rose petals, bits of satin, charred bones; a pale-skinned dog was crawling and sniffing through the petals and satin and charred bones.
>
> I looked at the ooze, and I looked at my mother's flexed foot, and I understood.

> This mud was holding her back: this big, swelling mound of black ooze. She was trying to fight the black mud; her toes were flexed and resisting; but the mud was sucking her in, sucking her in. It was so thick, and more of it was being created every moment as the river washed into the *ghat*. Soon she would become part of the black mound and the pale-skinned dog would start licking her. (15-16)

And his scathing comment is that nothing ever gets liberated here.

Bakhtin believes that carnival is "the feast of becoming, change, and renewal" and is "hostile to all that [is] immortalized and completed" (*Rabelais*, 10) therefore, in the true Bakhtinian sense, the novel debunks and demolishes grandiose ideas of India's past and present—Secular India, India of unity in Diversity, patriotic India of Mahatma Gandhi's followers, etc. The message is that ideological stances brought in from the past need to be re-examined and repositioned in response to new contexts.

Adiga presents the great secular India as one where honest, hardworking Muslims in order to feed their starving families have to take Hindu names like Ram Persad to get a job at the home of an "evil, prejudiced landlord" who does not like Muslims (109). Also, in this "fucked-up system" called parliamentary democracy thousands of people cast their vote but have never seen the inside of a voting booth (156). Moreover, in the world's greatest democracy, the protectors of law and the people, the judiciary and the police, both are equally corrupt. The much-touted cultural diversity of India is also shown to be "a fucking joke" for there are only two Indias—the India of the poor (Area of Darkness) and the India of the rich (Area of Light). However, in Adiga, always in the Bakhtinian strain, no idea is allowed to remain static and is continually subject to review—for that which is the area of Light is shown to be an area of Darkness as well. The rich appear to be happy in the eyes of the poor but they too are tired and sick of life. Having lost his way in life, Ashok is unhappy with his interfering family, his job of giving bribes, in fact his whole life. Totally discontent with his life, he says, "[m]y way of living is all wrong.... I let people exploit me, Balram, I've never done what I've wanted, my whole life, I..." (238). In his frustration, he thinks Balram is happy and desires to be a simple man like Balram and eat the food he eats.

Nothing exalted ever enters the world of *The White Tiger*. Roles are constantly being reversed. There is no completion in the true Bakhtinian sense, for new perspectives are continually emerging. In the novel, the exploiters become the exploited, masters become servants. The Great Socialist of Dhanbad towers over Mr. Ashok and the Mongoose, humiliates them and treats them like slaves to permit them to run their illegal coal mining business. When Balram brings the spittoon, the Great Socialist perversely insists on making the Mongoose hold it and as the Mongoose reluctantly holds the spittoon "with trembling hands" and a "face turned black with shame" he gets some diabolical pleasure in spitting into it three times. He has the perverse pleasure of knowing that the Mongoose is under his control. Similarly, Balram on discovering Ram Persad's real identity, which had been kept hidden in connivance with Ram Bahadur, the Nepali servant, uses this information to gain control over Ram Bahadur; he orders him to get him tea and biscuits and "clean those webs off the ceiling" (110). Ram Bahadur knowing Balram's power over him glares at him and reluctantly goes to get the broom and serves him "hot Nepali tea, and some nice sugar biscuits, on a porcelain platter" (110). In the city, Ashok becomes a stooge of the corrupt politicians, caught in their web, he cannot escape and is corrupted by them. The corrupt politicians cheat the businessmen and destroy them mentally, physically and emotionally. Businessmen, in turn, exploit their servants and oppress them mentally, physically and emotionally. Balram cheating on his master does not feel any guilt but only rage: "[t]he more I stole from him, the more I realized how much he had stolen from me", says Balram (230). In the novel, power games are played at all levels: within the family; the whole body of politics; servants and masters; and servants and servants. Rich or poor whoever can get the upper hand goes all out for it. "Servants need to abuse other servants. It's been bred into us", says Balram (130).

The great Indian joint family system too, comes under attack in the novel. Family traditions and loyalties are seen as pinning and smothering: they destroy a man in both the world of Light and the world of Darkness. Ashok's desires are always crushed by the allegiance he owes to his father and brother. He never could gather the courage to marry Uma, the woman he loved, nor have a say in the case of his own divorce and remarriage. He remains pinned and wriggling on the wall. Balram, a bright promising student, has to succumb to family pressures and give up his studies to pay for a loan taken for his sister's marriage.

Revered Muslim poets are praised in a tongue in cheek manner and their philosophy of love and spirituality, we are told, can be adapted and put to use in different contexts and it is "a mix of poetry and perversity in the potential killer that impels Balram to make the decisive stab by Mohammad Iqbal's great lines *I was looking for the key for years/ But the door was always open* (Lexmipappan).

One of the most fundamental disruptions to established inherent power structures is Adiga's granting linguistic ability to Balram, the narrator, which is an assault upon the long-established presumption of superiority possessed by those who can speak English. Balram's humiliation at the hands of Pinky madam and Ashok sir for not knowing how to pronounce Pizza is an incident worth quoting in full:

> "Ashok," she said. Now hear this. Balram, what is it we're eating?
>
> I knew it was a trap, but what could I do?—I answered. The two of them burst into giggles.
>
> Say it again, Balram.
>
> They laughed again.
>
> "It's not piJJA. It's piZZa. Say it properly." (154)

Going into the kitchen Balram because of the ridicule to which he has been subjected, tries out the correct pronunciation.

"Pijja."

"Pzijja."

"Zippja."

"Pizja." (155)

Not succeeding he gives up in frustration. In another episode, Ashok, exalted by self-importance, sees himself as a great intellectual, simply because he possesses education. His education has taught him to make fun of half-baked Indians who had to leave school under compelling conditions. His condescending attitude towards Balram when he stops the car to ask Balram a series of questions the answers to which amuse him and Pinky Madam to no end is both amusing and annoying and reveals a great deal about Ashok sir and Pinky Madam. Comparing the epic and the novel Bakhtin says that

> it is precisely laughter that destroys the epic, and in general destroys any hierarchical (distancing and valorized) distance. As a distanced image a subject cannot be comical; to be made comical, it must be brought close. Everything that makes us laugh is close at hand, all comical creativity works in a zone of maximal proximity. Laughter has the remarkable power of making an object come up close, of drawing it into a zone of crude contact where one can finger it familiarly on all sides, break open its external shell, look into its center, doubt it, take it apart, dismember it, lay it bare and expose it, examine it freely and experiment with it. ("Epic and Novel", 23)

Thus, much of carnival's power derives from laughter. Through laughter, and "the shift of the temporal center of artistic orientation", the author, his readers, and the world represented or narrated all exist on one plain (27).

Dialogics assumes "the inherent addressivity of all language" and "all language is addressed, never uttered without consciousness of a relationship between the speaker and the addressee" (Guerin et al. *A Handbook...*, 301). In the novel, Ashok's brother is seen to have objectified servants to such an extent that he cannot conceive of them as addressees in any genuine linguistic exchange. Therefore, there can be no dialogic interaction between him and a servant. When he speaks to a servant, the Mongoose hears nothing but his own voice. And, because the Mongoose will not allow for the possibility of dialogic interaction between himself and the servants, the intervening voice of the narrator reinforces the alienating effects of any discourse that denies the full subjectivity of the addressee ("Discourse in the Novel"). When Pinky Madam's car hits and kills a child, the Mongoose speaks and decides everything and Balram can only say "yes, sir", and "no sir". It is as if for the Mongoose he just does not exist.

Beyond its heteroglossia, however, *The White Tiger* embodies yet another distinctive trait of Bakhtin's theories about the genre of the novel and one that corresponds to Adiga's intentions in writing this book. That quality is the novel's creation of a sense of temporal immediacy, rather than the effect of events depicted within it belonging to a distant past. Bakhtin illuminates this quality of the novelistic form by contrasting it with another genre, the epic. In epic discourse, Bakhtin writes, "a national epic past...serves as the subject...national tradition (not personal experience) serves as the source", and "an absolute epic distance separates the epic world from contemporary reality" ("Epic and Novel", 13). In Adiga's novel, we are simultaneously presented with three levels of contemporary time: the immediate present—Balram writing the letters to the Chinese premier; the immediate past—the distributed references to sections of the wanted poster; and the not too distant past of Balram and his *bildungsroman* interspersed with episodes describing his life with Ashok sir and Pinky Madam. The contemporaneity of events strikes the reader on every page of the novel.

The epic according to Bakhtin, "does not permit an individual, personal point of view or evaluation", but instead relies on "a commonly held evaluation and points of view—which excludes any possibility of another approach—and therefore displays a profound piety toward the subject described" ("Epic and Novel", 16-17). Adiga through his novel approach of mocking and challenging hitherto revered subjects and romanticized ideals portrays the essential helplessness of people like Balram in a world controlled by the rich ruling class. In both the street and literary forms of carnival, language can be "made to disrupt authority and liberate alternate voices" (Selden and Widdowson, *Language and Ideology...*, 39). For the most part, human limitation prevents us from hearing any voices requiring liberation but those of our own kind. The novel depicts the inverted but instructive situations that might arise if oppressed classes were accorded power and the power latent in it. Thus, the novel subverts the usual authorities, brings down the pompous and "[strives] through gentle mockery to dismantle socially received ideas and replace them with their opposite, privileging weakness over strength" (*Language and Ideology...*, 121). The novel situates itself in positions of non-conformity. It expresses opposition to authoritarianism and seriousness. It makes extensive use of the abusive language or insulting words or expressions generally characteristic of the carnivalesque. In its breaking of the norms of official speech, it mocks and challenges authoritative figures and structures of the world. Balram's work of resistance against a totalizing, "centripetal" force, the dictatorship of the Stork, the Buffalo, the Raven, the Wild Boar and the Mongoose is evident in the transformation of the White Tiger. As he leaves the rule-bound world to subvert hierarchies and hegemonic structures, Adiga's protagonist is consciously immoral and the novel even goes so far as to interrogate set paradigms of morality. In this sordid jungle, where all are being eaten and consumed by each other, are there any norms of morality really existing? Is murder worse than the other heinous crimes being committed by other characters in the novel? In according moral relativism to murder, Adiga seems to be crossing all ethical limits, for although the voice that upholds murder is that of Balram, yet the reader cannot but feel that it has Adiga's approval. In the ending, there is an attempt to show regeneration and renewal in the spirit of the carnival but it sounds hollow. Balram, now Ashok Sharma (and this change of name to that of a higher caste is the last twist in the novel), a highly successful entrepreneur, runs a fleet of taxis, and employs other drivers. And when an accident takes place, he is shown to behave differently in comparison to the earlier incident pertaining to the killing of the child by Pinky Madam, but I see only a marginal difference. My own understanding is that Adiga gets so carried away by Bakhtinian ideology (conscious or unconscious) that a one-sided perspective emerges, which makes the ending of the novel, ironical and ambiguous—for the rooster who escapes now becomes a part of the power structure that he subverted—can we call this victory in any sense of the word?

REFERENCES

Adiga, Aravind. *The White Tiger*. India: Harper Collins, 2009.

Bakhtin, Mikhail Mikhailovich. "Discourse in the Novel." *The Dialogic Imagination: Four Essays* by M.M. Bakhtin. Ed. Michael Holquist. Austin: University of Texas Press, 1981: 259-422.

——. "Epic and Novel." *The Dialogic Imagination: Four Essays* by M.M. Bakhtin. Ed. Michael Holquist. Austin: University of Texas Press, 1981: 3-40.

——. *Problems of Dostoevsky's Poetics*. Ed. and trans. Caryl Emerson. Minneapolis: University of Minnesota Press, 1984.

——. *Rabelais and His World*. Trans. Helene Iswolsky. Bloomington: Indiana University Press, 1984.

Guerin, Wilfred L., et al. *A Handbook of Critical Approaches to Literature*. 3rd ed. New York: Oxford University Press, 1992.

Lexmipappan. http://www.epicindia.coin/magazine/Books/book-review-aravind-adiga-the-white-tiger

Selden, Raman and Peter Widdowson. *A Reader's Guide to Contemporary Literary Theory*. 3rd ed. Lexington: Kentucky University Press, 1993.

Stephens, John. Language and Ideology in Children's Fiction. Language in Social Life Series. London: Longman, 1992.

17

Aravind Adiga's *The White Tiger*: An Anti-religious Text

Sudhir K. Arora

> And indeed, Ram Persad—or Mohammad or whatever his name really was—came out of the mosque, took his sandals down from the window, slapped them on the ground, wriggled his feet into them, and began walking out. He saw me—I winked at him—and he knew that the game was up. (*The White Tiger*, 110)

Aravind Adiga, like his creation Balram Halwai alias white tiger is a rare genius who is born to differentiate himself from others by virtue of his superiority or to use Yeats' phrase "intellectual hatred" that has a right to defame or make the sweeping comment without considering the consequences that will result in hurting the religious feelings of a community. The novel *The White Tiger* is well-planned and well-constructed in the frame of Marxism, though it is a different thing that the protagonist Balram Halwai is neither purely a Marxist nor a Capitalist. He is rather an opportunist who changes not only the side but also the colour—sometimes white and sometimes red while the reality is that he is thoroughly black in spirits. An ideology, if it does not believe in a religion, never motivates its followers to spread the anti-religious feelings or create an environment of violence. To judge the whole community on the basis of a few cases shows only the mental sickness.

Adiga may be a Marxist or any. He has full freedom to propagate what he wishes but he has no right to do it at the cost of defaming or hurting others' religious feelings. *The White Tiger* is a text that mocks everything—be it religion, politics or social system or human beings. The white tiger is a tiger—an animal in the form of a man but inwardly he is not a human being from any angle. This animal-cum-man is a puppet in the hands of his creator—Aravind Adiga who has knowingly created him either to come into the limelight or propagate his agenda. The text remains silent on Buddhism. It is due to Adiga's fear of China where this religion still exists or his intention is to get favour because Delhi, where "the roads are good, and the people are bad" and Mumbai where "everyone goes in the films after they kill someone" (297) are not fit places in India where everyone "drinks and drives" (159). So, India is not a right place for him to live, however she is a good deal for him because of her salability in the Western market that showers gold, awards and rewards to see her nakedness.

Adiga's protagonist Balram Halwai does not spare any religion except Buddhism. His anti-religious feelings can be traced in the excerpt quoted here:

> Which god's arse, though? There are so many choices.
>
> See, the Muslims have one god.
>
> The Christians have three gods.
>
> And we Hindus have 36,000,000 gods.
>
> Making a grand total of 36,000,004 divine arses for me to choose from. (8)

Gods are not gods for him; rather they seem to be 'arses' for kissing. Touching feet or kissing them is not in his culture. Adiga may be an atheist or a staunch believer in the principles of communism but he has no right to call gods 'arses'. If the excerpt is minutely studied, he includes even Christianity and Islam and later Buddhism. For him, there are 36,000,000 Hindu gods, one Muslim god and three Christian gods making the total of 36,000,004 divine arses, among which he has to choose one. Later, he adds one more name to the list—Buddha when he answers to the question of the inspector about Buddha saying first that he was "An enlightened man", then, "An enlightened *god*." What Adiga writes in bracket is worth-noticing. (Oops! Thirty-six million and five--!) (34). He adds one more name—Buddha to the list that now has the total of thirty-six million and five. But what is worth-noticing is the hyphen after the word five. Is he afraid of the Chinese Premier or China where the followers of Buddhism reside? Has he no courage to fill the gap with the word 'arses'. Very cunningly he abuses as well as shows his respect for them. He laughs at Hindu gods or the names that are associated with them. He names his characters with the word Ram either in the beginning as Ram Dev (Stork), Ram Pandey (the Doctor). Ramanathan (a fixer) and Ram Bahadur (Nepali Guard) or in the end as Balram (the Protagonist) or Vikram (Father of Balram). The bearers of these names do not possess the qualities which their names suggest.

Balram Halwai considers himself to be a Hanuman in the service of Ram (Mr. Ashok) and Sita (Pinky Madam). But later, this Hanuman becomes a *rakshas* who kills his master. Then, he realizes that he should cut the mongoose's neck. The mongoose is Mukesh. Mukesh is the other name of Shiva, who killed Muka, a demon in the form of a wild boar. He himself admits that the name of Shiva is truth. In Bangalore, he becomes Ashok. But this Ashok Sharma does not follow any religion, rather keeps Dharam (i.e. religion) under his thumb and intends to kill him if he thinks of the family at the village. It seems that it is not Balram but his creator Aravind Adiga who feels inner satisfaction in seeing in pains or giving pains to the names that begin with Ram. The Stork whose real name is Ram Dev bows down before the Great Socialist. Dr. Ram Pandey gives a part of his salary to the politician to continue his private practice without going to the government hospital. He makes Ram Bahadur, the Nepali guard silent and bow down before him. Ram Persad is not Ram Persad but Mohammad who has taken the garb of Ram Persad only to get the job in a Hindu family. All these names beginning with Ram or ending with Ram are named not by chance but are preplanned by Aravind Adiga with the intention of mocking at the religion.

The White Tiger roars against the Muslims and wonders at their strange belief in the number 786—the number that can do miracle in life. This is the magic number that is associated with the religion. "Just before the movie got started, either the number 786 would flash against the black screen—the Muslims think this is a magic number that represents their god" (8). It is certain that the text is not written with the intention of showing unity between the Hindus and the Muslims. Ram Persad is not a Hindu but a Muslim in the disguise of Ram Persad for the purpose of a job in an orthodox Hindu family. If the text is decoded, a trap of showing a Muslim worshipping the idols can be seen. Muslims do not believe in idol worship. How a Muslim can begin his day by bowing down before the pictures of gods seems strange. There may be other ways of getting job. But job at the cost of religion is beyond understanding. Adiga's intention is not to show the religious harmony. He follows one religion—religion of mockery. He takes pleasure in creating a kind of disharmony showing the things that are very opposite to the particular religion. Here is an excerpt that shows how Ram Persad (actually a Muslim) begins his day:

> See, he began every day by bowing in front of at least twenty pictures of various gods he kept in his side of the room, and saying, "Om, om, om." As he did this, he looked at me through the corner of his eye, as if to say, *Don't you pray? What are you, a Naxal?* (77)

The chanting of Om and bowing down before pictures (not to talk of having them in one's room) are the activities that are not expected from a Muslim. "Mohammad denounced idolatry. No picture or idol of Mohammad is therefore available" (Rajeev, 87). It seems odd that a Muslim is scolding a Hindu calling him a Naxal for not praying. All these things are pre-planned; they cannot naturally flow to a mind whose mindset, if not anti-religious, is certainly not religious.

In *The White Tiger*, the Stork (Ram Dev) is anti-Muslim in his attitude while Mr. Ashok is cosmopolitan. When the

Stork's grandson calls himself that he is Azharuddin, he asks him to call himself Gavaskar, not Azharuddin. Mark the excerpt for the Stork's anti-Muslim feelings.

> Mr. Ashok joined thc game. He stood as the wicketkeeper while I bowled full tosses to the brat.
>
> "I'm Azharuddin, captain of India!" the boy shouted every time he hit a six or a four.
>
> "Call yourself Gavaskar. Azharuddin is a Muslim."
>
> It was the Stork. He had come into the courtyard to watch.
>
> Mr. Ashok said, "Father, what a silly thing to say! Hindu or Muslim, what difference does it make?" (70)

No doubt, people like the Stork suffering from narrow-mindedness are in India. If the people like the Stork are present, people like Ashok who oppose this mean mentality come to the front and create harmony through their humanistic attitude that all human beings are equal and children of the same god.

There is something common among Booker Prize winners. Sell India in the West-sponsored sale and get the prize. Indians are proud of these so-called sellers with tags. What an irony! Adiga also follows his sister Kiran Desai (not real but because of Booker Prize winner) who sells India and makes the inheritance of gains out of the inheritance of loss. "Wine is prohibited. The eating of pork is forbidden, because pig is a foul animal" (Rajeev, 87). But she presents a very disgusting picture in her novel. Mark the excerpt:

> Mrs. Sen: "More Muslims in India than in Pakistan. They prefer to multiply over here. You know, that Jinnah, he ate bacon and eggs for breakfast every morning and drank whisky every evening. What sort of Muslim nation they have? And five times a day bums up to God. Mind you," she put her sticky finger in her mouth and then pulled it out with a pop, "With that Koran, who can be surprised? They have no option but to be two-faced."

> The reasoning, they all knew from having heard this before, formed a central pillar of Hindu belief and it went like this: so strict was the Koran that its teachings were beyond human capability. Therefore Muslims were forced to pretend one thing, do another; they drank, smoked, ate pork, visited prostitutes, and then denied it.
>
> Unlike Hindus, who needn't deny. (Desai, 130)

The brother also follows the sister. The difference is that 'bum' becomes 'arse', whisky is named 'Black Dog', 'two-faced Muslim' is practically shown playing the two roles—of a Hindu as well as of a Muslim. In place of prostitution, a complete market with woman-wares is on sale. What Kiran Desai has said is practically demonstrated by Aravind Adiga. Ram Persad who is actually a Muslim goes to JACKPOT, an English liquor shop to purchase the Black Dog, the most expansive whisky for his master Stork and his sons. Mark the excerpt for the description of the liquor and Ram Persad's (a Muslim) imaginary satisfaction:

> Ram Persad would get the liquor, and then I would swat at the other servants and fight for some space for us to out while he cradled the bottle in his arms. It was the only time we were ever like a team.
>
> On our way back to the house, Ram Persad would always stop by the side of the road and slide the Black Dog out of its cardboard box. He said this was to check that Jackpot hadn't cheated us. I knew he was lying. He just wanted to hold the bottle. He wanted to hold the full, virgin bottle of first-class whisky in his hand. He wanted to imagine that he was buying for himself. (75)

Only a genius like Aravind Adiga can make a Muslim purchase wine for his master without considering the tenets and principles of the particular religion. Every Muslim is to follow the five rules which are:

1. A Muslim must declare the oneness of God and accept Mohammad as the prophet. This declaration is also known as recitation of 'Kalma'. The follower has

to say this that there is no other God except Allah and Mohammad is the Prophet of Allah.

2. He must say prayers five times a day and every Friday he must offer his afternoon prayer at the mosque.
3. He must offer charity (Zakat) to the deprived and the destitute.
4. He must observe fast in the holy month of 'Ramzan'.
5. At least once in his lifetime, in accordance with his means, he should go for pilgrimage (Haj) to Mecca. (Rajeev, 86)

A Muslim believes in one God. Ram Persad deceives his inner self by following the tenets of the Hindu religion. If he does not bow down before the idols, he is not a Hindu which he is only in name. If he worships the idols, he fails to be a true Muslim. The protagonist Balram Halwai finds out a secret about Ram Persad, the number one driver. He follows Ram Persad in the evening and finds him going to the mosque. Now he imagines the cause of Ram Persad's stopping eating either inside or the outside of the house. It is Ramadan (Ramzan), the religious month during which Muslims do not "eat and drink during the day" (109). This is the secret that he comes to know but it is also known to the Nepali guard. Mark the excerpt for Balram Halwai's way of exposing the scam.

> "I just saw a film, sir,"
>
> "Fuck off."
>
> "A great film, sir. Lots of dancing, Hero was a Muslim. Name of Mohammad Mohammad."
>
> "Don't waste my time, boy. Go clean the car if you've got nothing to do."
>
> "Now, this Mohammad Mohammad was a poor, honest, hardworking Muslim, but he wanted a job at the home of an evil, prejudiced landlord who didn't like Muslims—so, just to get a job and feed his starving family, he claimed to be a Hindu! And took the name of Ram Persad."
>
> The twig fell out of the Nepali's mouth.

> "And you know how he managed to pull this off? Because the Nepali guard at this house, whom the masters trusted absolutely, and who was supposed to check up on Ram Persad's background, was *in* on the the scam!" (109)

This is the way that Balram Halwai exposes the Nepali guard who has a hand in the disguise. This is the inner working of the mind of Aravind Adiga that he makes anything possible. Hats off to his creative mind! But he uses this creativity either for his commercial gains or for exposing someone. This unmasking makes his protagonist driver number one from number two. He is one step ahead from Kiran Desai who commented on Gorkhas. Here, he hits many with one arrow. Through the talks of the movie, he exposes Ram Persad, comments on the Muslim and doubts the integrity of the Nepali guard. Does it not indicate a conspiracy or a kind of trap in using the name of Ram Persad or Mohammad? He could use any other name but did not. He knows that the use of the name of Mohammad or Ram Persad will hurt the religious minded people. He wants to hurt and in this he succeeds though he makes his protagonist think: "I thought, *What a miserable life he's had, having to hide his religion, his name, just to get a job as a driver—and he is a good driver, no question of it, a far better one than I will ever be*" (110). Ram Persad goes away without saying any word leaving the scene for Balram Halwai for becoming the driver number one.

Adiga is prejudiced towards the Muslims who seem to be illiterate or the destroyer of buildings. He is also surprised that all the four great poets of the world are Muslims in spite of the lower literary ratio among the Muslims. He praises Iqbal for speaking the truth about slaves but the way he appreciates shows his mental attitude which is certainly anti-Muslim. Mark the excerpt:

> Iqbal, who is one of the four best poets in the world—the others being Rumi, Mirza Ghalib, and a fourth fellow, also a Muslim, whose name I've forgotten—has written a poem where he says this about slaves:
>
> That's the truest thing anyone ever said.

> A great poet, this fellow Iqbal—even if he *was* a Muslim.
>
> (By the way, Mr. Premier: have you noticed that all four of the greatest poets in the world are Muslim? And yet all the Muslims you meet are illiterate or covered head to toe in black burkas or looking for buildings to blow up? It's a puzzle, isn't it? If you ever figure these people out, send me an e-mail.) (40)

Why can a Muslim not be a great poet? Is there anything to wonder at? It can be bypassed to some extent saying that this remark is the outcome of the mental sickness or prejudice. But what about the sweeping statement that he offers within brackets? Are black burkas and blowing up the buildings associated with Muslims? All Muslims are not the destroyer of the buildings? Black burka is their dressing culture with a religious leaning.

Adiga also used the derogatory words for Urdu. Urdu is a language known for sweetness and lyricism. It is the language which is spoken and understood by the Muslims as well as the Hindus. But what makes Adiga say through Balram Halwai is again beyond understanding. Mark the words that he uses for Urdu: "Some books were in Urdu, the language of the Muslims—which is all just scratches and dots, as if some crow dipped its feet in black ink and pressed them to the page" (253). Is Urdu merely scratches and dots? Is it crow that writes it with its feet in black ink? The crow is nowhere; it is in the mind of Adiga who makes it write such. He is a sadist who takes pleasure in hurting others. He is not satisfied with this and, so, makes Balram Halwai ridicule the Muslim bookseller. Mark the excerpt for the way he requests to the Muslim bookseller for telling him about poetry:

> "Please Muslim uncle," I begged. "I'm just a rickshaw-puller's son from the darkness. Tell me all about poetry. Who wrote that poem?"
>
> He shook his head, but I kept flattering him, telling him how fine his beard was, how fair his skin was (ha!), how it was obvious from his nose and forehead that he wasn't some pigherd who has converted but a true-blue Muslim who had flown here on a magic carpet all the

> way from Mecca, and he grunted with satisfaction. He read me another poem, and another one—and he explained the true history of poetry, which is a kind of secret, a magic known only to wise men. (253-54)

What is noticeable here is the way he flatters. He praises him for his beard and fair skin while the reality is that his beard is white and skin is black. Earlier, he describes his face as "a pitch-black face that was bedewed with sweat" (253). The word 'ha' within bracket makes his intention clear that it is not his praise rather it is hatred that he has for the Muslims. To call him that he is a true Muslim who has directly come from Mecca is nothing except the emotional blackmailing. The use of the word 'pigherd' needs no explanation as it reveals the inner pattern of his mind.

Adiga thinks that he has dissected India so that she may transform herself into a better society. Is it really so? What has he displayed in the name of "greater process of self-examination"? Will the mockery of religion make him a Flaubert, a Balzac or a Dickens? Religion binds the people in one thread. He thinks that he has done a good job for India by breaking this thread because of his communistic mindset that never includes religion in its philosophy. A genius like Adiga can make his characters Muslim or Hindu without taking the parameters of the particular religion into consideration. He makes his characters do the things that are not followed in their religion. It does not matter whether he names his characters Ram Persad or Mohammad. He makes his character slap the ground of the mosque with sandals. He could use the proper word but he uses slap. What he wants to convey is clear enough to surmise. Balram winks at Ram Persad who is really a Muslim to make him feel that his game is up. What's about the game that the creator of Ram Persad is playing with religion? It is not a sign of healthy literature. How *The White Tiger* can be healthy literary text is beyond understanding. But he has done a right thing for the West who has also performed her duty by awarding the Booker Prize to *The White Tiger* who is indeed white outwardly but black inwardly. His statement that he is himself disturbed with the character of Balram

Halwai seems to be ridiculous. How can he disassociate himself with Balram when he himself is his creator? It is possible that the West may believe in Balram Halwai's story but one day God will come to take him to His Court where he will accept the complete truth. The robotic atheistic white tigers from the school where no one is allowed to corrupt one's head with the stories about God and Gandhi will fail to save this boss of Bangalore from the clutches of the boss of bosses—God.

WORKS CITED

Adiga, Aravind. *The White Tiger*. New Delhi: Harper Collins, 2008. All the pages in brackets are from this book only.

Desai, Kiran. *The Inheritance of Loss*. New Delhi: Penguin, 2006.

Rajeev, Rajendra Kumar. *World-famous Religions, Doctrine and Sects*. New Delhi: Family Books, 1988. Rpt. 1989.

18

Aravind Adiga's *The White Tiger*: An Overview

A.S. Rao and *Pawan Kumar Sharma*

Aravind Adiga by his first novel, *The White Tiger* shot to fame and as a result got the Man Booker Prize in 2008. Written in epistolary form, it raises protest against numerous social, cultural and economic ills spread over the contemporary India. To put it otherwise, it looks down social, political and economic set-ups. It consists of seven long letters written by Balram Halwai, the protagonist and narrator to the Chinese premier, Wen Jiabao who is supposed to visit India. When Balram came to know about Chinese official's forth coming visit to India on the All India Radio, he is inspired to write to Wen about Indian entrepreneurship. Balram was a son to a rickshaw puller and his mother died in his childhood days. And therefore, he has to do several odd and menial jobs to meet both the ends.

Adiga, in the novel, is primarily interested in shooting at dark side of contemporary Indian society. And therefore, he divided India metaphorically into India of darkness and India of light. Impatiently, he counts down problems facing India and Indian people like corrupt politics, illiteracy, poverty, unemployment, pollution, prostitution, fundamentalism, naxalism, and above all Machiavellism. He finds pre-independence India in a zoo where all animals and birds live in their respective houses. Similarly, before independence everything was systematic and strategic. But after independence Indian looks preoccupied with and running after social, cultural and economic exposition. Balram, the protagonist and The White Tiger of this novel, is a typical character. Like a white tiger which is quite rare and is found once in a generation, Balram feeds on other fellowmen's life.

The narrator has chosen Chinese premier to narrate his story because he is of the view that Chinese people love freedom and liberty and that only they can understand the reason of murdering his master. He points out that "only three nations have never let themselves be ruled by foreigners: China, Afghanistan and Abyssinia. These are the only three nations I admire." And he considers that the future "lies with the yellow man and the brown man now that our erstwhile master, the white-skinned man, has wasted himself through buggery, Mobile phone usage, and drug abuse".

After a few months' service as a taxi driver to Ashok Sharma, Balram felt an urge of power and money. He soon got fed up with the life of slavery and humiliation and decided to avenge his master. Consequently, one day he plotted to murder his employer and to become a part of the India of light. When Ashok was carrying bag of seven lac rupees to bribe a politician, Balram cuts Ashok's throat and flees to Bangalore. There he launches a taxi company named "The White Tiger Drivers" and assumed his master's name. This was the scintillating and successful story of Balram Halwai. Associated strands with this story of Balram Halwai are dishonesty, insincerity, immorality, opportunism, exploitation of down casts, etc.

In the centre of these glaring problems, main motif is to gain in material growth by hook or by crook. Adiga criticizes the hollowness of government welfare programme and has tried to show that the democratically elected government seemingly does nothing to bridge the yawning gap between the rich and the poor. In the first part of the book, Balram sarcastically calls his village as Indian paradise lacking basic amenities like drinking water, electricity, health education, transport, communication and other facilities. He takes up another shortcoming of police system. The whole system is involved in filling the pockets. The other problem is water pollution. The Ganga adorned in India as mother, is blackened by limitless flow of industrial acids, dead human bodies and animals into it. Next to water pollution, Aravind Adiga turns to air pollution as he writes: "The air is so bad in Delhi that it takes ten years off a man's life." Smokes emanated by both high and heavy vehicles cause cancer and other breath related diseases. The Mall culture has ushered in a new era of slums, beggars and street vendors. Prostitution is another blot to shining India. The problem of poverty has forced many women to adopt the profession of prostitution. In India family break-down is another serious problem. The growth rate of divorces every year is in probation as Balram for material advantages manages distance from his family.

Indian Zamindari which was abolished long back by our constitution, can be still persisting in certain parts of India. Adiga has named the four landlords of village metaphorically, according to their appetite, as Buffalo, Stork, Wild Boar and Raven. Here, the landlords hold the sway. The Buffalo owned the river, the wild Boar owned the good agricultural land and the Raven owned the rocky hillside around the fort. The villagers have to pay them revenue if they want to use their property. Adiga in this part shows how the landlords suck up the blood of people to fill their big bellies.

In Indian villages poor-rich divide is very critical and grim where the poor are oppressed and exploited by the rich as Balram's father says: "My whole life, I have been treated like a donkey." Balram metaphorically calls poor people as stick-men with thin bodies and dirty faces whereas rich men's bodies as premium cotton pillow, white and soft and black. Usually poor, in search of food and work, migrate to big cities and live there on roads and under fly-overs.

Aravind Adiga castigates voting system also. In India every citizen above the age of 18 years has the right to vote but poor people are not allowed to cast their votes as the rich ones sell their votes. Adiga identifies three main diseases of this country. Election fever is one of them.

Aravind Adiga does not leave even educational system. He calls school teachers a Paan-and-spit man who are involved in muzzling school lunch money and uniform expenses. This adverse situation led Adiga to comment: "You can't expect a man in a dung heap to smell sweet."

The White Tiger, is in the first person narration and from Balram's perspective. Mostly Adiga has used simple words but here and there he has employed figures of speech as similes, metaphors, etc. He even does not hesitate to use Hindi words like namaste, daal, chapattis, paan, mandals and ghat. And at times, he has applied the technique of analogy to prove his stand. The Rooster cook is exemplary. Moreover, he has taken the course of some myths like Hanuman, Shankar Shiv, etc. to lend charm to the story.

Thus, we can put it on the writing on the basis of above observation that Adiga by his interesting exposition of hollowness of India and Indian society proved that life in metropolitan cities especially cannot remain free to corruption. Life here corrupts being itself corrupt. Adiga firmly opines that it is almost impossible to bring about justice and equality for commoners unless they come forward and ask for their dues.

REFERENCES

Ahuja, Ram. *Social Problems in India* (Rawat Publications, Jaipur, 2004).

Chandra, Snehlata. *Marginal Communities and Social Development* (Kanisha Publications, New Delhi, 1998).

Davis, Kingsley. *Human Society* (Surjeet Publication, New Delhi, 1995).

Dube, Siddarth. *Words Like Freedom: The Memoirs of an Impoverished Indian Family: 1947-1997* (Harper Collins Pub., India, 1998).

Keith, A. Berriedale. *Indian Mythology* (Mittal Publication, New Delhi, 1998).

Mahajan, V.D. *Modern Indian History: British Rule in India and After*, 7th edition (S. Chand & Co., New Delhi, 1999).

19

An India of Light and an India of Darkness: Reality Check in Adiga's *The White Tiger*

Anjita Singh

Aravind Adiga became the fourth Indian novelist to be awarded the prestigious Man Booker Prize for his debut novel, *The White Tiger* in 2008. This novel, about the emotions, sorrows and aspirations of a hitherto invisible class of society, has attracted attention not merely for the social ethos it portrays but for the manner in which it portrays it. It is arguable whether the achievement of Adiga, in capturing something new, is in his choice of subject, or in his manner of portrayal. Initially, the novel was praised for bringing into focus the injustices and poverty present in the rapidly changing India. It was considered almost a stirring, in the hint of refusal by the poor to accept the fate ordained for them by their masters. But outrage soon gained ground at the Booker panel's decision in selecting this particular novel which presents the imaged country in a poor light thereby coming under suspicion of pandering to Western prejudices. It was seen as a subversive act on the part of the nominators, in subtly highlighting the supposed inferiority and darkness of Indian culture as compared to the assumedly superior European one.

Literature does not occur in a space separate from other concerns of life. The reflection theory of Gyorgy Lukacs stressed literature's reflection, "conscious or unconscious of the social reality surrounding it",[1] and more importantly, not just as a reflection of a flood of realistic detail but as a reflection of the essence of a society. At the same time, while it is truc that every work reflects, to some degree, the age of its composition and thus the conditions of society, there is more beyond mere concern with the disclosure of tensions and contradictions within a society. Here we encounter the production theory of Louis Althusser. Literature is not mere narrative or a picture of the real, because it cannot define itself simply as a figuration of reality. By a complex process, literature is the production of a certain reality. Hence, the meaning of any literary text can never be fixed by any universal criterion but is subject to specific appropriations. All works of art carry their hidden agenda.

This brilliantly experimental first novel by Adiga too carries its agenda. It is in the form of a series of letters addressed to Wen Jiabao, the Chinese premier, by Balram Halwai the self-styled 'White Tiger' of the title. On hearing of Jiabao's impending visit to India to know about Bangalore, the silicon valley of India, through a meeting with some Indian entrepreneurs, Halwai offers to tell him, 'free of charge, the truth about Bangalore'.[2] He wishes to impart the essence of the new India to the Chinese premier—out of respect for the love of liberty shown by the Chinese people and also in the belief that "the future of the world lies with the yellow man and the brown man now that our erstwhile master, the white skinned man has wasted himself thru buggery, mobile phone usage and drug abuse...".[3]

Over a period of seven nights, in a 150 square foot office, with no one else but himself and a chandelier, "...a huge thing, full of small diamond shaped glass pieces just like the ones they used to show in the films of 1970s...with...a personality of its own"[4] for company, Balram Halwai tells his story by the scattered light of the outlandish chandelier. This, the first meeting with Halwai; servant, philosopher, entrepreneur, murderer in turns, holds promise of a good tale to follow, about himself and thousand other half-baked fellows like him, in this country of 36,000,004 gods.

Born to a rickshaw puller in Laxmangarh, a village in the dark heart of India, Balram, is pulled out of school and made to work in a tea shop. His short stint at school, however, gifts him the most invaluable part of his life, his name "Balram", given to him by his class-teacher simply because he had never been given a proper name by his parents other than a non-committal 'Munna'—"...now what kind of place is it where people forget to name their children...?"[5] As Balram crushes coal and wipes tables at the tea shop, he determines to make it a profoundly enriching experience, using his time to spy on every customer at every table and overhearing everything they said, thus keeping his education going. And it was at another tea shop in Dhanbad, the city of coal, where his brothers had brought him after he was fired from the one in his village, that his life changed—he learnt of a way to escape—of breaking away from the banks of Mother Ganga, which is overflowing with "a rich, dark, sticky mud whose grip traps everything...".[6]

The lesson Balram Halwai proposes to impart to the Chinese premier about the new India is drawn from his own rags to riches story. This son of a rickshaw puller is brought away, by his own entrepreneurial spunk, from the Darkness which constitutes at least a third of the country, "a fertile place full of rice fields and wheat fields...and water buffaloes wading through the ponds..."[7] to the Light. "Please understand your Excellency, that India is two countries in one: an India of Light and an India of Darkness. The ocean brings light to my country. Every place on the map of India near the ocean is well off. But the river brings darkness to India—the black river."[8]

Balram Halwai's big chance comes when a rich village landlord hires him as a chauffeur for his son, daughter-in-law and their two Pomeranian dogs living in the capital. From behind the steering wheel of a Honda, Balram sees Delhi. It is a revelation and a re-education for the poor village youth. The cockroaches and call-centers, the slums, the shopping malls and the crippling traffic jams, all join in his orientation. However, the one emotion he feels strongly all the time is the sense of loyalty to his master. He is caught between his instinct to be a faithful son and servant and his desire to better himself, and step by step, learns of a new morality at the heart of the new India. Gradually, he starts doing things he is ashamed of admitting, like cheating his employer, but the strange thing was that each time he cheated he felt, instead of guilt, rage. The final step he takes towards his liberation is fraught, not with remorse but with anxiety to make it succeed and succeed it does. The whole story from the point where he gores his master to death with the broken bottle of Johnny Walker to his escape to Bangalore with his master's red bag full of cash (which was the catalyst to his deed), is an "amazing success story...from being a social entrepreneur to a business entrepreneur".[9]

The White Tiger becomes thus, a vivid exploration of India's class struggle, anatomizing the fantastic cravings of the rich and evoking, with startling accuracy, the even more desperate struggles of the deprived. The novel which is apparently straightforward, gives a dazing account of the realities of life of India's poor. The sharp and satirical eye of the narrator draws the reader into dark regions. Adam Lively in *The Sunday Times* remarks that Adiga is playing 'a bigger game'. *The White Tiger* is contradictory to those representations (where the images of doe-eyed children dominate the electronic media), which sentimentalize poverty and suggest that there may even be something ennobling in it. Balram Halwai's story illustrates that poverty creates monsters and he himself is such a monster. Cultural critics place themselves in opposition to the power structures of society, "questioning inequalities within power structures"[10] and seeking to restructure. Adiga is in the same role, bringing together subjectivity—culture in relation to individual lives—with an engagement that is a direct attack on class inequalities in society.

The reality of the class divide in Indian society hits hard through this tale. Following Marx, it can be said that the struggle between oppressor and oppressed has been carrying on uninterruptedly, sometimes open, sometimes hidden, in all societies. The two have stood in constant opposition to each other and their light has brought on either a revolutionary re-constitution of society or the common ruin of the contending classes. The inhumanity shown by the rich towards their domestic staff in *The White Tiger* is something of which many Indians will realize they too are guilty. The fearful crime committed by the protagonist Balram Halwai sends a palpitation of fear into the heart of that class which remains complacently unmoved by the social inequality perpetuated by itself. Adiga comes across as a writer with a 'real' sense of social commitment and an original voice and vision in his novel. He has a sharp and satirical eye for the realities of life in the feudal-bourgeois set-up of India. The world of the rich with their tinted windows up, and the lives of the poor—"...go to old Delhi...and look at the ways they keep chicken...the very same thing is done with human beings in this country"[11] affords a disturbing contrast, and the truth of it is driven home forcefully "In the old days there were 1000 castes...in India. These days there are just two castes: Men with Big Bellies and Men with Small Bellies."[12]

The White Tiger is an unexpected journey into a new India, an unforgiving story about modern India, horrifying in its details about the desperate acts it takes for one man to rise above poverty, caste system, corruption and brutal social contract. Indians fear Adiga's novel says too much about them. William Green, former *Time Asia* Editor understands that the book has raised Indian hackles because it is an unsettling novel and touches raw nerves but captures the complexity and subtlety of Indian fiction amazingly. This is a more justified view—that *The White Tiger* has attracted attention not merely for the social ethos it portrays but for the comportment of this portrayal.

At the reception of the Booker Prize for his novel, Adiga said his book was "an attempt to catch the voice of men you meet as you travel through India—the voice of the colossal underclass".[13] Born in India but brought up partly in Australia and educated abroad, Adiga looks at India with the perspective both of an insider and as outsider. He confesses "as an immigrant in the US and England, I was an outsider. I spent a lot of time being confused, trying to figure things out. That was how I understood how Indian villagers feel when they move to the big cities for work. The middle class is paranoid about servants and their 'laziness', greed and thieving tendencies. However, the fact is that in spite of the huge disparities of wealth, and the intimate access that servants have to their masters in their homes, very few actually commit any crime."[14]

The focal point of the novel is the glaring question of inequalities within power structures in Indian society. *The White Tiger* provides a darkly comical view of modern life in India through the narration of Balram Halwai. The overall theme is the contrast between India's rise as a modern global economy and the state of the working class people who live in demeaning, acute poverty. The modern bourgeois society born out of the ruins of the feudal set-up has inflamed class antagonism in a subtle but larger way—"it has established new classes, new conditions of oppression, new forms of struggle in place of the old ones".[15] There is social justification in the rebellion of the underclass against their masters, but it is amazing that given all the paraphernalia of a social revolt, there are actually very few murders or attacks. On reading the novel, one is compelled to wonder why there isn't a continuous violent insurgency by the servant class. That desperation can lead to crime is exemplified in Balram's story.

The White Tiger, marks a new beginning in Indo-Anglian fiction by presenting the situation as seen, not merely through the eyes of a social reformer, but by one of themselves subject to the inequality. Adiga clearly reiterates that his aim is only an indictment of the injustice to which the servant class is subjected. The current social order reinforces that the poor slave as cooks, cleaners, drivers and maids so that the rich can feel comfortable. Adiga's voice which is a flash of an arousing cannot bring to an end this arrangement but it does make the affluent uncomfortable. For exactly this reason the novel is seen as appalling regression by some Indians. Author and playwright, Manjula Padmanabhan dismisses the book as a "tedious, unfunny slog". She admits that the hype about India as an emerging superpower, is dishonest, but the novel does no more than effect a schoolboyish sneering.

Comparing the novel to earlier writings *The White Tiger* is seen by Indian critics and defenders of the system as a step backward in terms of the deplorable picture it presents of the country. Indians thought that the old image of their country as a land of poverty, cows and snake-charmers had been finally shed and had started being respected as a high-tech prosperous nation, Adiga's novel arrived (with a Booker) to rub their noses in the dirt again. V.S. Naipaul, the first Booker Prize winner of Indian origin, had received criticism for talking contemptuously about India, how cleaners mop the floor in restaurants by crunching and moving like crabs and about Indian defecating in the open and Adiga is now held in the same view, focusing on everything that is bad and disgusting.

Cultural materialists perceive that ideology is actively constituted through social struggle and dominant ideologies sustain and keep social structures in place. Moreover, ideology is firmly situated within material institutions as a body of discursive practices which have no universal validity but are potent method of controlling and preserving social relations of exploitation. Adiga's act may be viewed as a challenge to the existing ideologies in the familiar privileged text which do no more than uphold the existing dominant social order. *The White Tiger* throws them into a new perspective opening up postcolonial Indian society to a fresh analysis.

The White Tiger is unmistakably, an unsettling novel which touches raw nerves but it captures the complexity and subtlety of India in fiction in an admirably potent way. It combines the journalistic account with a human eye for the reality of class distinctions saving the novel from becoming a racy thriller. The novel prevailed with the judges of the Booker panel because it shocks and entertains in equal measure. It is a difficult task to gain and sustain the readers' sympathy for a character who apparently is a thorough-going villain (which is how Balram Halwai appears on the surface) but the book has gained from dealing with pressing social issues and significant global developments with amazing tact and humour and offering a critique that is devastating. By an exploration of the complex totality of Indian society with the focus on its marginalised members and subversive practices, Adiga is only reiterating that "every history of subjection also contains a history of resistance",[16] and resistance other than being only a symptom and justification for subjection is the marker of a difference which ushers in a change. What he is doing is adopting the perspective of change, cultural difference and relativity of truth. The voice of dissenting critics can be silenced by this recognition of the task effected by Adiga that of giving priority to the production of alternative knowledge. "The idea of a uniform and harmonious culture is a myth imposed and propagated by the ruling class in their own interest"[17] and Adiga has made a move towards busting this myth.

REFERENCES

1. Guerin, Wilfred, et al. *A Handbook of Critical Approaches to Literature*, fourth edition. New York: Oxford University Press, 2003: 328-29.
2. Adiga, Aravind. *The White Tiger*. India: Harper Collins, 2008: 6.
3. *Ibid.*
4. *Ibid.*, 7.
5. *Ibid.*, 14.
6. *Ibid.*, 15.
7. *Ibid.*, 14.
8. *Ibid.*
9. *Ibid.*, 299.
10. Guerin, 241.
11. Adiga, 173.
12. *Ibid.*, 64.
13. Young, Victoria. *Novel about India Wins the Booker Prize.* NY Times: October 14, 2008. NYTimes_com.mht.
14. Interview with Adiga on "You Tube" on Oct. 15, 2008.

15. Marx, Karl and Engels, Friedrich. *Bourgeois and Proletarians*. Trans. Samuel Moore. *From Modernism to Postmodernism: An Anthology*. Ed. Lawrence E. Cahoone. Great Britain: Blackwell Publishers, 1996: 92.
16. Seldan, Raman and Widdowson, Peter. *A Reader's Guide to Contemporary Literary Theory*. Third edition. Great Britain: The University Press of Kentucky, 1993: 165.
17. *Ibid*., 163.

20

Reflection of India in Aravind Adiga's *The White Tiger*

Ansul Chandra

The White Tiger is the debut novel by Indian author Aravind Adiga, which was published in year 2008 and won the Man Booker Prize. It has become a well-known novel for its lucid depiction of India as two countries, the light and the darkness. In this novel, Adiga uses the back drop of present-day India to show the degradation of Indian values through the story *of the* protagonist, Balram Halwai. The main theme of the novel is the contrast between India's rise as a modern global economy and the working class people who live in crushing rural poverty.[1] Corruption in Indian society and politics, familial loyalty versus independence, the experience of returning to India after living in America, globalization and tensions between India and China as superpower countries in Asia are the other themes of the novel. The novel takes the form of a series of letters written by Balram to Wen Jiabao, the Chinese premier. Wen is poised to visit India to learn why it is good at producing entrepreneurs. So Balram presumes to tell him how to win power and influence people in the modern India. Balram's story is a tale of bribery, corruption, toxic traffic jams, theft and murder. Adiga himself says about his novel, "at a time when India is going through great changes and with China, is likely to inherit the world from the west, it is important that writers like me try to highlight the brutal injustices of societies—it's not an attack on the country, it's about the greater process of self-examination".[2]

Balram Halwai is a complicated man, servant, philosopher entrepreneur and murderer. He has divided India in the "India of Darkness" and "India of Light". He writes in his letter, "please understand your Excellency that India is two countries in one, an India of Light and an India of Darkness" (14). The area near the ocean is the India of light while India near the dark river "Mother Ganga" is the area of Darkness.

The protagonist Balram lived in village of Laxmangarh, a fictional village in Bihar, a community deep in the "Darkness" of rural India. The son of a rickshaw-puller, his family is too poor for him to be able to finish school. There is a reference to the poor facilities in a village; from which one can surmise how pathetic the predicament would have been for the villagers "Electricity poles—defunct. Water tap broken. Children too lean and short for their age and with oversized heads from which vivid eyes shine" (20).

The pathetic situation of poor people is described by the novelist when Balram's father was suffering from tuberculosis. When his father began spitting blood Kishan and Balram took him by boat across the river. They kept washing his mouth with water from the river, but the water was so polluted that it made him spit more blood (48). When they went to government hospital there was no doctor in the hospital and he died due to lack of treatment. There was corruption in hospital and bribery between politician and doctor. They bribe for the post and then keep practice in private hospitals because there's good money in public service.

In his childhood Balram was smart and brilliant, a school inspector notices and he was given the moniker White Tiger, a rare creature that comes once in a generation soon after, he's pulled out of school to work in a tea shop where people like him work as spiders. He writes to premier, "Go to a tea shop anywhere along the Ganga, Sir and look at the men working in that tea shop. Men, I say but better to call them human spiders that go crawling in between and under the tables with rags in their hands, crushed human in uniforms, sluggish, unshaven, in their thirties or forties or fifties but still 'boys'. But that is your fate if you do your job well—with honesty, dedication and sincerity the way Gandhi would have done it, no doubt, I did my job with near total dishonesty, lack of dedication and insinccrity—and so the teashop was a profoundly enriching experience" (51). Adiga uses Gandhi to show how Gandhian principles and his ways of life is missing in our life. This is a kind of degradation of our country.

The oppression of the lower-class people is everywhere throughout the novel by rich. Adiga has employed a strange technique of assailing the rich by addressing them only by names of animals like buffalo, stork, wild boar, and raven. S. Prasannarajan says that, "there is protest, anger, disgust and a sense of compassion".[3] The life in Laxmangarh revolves around the landlords and they in their greed for power and money suck the marrow from the bones of the poor labour class.

While working in Dhanbad Balram learns to drive and he gets his break when a rich man from his village known simply as "The stork" hires him as a chauffer from his son Ashok and his wife Pinky Madam who live in the city of New Delhi, the light. Ashok is a gentleman and his soft behaviour with his servants is resented by his brother Mukesh and father. When his father hit Balram when he was doing his massage Ashok asks ".... Do you have to hit the servants, father?" and he replies, "This is not America, Son. Don't ask question like that" (72). It is horrible to find that there is casual human right violation perpetrated by the rich landlords on the poor. Facing physical as well as mental discomfort is a part of poor in rural areas in India. The gap between the rich and the poor became wider and Ashok becomes the victim of this.

Stork and his sons involve in the coal trading and they give money to the politicians so that during an election the campaign and victory will be assured. In return, they are thanked by exemption from paying taxes. Ashok is conflicted by the corruption and harshness of life in India but he is caught in this foul maze. Ashok also has to deal with his family's unhappiness for marrying his current wife Pinky, as the two of the married in the US. They do not believe in caste system but Ashok's father does approve of the marriage because she is of another caste.

Balram's experience in New Delhi is a revelation of 'Light India'. As he drives his master to shopping malls and call centers, Balram becomes increasingly aware of immense wealth and opportunity all around him. It reflects the economic progress of country. It's in Delhi that Balram comes to the realization that there's a new caste system at work in both India and world and it has only two groups those who are eaten and those who eat prey and predators. Balram decides to be an eater. A key metaphor in the novel is the Rooster coop. Balram compares the life of Indian servants to that of chicken in rooster coop. Balram also recognizes that those who are eaten are trapped inside a small and closed cage the rooster coop—that limits their opportunities. Even worse they begin to internalize the limitation of the coop, so that after a while they're unable to image they deserve any other world than the cramped one in which they exist. He calls this coop, "the greatest thing to come out of this country in the ten thousand years of its history" (173). He also says that the trustworthiness of servants is the basis of the entire Indian economy. The following lines in the novel glorify the honesty of poor people, "He (rickshaw-puller) unloads all this furniture for you and you give him the money in cash a fat wad of cash, the size of a brick. He puts it into his pocket or into his shirt or into his underwear and cycles back to his boss and hands it over without touching a single rupee of it" (174).

He has also presented the honest deeds of the chauffeurs, taxi drivers and servants of the diamond merchants.

As there is always exception everywhere, it is quite natural in poor to feel irate to change their social and economic status. When the torture imposed on the poor crosses its limit, the poor are desperate enough to attack on the rich. This situation leads to the birth of critical crime like murder. The prolonged inner struggle going on in Balram's mind to murder or not to murder Ashok, his master is very well brought out by Adiga. The feeling of revenge after the car accident where he had to take up the blame for his mistress Pinky Madam was held up against the goodness of his master. Finally, he decides to murder him. Balram slashed his throat and fled to Bangalore with Dharam. He steals seven hundred thousand rupees and creates his own taxi company and changes his name to Ashok Sharma. Now he becomes a wealthy entrepreneur in new technological society, i.e. India of light.

Adiga has also touched upon the current political scenario and showed there is, bribery between politicians and wealthy businessman. Ashok gives money to the politicians during an election and in return he is thanked for his effort by being exempted from paying taxes.

The party of Great socialist keeps getting elected over and over again. He is progressing from the Darkness to Delhi and then onto Bangalore which is the India of light. However, the condition of the people of Darkness do not improve and rich people continue to live in the lap of luxury.

The police are also corrupt. Balram gives the police more than ten thousand rupees for raiding a taxi service so that he could start-up (301) his own taxi company. The police can also be brought off by rich and powerful persons. Once Balram gives the police an envelope of rupees to smooth over the situation when his driver Mohammad Asif accidentally runs over a boy.

In his simple and lucid language, Adiga describes the innermost thoughts of a driver, a real Indian who dreams to be a rich man. As Uma Mahadevan-Dasgupta says, that *The White Tiger* is the story of this underclass and its life begging for food, sleeping under concrete flyovers, defecating on the roadsides, shivering in the cold, struggling in the twenty-first century for its freedom. *The White Tiger* gives this underclass a voice one that is intelligent, savagely funny and unforgettable. It is a voice that seeks out and understands the power of beauty.[4]

Aravind Adiga has focused his attention much on the poor in the India of Darkness as well as India of Light. One can easily measure the ocean of difference between the rich and the poor. By presenting Balram as a great entrepreneur, Adiga has ended the novel with a optimistic thought that it is possible for a person of economically poor status to bring about better economic condition by hook or crook in India.

NOTES

1. Review: *The White Tiger* by Aravind Adiga. *The Telegraph* 09/08/2008.
2. S. Prasannarajan, Review "Books—Driving out of Darkness".
3. *Ibid.*
4. Uma Mahadevan-Dasgupta, "Profoundly Indian", *Frontline*, Nov. 2008: 128.

21

Politico-social and Cultural Image of India in Kiran Desai's *The Inheritance of Loss* and Aravind Adiga's *The White Tiger*

Krishna Singh

The paper endeavours to analyse the politico-social and cultural consciousness in Kiran Desai's *The Inheritance of Loss* and Aravind Adiga's *The White Tiger*. Both the novels bagged the prestigious Man Booker Prize in 2006 and 2008 respectively explore various facets of India. *The Inheritance of Loss* (2006) explores colonial neurosis, multiculturalism, modernity, immigrants' bitter experiences, insurgency and the game of possession, gender-bias, racial discrimination, changing human relations, impact of globalization, *Isthal Puran* type delineation of the North East of India, post-colonial chaos and despair, ethno-racial and historical relationships between people from different cultures and backgrounds. Love, longing and losses are dexterously handled in a humane manner articulating diasporic experiences of the novelist who is an Indian citizen but a Permanent Resident of America. Kiran Desai is deeply interested in India—the India of 1980s—honestly and consciously represents the mixed image of India. Desai observes everything through the "lens of being Indian", without that perspective, she acknowledged, "she can't write" ("wiki/kirandesai"). It was only when she began to writing about the immigrant experience in New York that she realized she would have to return to India. But she finds India has changed, it belongs to the Indian author living in India. The subjects belong to them. She goes back to India of the 1980s. It is this feeling of being caught between two continents that infuses the novel. Consequently, she makes the novel an Indian treating subjects concerning Indian life in India as well as in abroad. Aravind Adiga's debut novel *The White Tiger* creates two different Indias, i.e. India of Light and India of Darkness. It was Adiga's journalistic experience working with the *Time* which allowed him to make frequent visits to India and make reports for the paper which prompted Adiga to transform this accumulated knowledge and experience about India into a tale—a tale of two Indias. It is from the desk of the protagonist Balram Halwai, Seven Nights' epistolary communiqué to the Chinese Premier Wen Jiabao—political culture, social milieu and entrepreneurial success of India in a globalized world of twenty-first century is reported; simultaneously India has been contrasted with the emerging second world power China. Though India has already figured in the Booker novels of V.S. Naipaul, Salman Rushdie, Arundhati Roy, yet Desai and Adiga have made conscious efforts to highlight the politico-social and cultural issues which constitute the very fibre of Indian life. This bold attempt endorses their keen interest and involvement in Indian life and aims to introduce corrective measures. Balram's journey from the darkness of village life to the light of entrepreneurial success is amoral altogether, brilliantly irreverent, deeply endearing and completely unforgettable. Balram is a typical voice of underclass metaphorically described as "Rooster Coop" (173) struggling to set free from age-old slavery and exploitation. His anger, indulgence in criminal acts, prostitution, drinking, chasing, grabbing all the opportunities and means fair or foul endorse deep-rooted frustration and its reaction against the "haves". Bloody revolution, use of barrel and guns, emergence of the Socialists in India alarm that the voice of the underclass cannot be ignored for long. Though the novel centres on Munna Halwai, son of a rickshaw-puller, destined to make sweets becomes Ashok Sharma (transformation from Munna—

Balram Halwai—White Tiger—Ashok Sharma), North Indian entrepreneur settled in Bangalore—other issues, i.e. political, social, cultural, economic are also incorporated throughout the novel making it a complex work of fiction.

In *The Inheritance of Loss*, politically, India was hit by insurgency. It imposed a big threat to law and order. Entire novel is set in the backdrop of insurgency rising in the North East, i.e. GNLF movement which disrupted the normal life, tourism, business and peace. Out of fifty-three Chapters of the novel more than eighteen Chapters are exclusively devoted to describe insurgency to highlight the dismal picture of the region. Poverty, unemployment, socio-economic backwardness, xenophobia, discriminatory policies and the government's apathy to seek remedies are deeply rooted in the separatist movements rampant in the whole country. No part is spared; it's alarming and anticipates disastrous consequences: "Separatist movement here, separatist movement there, terrorists, guerillas, insurgents, rebels, agitators, instigators, and all they learn from one another, of course—the Neps have been encouraged by the Sikhs and their Khalistan, by ULFA, NEFA, PLA; Jharkhand, Bodoland, Gorkhaland; Tripura, Mizoram, Manipur, Kashmir, Punjab, Assam..." (128-29). Desai curtly blames the policymakers for these violent movements: "This state making, the biggest mistake that fool Nehru made. Under his rules any group of idiots can stand up demanding a new state and get it, too...it all started with Sikkim. The Neps played such a dirty trick and began to get grand ideas—now they think they can do the same thing again" (128). "Gorkhaland for Gorkhas" (7) is the motto of the movement; the activists work on universal guerilla fashion. Socio-cultural and political identity and quest for autonomy furthers and kindles the fire of agitation. Indian Nepalese are "fed up being treated like the minority in a place where they were the majority. They wanted their own country or at least their own state, in which to manage their own affairs" (9). Gyan's involvement in the separatist movement is the reflection of young Indians' deep-rooted frustration, for which Gyan even sacrifices the love of Sai. The novel opens and ends with insurgency. The partition of India and the emergence of Pakistan is indeed, Desai poignantly reacts: "First heart attack to our country...that has never been healed" (129). In *Hullabaloo in the Guava Orchard*, Desai exposes political bankruptcy: "Not one truthful politician in the whole country. Yes, our parliament is made of thieves, each one answerable to the prime minister, who is the biggest thief of them all" (20).

The novel portraits the Indian society as poverty-stricken; moreover illiteracy, unemployment, xenophobia, cultural conflicts, traditional values, customs, practices; and multiplicity of languages, religions, faiths constitute the very structure of the society in which the novelist is deeply interested. Though she draws a dismal picture of the Indian society, she has a humanistic approach—even characters, i.e. Jemu, Sai, Gyan, Biju, Cook, Lola, Noni, Booty, Potty and Bela all are helpless and feel inferior by their subject position—Desai, very candidly and in an inhumane manner treats them. Poverty is the root cause of GNLF movement and migration. Gyan's involvement in GNLF movement and frustration caused by the extreme polarities he witnesses between the poor and the rich brings drastic changes in his attitude and love. He is upset to undertake long walk in the cold for the small amount of money the judge paid him. It maddened him that: "People lived here (Cho Oyu) in this enormous house and property, taking hot baths, sleeping alone in spacious rooms...cutlets and peas dinner..." (162). Cook and Biju epitomize the distress of common men. Sai's journey from Dehradoon to Darjeeling notices the panorama of village life and India looks as old as ever; realistic description arrests our attention: "Women walked by with firewood on their heads, too poor for blouses under their saris.... It was early in the morning and the railways tracks were lined with rows of bare bottoms...defecating onto the tracks, rinsing their bottoms with water from a can" (30). *Chapatis, jalebis, samosa, fish, chips, pakora, tea, chhang, laddoos, chooran, srikhand, fresh milk*, etc. figure in regular meals of the society gradually experiencing transition and replacing them with *Angrezi Khana*. But all over Kalimpong modernity began to fail.

The novel is a brilliant study of Indian culture—the culture in its transitional phase. Changes are brought out by "colonial neurosis", craze for the Western values, manners, language and glamorous lifestyle; impact of modernization, consumerism, globalization and deep-rooted reaction to indigenous values which failed to sustain life. Characters feel inferior, bounded and defeated by their Indian heritage confronted with colonialism; consequently, they develop grotesque complexes which mar their mutuality and reciprocal relationship. Jemu, Lola, Pixie, Noni, Biju, Cook, Sai, Gyan all are generic, reflect the pain of transition. Despite political freedom, cultural slavery is directly manifested through these characters. They fail to assimilate new culture and give up original culture in totality. There remains identity crisis which most of the Indians face despite postcolonial reactions in which endeavour is to revitalize indigenous culture and its values. Jemu originally belongs to Piphit, goes to Cambridge for higher studies, selected in I.C.S.; becomes a judge. In this entire process of making, he goes on adopting the West as a model of excellence; he sacrifices his native values. He even changes the name of his desi wife Bela to Nimi; condemns her for her socio-cultural practices; whereas, Sai, the granddaughter is commended because she is Westernized Indian brought up by English nuns. Jemu is the finest example of an Anglophile—"being a foreigner in his own country..." (29). Jemu and Sai are type of "estranged Indian living in India" (210). Gyan also satirizes: "You (Jemu and Sai) are like slaves, that's what you are, running after the West, embarrassing yourself" (163). Biju stands for young crazy men of the Third World who dream a plan to go to the West for money making; unflinchingly, they sacrifice original culture and social conventions. Lola, Noni, Pixie and Mrs. Sen are also camouflaged by British ways. Lola advises her daughter Pixie to leave India because "India is a sinking ship...*the doors won't stay open for ever...*" (47). Multiculturalism is an important feature of Indian society. Jemu, Sai, Biju, Cook, Lola, Noni, Booty, Potty, Gyan, Mr. and Mrs. Mistry belong to different cultural backgrounds. She maintains convivial attitude to all cultures and mildly exposes the vanity and hypocrisy imbibed in them.

Nature and landscape description occupies large canvas of the novel; though it extends from Manhattan to Himalayas, it is central to Piphit, Kalimpong, Cho Oyu, and Darjeeling. Topography, scenic beauty, variety of vegetation, changing colours of the sky, patches of clouds, rain, mist, mountain tops, Teesta river, thick forests, cluster of houses, vapour, ice, zig-zag roads and seasonal changes, etc. define nature in the novel. It is sensuous beauty, which delights the novelist very much, simultaneously; it is contrasted with rising insurgency and its violent outbreak disrupting normal life. Her treatment of nature is highly poetic and Wordsworthian finding deeper import in it. She investigates parallel development in changing seasons and incidents of violence:

> *The incidents of horror grew,* through the changing of the seasons, through winter and a flowery spring, summer, then rain and winter again. Roads were closed, there was curfew every night, and Kalimpong was trapped in its own madness. You couldn't leave the hillsides; nobody even left their houses if they could help it but stayed locked in and barricaded. (279)

The novel is essentially a study of losses—loss of culture, loss of identity, loss of human relations. Loss of emotional binding, loss of human values, loss of rationality, loss of peace and harmony, loss of human beings' faith in each, etc. Sense of loss is an integral part of every character's life; they are insecure, and unmoored, struggling to survive in the modern world, unsure of whether they will ever see the benefits of globalization; characters unnecessarily feel inferior due to their Indian heritage. Historical events have deep personal import that last people's lifetime and even beyond. Jemu who originally hails from Piphit; goes to Cambridge for higher studies, he is selected in I.C.S. and becomes a judge. He is so much impressed and immersed in Western values, he loses his original Indian identity and feels "foreigner in his own country" (29). These Indians are also unwanted anachronism in postcolonial India, where long-suppressed peoples have begun to awaken to their dereliction, to express their anger and despair; GNLF movement is an outburst of that reaction and

Gyan's xenophobia is rooted in it. Jemu cannot free himself from "colonial neurosis" (46). Jemu loses peace by the arrival of Sai and Biju and GNLF activities; strongly misses the glorious past and Mutt for whom he laments loudly. Due to insurgency North East loses three Ts: "Tea! Timber! Tourism" (225). Sai also loses indigenous cultural values. In the process of academic learning in a convent school, Western Christian values enter into her blood. Though she remains "full of contradictions" (30) she also suffers from identity crisis. The biggest loss she feels profoundly is the love of Gyan. Biju who goes to New York with bright hopes, soon discovers authentic colonial experience how Third World poor natives are exploited and humiliated in the West: "They drew the lines at crucial junctures" (23) and "on the top, rich colonial, and down below, poor native; Columbian, Tunisian, Ecuadorian.... Above all, the restaurant was French, but below in the kitchen it was Mexican and Indian" (21). White men also shout: "*Uloo ka Patta,* son of an owl, low down son-of-a-bitch Indian" (23). Even the glamorous picture of the West changes into hatred: "There was a whole world in the basement kitchens of New York" (22). He also faces tough and discriminatory Immigration laws in America, fails to procure green card; listed "shadow class" (102) of illegal immigrants in New York and spends thirty years time dodging the authorities, moving from one ill-paid job to another. His bitter experiences in America and homesickness compel him for homecoming. Even in his own country he finds total loss of peace, law and order. He is robbed by GNLF activists and chased by dogs. Lola, Noni, Pixie and Mrs. Sen are also trapped by British ways. Lola advises her daughter Pixie, a BBC reporter: "Better leave (India) sooner than later...India is a sinking ship. Don't want to be pushy, darling, sweetie, thinking of your happiness only, but *the doors won't stay open for ever...*" (47). Lola and Noni are publicly humiliated by *Pradhan* of GNLF, violate the dignity of genteel women while both the sisters go to complain against encroachment in Mon Ami. Loss of dignity and dreamland (Mon Ami) make them helpless. Father Booty, who runs a dairy in Kalimpong, spends forty-five years as an illegal immigrant, while he has the visa for two weeks only. Later he is forced to leave the country. Consequently, he lost "every thing but his memories" (257). Gyan sacrifices the love of Sai for his Gorkhaland. Cook loses his honour when Jemu cruelly beats him on the missing of Mutt. Almost all of Desai's characters have been stunted by their encounters with the West.

Binnie Kirshenbaum has rightly commented about the novel: "A nation's tragedies, great and small, are revealed through the hopes and the dreams, the innocence and the arrogance, the love betrayed and the all, too, human failings of a superbly realized cast of characters. Kiran Desai writes of Postcolonial India, of its poor as well as its privileged, with a cold eye and a warm heart" ("*The Inheritance of Loss:* Reviews"). Sunita Sinha observes, "Desai's novels are full of wisdom and subtle parallels; it is both funny and bitterly sad, but generally optimistic. Never preachy, never predictable, Desai's scope is broad looking at the consequences of large cultural and political forces for both people and individuals" ("Introduction", xxv). Political, social and cultural aspects are dealt in and described in a comprehensive manner, which is not only entertaining but also highly informative.

The novel *The White Tiger* is structured as a series of letters written to the Chinese Premier by a former car driver from Laxamangarh, Bihar. Why the Chinese Premier? "Because" the narrator Balram Halwai, based in the city of Bangalore acknowledges, "the future of the world lies with the yellow man and the brown man now that our erstwhile master, the White skinned man has wasted himself through buggery, mobile phone usage and drug abuse" (5-6). India of Light with access to education, health care, transportation facilities, electricity, running water, hope, justice, emerging entrepreneurial power in the world surpassing China; India's rapid advancement in the field of science and technology, space, real estate, yoga and meditation, hotel and tourism industry, expansion of cities and mall culture, Delhi is adulated as Young America in India; the voice of the underclass is strongly articulated and attempts to give them proper recognition in the society. Entrepreneurial success is the hallmark of India: "You Chinese are far ahead of us in every respect, except that you don't have entrepreneurs.... Especially in the field of technology. And these entrepreneurs—*we* entrepreneurs have set up all these outsourcing companies that virtually run America now" (4). The narrator explains the reasons for entrepreneurial success: "My country is the kind where it pays to play it both ways: the Indian entrepreneur has to be strait and crooked, mocking and believing, sly and sincere, at the same time" (8-9). The secrets of success in a modern globalized world has summed up in the last section of the novel. Murder, manipulation, malpractices, opportunism, bribery, absconding police and judicial proceedings all are justified for success and teaching based on the facts of life:

"A school where you won't be allowed to corrupt anyone's head with prayers and stories about God and Gandhi—nothing but the facts of life for these kids. A school full of White Tigers" (319). Adiga makes humble prediction: "In twenty years' time, it will be just us yellow man and brown man at the top of the pyramid, and we'll rule the whole world" (305). Ashok, the employer of Balram also observes shining India: "things have changed so much in India. There are so many more things I could do here than in New York...the way things are changing in India now, this place is going to be like America in ten years" (89). The voice of Dark India—the under class that is, comments Uma Mahadevan-Dasgupta, "intelligent, savagely funny and quite unforgettable—it is also a voice of anger and protest, and it is almost completely unsentimental. It is a voice that seeks out and understands the power of beauty" (128). The novel can also be assessed as a socialist manifesto trying to dismantle the discrimination between the "Big Bellies and the Small Bellies" (64) and evolve an egalitarian society.

The larger canvas of the novel discusses the Dark pictures of India. Some critics have raised suspicion over his undue emphasis to this dismal portrayal. Adiga has reacted: "At a time when India is going through great changes and with China, is likely to inherit the world from the West, it is important that writers like me try to highlight the brutal injustices of society...the great divide" (*Sunday Times of India,*

Oct 19, 2008). Just when we thought that the world has raving about the economic miracle of India, a brutal confession by *The White Tiger* protagonist exposes the rot in the three pillars of modern India—democracy, enterprise and justice—reducing them to the tired clichés of a faltering nation. And the author of this tragic tale grabs the prestigious Booker, with the head of the jury, Michel Portillio, calling it a work that shows the "dark side of India—a new territory" (*Sunday Times of India*).

Ever widening gap between the rich and poor, rural and urban, and the brutal reality of an economic system that allows a small minority to prosper at the expense of the silent majority; political culture of India, voting behaviour, social milieu, caste and culture conflict, superstition, social taboos, exploitation of underclass, Zamindari practice, emergence of Naxalism, unemployment especially in rural India, prostitution, master-servant relationship, nexus between the politicians, criminals and the police, mockery of education system, hollowness of government's welfare schemes, poor medical services, harmful impact of scientific, technological and industrial development, etc. mark off the novel. The final impression of the novel is that it justifies every kind of trick to succeed in life. Balram Halwai, the protagonist and his rise from Munna to Ashok Sharma verifies this proposition. Adiga's exposure of the dark areas of India can be taken positively to cure the sick image of it—if we focus on those areas and work sincerely, undoubtedly a new India will emerge.

Political system and bureaucratic set up, according to the novel refer to the darkest areas of our country which breed, "rottenness and corruption" (50) in our society and hamper all developmental and welfare schemes. It restricts half of this country from achieving its potential. Most of the politicians are "half-baked. That's the whole tragedy of this country" (10). The story of Balram's emergence is the story of how a half-baked fellow is produced. Politics is the last refuge for scoundrels. Government doctors, entrepreneurs, taxpayers, industrialists all have to befriend a minister and his sidekick to fulfill their vested interests. Mukesh and Ashok also bribe the minister to settle income-tax accounts. Election, though we feel proud of glorious democracy of ours, are manipulated; power transfers from one hand to another but the common man's fate remains unchanged. Adiga considers, "Typhoid, Cholera and election fever the three main diseases of this country and the last one the worst" (98). Voters discuss about the election helplessly as "eunuchs discussing the *Kama Sutra*" (98). Balram reports: "I am India's most faithful voter, and I still have not seen the inside of a voting booth" (102). Adiga observes that we are lagging behind China because of "this fucked up system called parliamentary democracy. Otherwise, we'd be just like China" (156). This rotten system has created new distinctions and classes. In the old days there were one thousand castes and destinies in India now just two castes: "Men with Big Bellies, and Men with Small Bellies. And only two destinies: eat—or get eaten up" (64). It did not "matter whether you were a woman, or a Muslim: or an untouchable—anyone with a belly could rise up" (64).

The novel gives the detailed accounts of the Indian society—rural as well as urban and its various facets. Laxmangarh, Gaya, Dhanbad, Delhi and Bangalore are generic, represent the portrait of India. Poverty, illiteracy, unemployment, caste and culture conflict, superstition, dowry practice, economic disparity, Zamindari system, and exploitation of marginal farmers and landless labourers, rise of Naxalism, corrupt education system, poor health services, tax evading racket, embittered master-servant relationship, prostitution, weakening family structure, entrepreneurial success and its fallout, etc. constitute the basic structure of Indian society which largely forms the Dark image of India. Adiga was curious and troubled by the sight, and during his travels in India as a journalist, he wanted to explore more. *The White Tiger* is a tale of this underclass and its life—begging for food, sleeping under concrete flyovers, defecating on the roadside, shivering in the cold, struggling in the 21st century, for its freedom. V.S. Naipaul has also highlighted the Darkness of India in his *Area of Darkness* (1964): "rigid caste distinction" (53), "English mimicry" (55), "Indian lavatory and kitchens—the visitors' nightmare" (58), "clubs of Bombay and Delhi...poverty" (62-66), "misfortunes of refugee family" (68), underclass denied of opportunities; lack of hygiene and sense of sanitation: "Indians defecate everywhere" (70), "labour is a degradation" (73), businesman: "all his duty is, by whatever means, to make money" (77); "symbolic actions" (80); irrational "reservation policy [which] places responsibility in the hands of the unqualified" (82). It is extreme poverty, which creates Darkness in the life of the rural as well as urban people, and it perpetuates the sufferings of the underclass. It is poverty in Laxmangarh, Gaya there is an exodus of jobless youths towards big cities and the protagonist Balram Halwai and his brother are no exception. It is poverty, which compels Balram—The White Tiger to leave the school and work in a tea stall washing utensils and doing every kind of menial jobs.

While the novel moves from country to city, the whole world of underclass also migrates—their exploitation and sufferings. With the labourers working in the industrial set-up, taxi and auto drivers, servants, prostitutes, beggars, poor and shivering lots hiding under flyovers, slum-dwellers, corrupt police, legal and administrative structure, unfriendly master-servant relationship underclass emerges. Big cities like Delhi and Bangalore witness both kinds of India. Balram's journey from Laxmangarh to Dhanbad then Delhi and finally to Bangalore endorses that the socio-psychological condition of the underclass remains unchanged. Though the cities provide ample opportunities of job, social behaviour and psyche of the upper class is identical everywhere—whether it is a landlord or politician, police official, bureaucrat, upper caste people, rich-man, industrialist or entrepreneur. Everywhere underclass is trapped in Rooster Coop, struggling to come out of the cage. Balram is the conscience of underclass—its anger, frustration, protest and revenge, ready to adopt a new moral code of conduct to succeed in life. Murder of Ashok by Balram is the reaction of deep-rooted frustration of underclass experiencing the polarities between the upper class and lower class. Apart from these, pollution, hectic routine of life, harmful effects of mobile, impact of city culture, etc. create new territories of Darkness in India.

India is shown as an emerging entrepreneurial power in the world. Advancement in the field of science and technology, space, transportation, hotel industry, tourism, real estate, expansion of cities, mall culture, industries and outsourcing, etc. characterize the image of India. But all these developmental activities depend on underclass with distinct identity. Auto and taxi drivers constitute a big fragment of underclass inhabiting in the cities. Balram is a true prototype of this class manifesting miseries of their life, humiliation, struggle, dreams and involvement in criminal and illegal activities. There is no space for the poor in the malls of New India. Drivers and servants are also forced to confess the crime their masters have committed. Balram is so much disgusted of the life of a slave that he never feels guilty of Ashok's murder. He wants to experience "just for a day, just for an hour, just for a *minute*, what it means not to be a servant" (321).

Adiga has successfully portrayed the different images of India—India of Light and India of Dark. But his focus is on the latter and he tries to give it a literary voice. Adiga in conversation with Hirsh Sawhney explained the nature of progress: "technology is one aspect of progress; it is not progress in itself. Progress is holistic—its water and cell phones" ("India: A View from Below"). Deirdre Donahue considers the novel one of the most powerful books she has read in decades with, "No hyperbole...an amazing and angry novel about injustice and power" ("Complete Review"). Lee Thomas has reviewed the novel in *San Francisco Chronicle* (April 27, 2008): "Adiga's first novel *The White Tiger,* delivers an indomitable central character and an India bristling with economic possibility, competing loyalties and class struggle" ("Complete Review"). Sudheer Apte finds the most enjoyable part of the novel, "is richly observed world of have-nots in India...with his keen observation and sharp writing Adiga takes us into Balram Halwai's mind, whether we want or not" ("Mostly Fiction Book Reviews").

Adiga in the second novel *Between the Assassinations* has further elaborated the political, social and cultural milieu of India (Kittur). Kittur is a multi-religious, multi-ethnic and multi-lingual town. Underneath the assured richness, diversity and scenic topography, Kittur proves a backdrop for communal hatred, casteism, corruption, social evils and political rottenness. The "old bad India" still exists, "India of caste and class privilege—the India of child marriage; of ill-treated widows; of exploited subalterns" (267). Corruption engulfs the whole Kittur. Adiga sarcastically comments, "when it comes to three areas—'black-marketing, counterfeiting, and corruption', we are the world champions" (31).

Kiran Desai's *The Inheritance of Loss* and Aravind Adiga's *The White Tiger* are remarkable studies of politico-social and cultural life of India; they cannot be dismissed as merely traveller's accounts. The minute observation and close understanding of both the novelists are manifested in their fictions, which facilitate us to concentrate on them and evolve corrective measures. The dark areas of our polity, culture and social milieu have been targeted by both, simultaneously, the bright image of India, hope for entrepreneurial success find place in both the novels.

WORKS CITED

Adiga, Aravind. *The White Tiger*. New Delhi: Harper Collins Publishers India with India Today Group, 2008.

——. *Between the Assassinations*. London: Pan Macmillan Ltd., 2008.

——. *The Sunday Times of India*. New Delhi: Oct. 19, 2008.

Apte, Sudheer. "Mostly Fiction Book Review", 22.04.2008.

Desai, Kiran. *The Inheritance of Loss*. New Delhi: Penguin Books India, 2006.

——. *Hullabaloo in the Guava Orchard*. London: Faber and Faber, 1998.

Donahue, Deirdre. "Complete Review", 23.04.2008.

Kirshenbaum, Binnie. "*The Inheritance of Los:* Reviews", 10.10.2008.

Lee, Thomas. "Complete Review", 27.04.2008.

Mahadevan-Dasgupta, Uma. *Frontline*. November 7, 2008.

Naipaul, V.S. *An Area of Darkness*. London: Picador, 1995.

Portillio, Michel. *The Sunday Times of India*. New Delhi: Oct. 19, 2008.

Sawhney, Hirsh. "India: A View from Below Aravind Adiga with Hirsh Sawhney", 11.11.2008.

Sinha, Sunita (Ed.). *Critical Responses to Kiran Desai,* New Delhi: Atlantic Publishers & Distributors (P) Ltd., 2009.

Wikipedia. "Wiki/kirandesai", 20.10.2009.

22

India—Constructed or Incidental

Smita Verghese

> When *Midnight's Children* came out in 1981, it seemed all but impossible for subsequent writers to go back to the referential mode of Mulk Raj Anand, Kamala Markandaya and Khushwant Singh. And yet, ten years later, Seth writes a decidedly referential work, traditional in its linearity, unpretentious in its subject matter, and conventional in its prose. It is a work that grows out of the sensibility of an insider. While Rushdie's work is concerned with history, historiography, and the collapse of identity, Seth's concern in *A Suitable Boy* is with consolidation of family, community, and the nation.[1] (207)

Trying to figure out the nation or nations—be those the one(s) you are born to or the one(s) you end up being a part of—has been a challenge for many writers over the years. As readers and interpreters of literature, our challenge has been similar. When in the process of understanding texts which are rooted in different nations or countries there are so many arguments that we have to face, so many details we have to take into account, so much of information that we are forced to seek out. It gets just that much more complicated when the nation or nations involved or discussed are familiar to us.

Chelva Kanaganayakam's reading of Rushdie's work (the lines quoted above) becomes significant because his observation for writers holds good for readers of literature as well. Perhaps, India and the concept of the formation of a nation could never be the same after *Midnight's Children* and every reader attempting to understand the phenomenon called India would have to refer to how much of a "Midnight's Child" she/he was or is.

Twenty-nine years after the appearance of Rushdie's novel much has changed and evolved in the literatures across the world. Theories have formed exclusively to discuss writings from nations that have been termed postcolonial. Writers and works produced have been studied in order to understand the confusion, complexities, and problems of hailing from a postcolonial position. Kanaganayakam, in his essay "Exiles and Expatriates", discusses the perplexity of the situation in the following manner, "...dozens of...post-colonial writers continue to write about the land they left rather than the one in which they live problematizes the experience of exile and creates the distinctive texture of this corpus" (201). He further says, "Even the fundamental definitions of exile, expatriate, refugee, and immigrant have now become increasingly problematic" (202). Kanaganayakam ventures into citing examples of writers who are born to one nation, move to another by choice (questionable choice) or exiled by force and wonders how one could classify these writers. He discusses the works of writers like Ngugi, David Malouf, Vikram Seth, Dennis Brutus, Satendra Nandan, Zulfikar Ghose, Salman Rushdie and others. Amongst the list of writers featured, Salman Rushdie's "situation" seems to be the "even more complex" one.

It is fascinating to note that the arguments placed in Kanaganayakam's "Exiles and Expatriates" are more than relevant for the authors studied, discussed, heralded and sometimes declared controversial. However, the ultimate necessity to "classify" writers, in this case postcolonial writers, as "insiders" and "outsiders" is problematic in itself. Be this as it may, the interest in the arguments gathered so far is not necessarily to understand Kiran Desai as a writer, in terms of where she hails from or where she has settled (although that could form a very important argument and may be taken up at some other point in time), but that Kanaganayakam's points of view may be extended to understand the characters from Desai's novel as well.

The classic example from Kiran Desai's *The Inheritance of Loss*, which attempts to look at the problem of finding yourself in a nation that is not "yours" to start with, is Biju's narrative. Alienated from everything that is familiar—the cook's son makes it to America, living a life that is on the edge of truth and lie, a life that is part reality and part fiction. He constructs a country, time and again from fractured memories only to revisit them and find them wanting. Rich village life with plenty to eat, no idea of what the face of true poverty looks like, the happy moments with family, the necessity to stick to family values and not bother with steaks, the urge to go back, the fear you'll never see loved ones again, the need to prove yourself, the frustration with failures, the imagination that paints one picture and harsh reality, an everlasting contrast—all these and so much more that Biju experiences are at once familiar as well as foreign.

Biju's experiences when encountered for the first time, remind one of Kanaganayakam's quest to discover the differences between exile, expatriate, and refugee experience which then reflects in the resultant writing. He states that, "One cannot gloss over or underestimate the differences among exile, expatriate, and refugee although convenience dictates that they be seen together as one corpus. The sensibility that informs these conditions results in very different thematic preoccupations" (202-03). In the context of the refugee experience and what inspires a refugee to write, Kanaganayakam cites Nuruddin Farah's essay "Homing in on the Pigeon"[2] and makes the following observation, "For the refugee the notion of home brings to mind disintegration rather than nostalgia" (203). Kanaganayakam's statement quoted above is a sharp reminder of Biju's vacillation from disintegrating memories to nostalgia of a home he's left behind to come to the United States of America.

While discussing expatriate writing Kanaganayakam claims that for those writers who chose to leave their homelands, sans the satisfaction of leaving, the writing is not easy to characterize. He goes on to state the reason why. "They [expatriates] remain outsiders, for the conditions that alienated them do not always change, and their memory creates images that are divorced from immediate realities, thus creating a more fluid space. And it leads to a very different kind of writing" (207). While the statement maybe considered for a better understanding of Desai as a writer, Kanaganayakam's claim inadvertently places Biju's life in sharp perspective.

For, Biju becomes an outsider with a memory that has created various images that do not seem to be based in reality. The condition(s) that have brought him to America have not altered and a "fluid space" has been created—a bubble in which Biju floats along the course of life, asking various questions whenever the urge arises. However, Biju's floating in the bubble is not a fantasy, dream-like situation—rather the opposite, where his utter misery seems to define him and the questions he asks happen to be the only straws he can grasp in order to survive a horrific situation. It is sheer irony, however, to note that while Kanaganayakam states that that there is a "sense of dissatisfaction" the expatriate carries with her/him when she/he leaves and which invariably gets expressed in expatriate writing, Biju leaves to America with very high expectations of success. There seems to be no real dissatisfaction initially just a high level of elation at the opportunity that has come his way, when Biju makes his way out of his nation in order to reach another. In addition his father, the cook, is ecstatic of his son's making it to America.

And then the events of Biju's life start to unfold startling him into bewilderment at times, surprise at other times and reducing him to pure anger at other times. In addition, it is interesting to observe the trajectory of Biju's anger which is directed towards his *situation* most of the time. And yet, on one occasion he does get angry with his father for sending him to this strange land all on his own. Ironically, he also knows that he would have hated his father for not trying to send him having the opportunity to do so.

This reaction of Biju's is interesting because it raises the fundamental question of desires and choice. What is it that one desires and chooses? Are the choices always our own to make or are they made for us? Is one forced to choose something in the absence of any other choice? The questions echo Ammu's situation from *The God of Small Things*, where she is forced to go back to Ayemenem when her choices run out. Further when she falls in love with Velutha and is punished for doing so the question of choices raises its ugly head. Are we indeed free to make our own choices? And even in the category of choices are there acceptable choices and unacceptable choices? These questions are answered rather innocently by Rahel when she observes that she, Amu and Estha seem to have broken some unknown law and "crossed into forbidden territory".[3] In fact, it was not the three of them alone but human beings all over who were being condemned because, "They all tampered with the laws that lay down who should be loved and how. And how much. The laws that make grandmothers grandmothers, uncles uncles, mothers mothers, cousins cousins, jam jam, and jelly jelly" (31). Quite simply put uncles could not become fathers, mothers could not be lovers and cousins could not die and have funerals. And thus when these events happen, the laws are transgressed and "the unthinkable" becomes "thinkable" and "the impossible really" happens.

Interestingly, Biju chooses to come back to his country unlike, Amu who is forced back to Ayemenem when she divorces her husband; a familiar place to be. He imagines what his homecoming will be like and the meeting up of father and son after a long time. Reality has something else in store for Biju, though. He comes back to find the picture he has carried with him all those years ago ruptured. He is suddenly a non-Nepali from a foreign country, stripped of not only his clothes but his pride as well. Can he recognize home?

A similar question may be posed to the judge Jemubhai Patel about recognizing home on returning from his sojourn in England. It is important to note here the near parallel experiences Jemubhai and Biju share. Jemubhai Patel, who goes to England to study law, discovers that he is not successful at making friends nor is he successful at the vocation that is chosen for him either. Coupled with his failures Jemubhai also faces racial prejudice of the worst kind. Finally, in an effort to hide his inadequacies he changes entirely. He turns into a person he cannot recognize nor associate himself with. Unable to understand where he belongs or who he is, he ceases to understand his nation, the people living in his country, his home, the members of his family, the food they eat, the woman he marries, or the child she bears him.

The interesting parallel once again is that Jemubhai's profession is chosen for him and the decision to study in England is also made by Jemubhai's family. Further, he does not get to choose his wife either. Although initially there seems to be a spark of attraction between the young couple, Jemubhai's stint in England helps him realize that his wife is probably the only one towards whom he can vent his frustrations and anger. Controlling her gives his existence meaning and helps him succeed in hiding his inadequacies from the world. Sadly though he begins to find her mere presence detrimental to his image of what and how a person should be. Her unsophisticated, village ways go against his more "refined" notions of class, standard, polish, and culture.

In many ways then Biju and Jemubhai share similarities in their experiences. However, while Biju yearns for a home he can associate himself with Jemubhai is alienated in his very own nation/country. Interestingly in order to deal with his constant estrangement from the people and the land around him Jemubhai moves to Kalimpong. Not only does the sprawling house and the location answer his need for power and control, but also helps him keep away from anyone who can lay claim on him as their own. It is the entrance of Sai, his granddaughter, into his life that changes him once again. Jemubhai realizes, reluctantly perhaps, that he does like Sai in spite of the inevitable connection between his past and his granddaughter.

In an initial reading of the text, Sai appears to be the protagonist of the novel. This dreamy child could be familiar to most readers. Lost in her comfortable world of youth and National Geographic, Sai reflects a sense of loss all the time. From the boarding school in Dehra Dun to Cho Oyu her journey lacks any sense of belonging. She has no idea how to grieve the loss of parents she never really knew. The only real feeling that assails her on learning about their death is that she now will be termed an 'orphan', a title she would have liked to avoid if she could. She arrives in Cho Oyu to stay with her grandfather and gets absorbed into the way of life of the place. Sai comfortably makes friends with Noni, Lola, Uncle Potty, and Father Booty, the not so young residents of Kalimpong and her world revolves around her new found friends as well as the judge, the cook and Mutt (her grandfather's dog). Until the elders decide that she should meet someone young. And so it is that when Noni declares her lack of knowledge in teaching Sai mathematics and science a new tutor is hired (Gyan).

The meeting of the new tutor and student starts a whole new phase in their young lives; one that was anticipated could end in a well-known happy ending or at least a recognizable tragedy. However, the romance does not go very far, for too long or culminate with any kind of high drama. It just dies out with the change in sensibility that envelopes them in Kalimpong. Interestingly, the writer leaves a note of possibility with Gyan's wanting to go back to Sai, with the added perception and understanding that he does not belong to those (people/persons) perpetrating violence. What he seeks beyond this in terms of his identity and the nation he wants to belong to is yet to be determined by Gyan. The reader's understanding of the text may well give Gyan's search various interpretations which may be addressed at a more opportune moment. What does become important for the argument in this context is the contrast he brings to the narrative. Hailing from a poverty-stricken neighborhood Gyan is caught in the emerging nation, the arguments, the unrest, the debates and discussions, the right and the wrong and his position in the midst of it all. He happens to be the one marginalized in his own land.

Thus, the narratives of the judge, Jemubhai Patel, his granddaughter Sai, her tutor Gyan, his cook Panna Lal, and the cook's son Biju intercept one another to form a lattice that is only an attempt at answering the larger questions of the future of an emerging nation. The other characters like Noni, Lola, Father Booty, Uncle Potty, and others add their bit about whether the arguments are valid, whether a separate nation should even be asked for/demanded for by the "insiders" and where they will be if a new nation is created and they, inevitably, become the outsiders.

To address the question of the construction of the nation then becomes unavoidable and all important. Before addressing the question of the text, it is imperative to ask the question, what does India mean to us? Lunchroom conversations that involve places, foods, tastes, colors, landscapes, sharing of experiences of travel to various places within the country, conversations revolving around concerns like whether systems in India are effective or not, like the railways, postal systems, the system of reservation, etc. whether one is pro/anti the caste system, pro/anti the Northeast, pro/anti Muslim or pro/anti neighboring countries and so much more—the sky is the limit!

What then of India does Kiran Desai manage to portray or capture effectively in her writing? The first clear aspect would be that of class—the difference between those who have achieved a top position—either because of money, or the jobs they have done—reflected in the large sprawling houses they live in or the gardens they grow around the house. The abundance that a few are privileged to while the majorities starve is a theme that shadows the narrative rather significantly from the start to finish.

A second aspect of India that Desai manages to capture magnificently wed is the way things are taken for granted in India and are ignored rather than addressed. One such example has already been discussed earlier in this paper about choices that are made by social systems for people; as well as external factors that the person involved has no say/control over. The other examples Desai hints at are the homosexual relationship between Father Booty and Uncle Potty, the single woman's angst in Noni, the budding love between Sai and Gyan that is expressed in the touching and feeling that is unacceptable without social sanction/endorsement, and families that make decisions without finding out what one wants or realizing the true capability or capacity of an individual. In our intellectual discussions, however, we do come up with having an urge to address issues that are ignored because of a visible lack of strength to address them in society or real life on a daily basis. It is this weakness that Desai captures in her narrative with aplomb.

Desai steps up her art of capturing the lack of visible strength through her characters when she portrays the true high point in terms of a climax in the novel, which may be noted in the disappearance of the judge's dog Mutt. The loss of Mutt may well be the last straw. The judge, haunted by his mistakes from the past, reacts violently once again towards his cook; much like his reaction to a wife he never could stomach or understand. His cook is at a loss anyway, because in reality he does not much care for Mutt. The cook's love, his whole life in fact, is focused around his son Biju, who ironically enough is conspicuous in his absence. Willing to take a beating, the cook faces the judge's wrath. Sai, on the other hand, does not want the cook to be beaten up at all. For her the loss of Mutt is the ultimate culmination of everything that she has lost in the short span of her life—the loss of her parents, the loss of love newly found, the loss of Father Booty, the true loss of innocence.

Each character then plays out her/his part and each chapter of the book is like a kaleidoscope where the pattern changes every time you turn the page. As the pattern changes the different points of view of the characters and their interpretations—of being an Indian in India or abroad, being rooted or a complete outsider within the country, returning after journeying and residing in foreign lands—emerge in very many layers or in a layered manner. Further, the ending of the novel is abrupt. The effect is perhaps a little on the anti-climax but with an impact. The fact of real life is that the worst part of war, unrest, uprising, is that life goes on—it has to. And so the novel ends because the judge, Sai, Gyan, Panna Lal, Biju,

Noni, Lola, etc. will continue to survive. A part of each of them has perhaps died because of the disintegration of dreams. But life does not cease and that is true tragedy.

In conclusion, Kiran Desai's nation is an invisible shadow that stalks the narrative, only to suddenly make an appearance of blinding clarity in "messy maps", borders drawn, nations born "boldly overnight", in hatred, anger, in gaps, in the mist, in confusions, debates and questions, in "imagined" constructions and so much more.

NOTES

1. Chelva Kanaganayakam, "Exiles and Expatriates." *New National and Post-Colonial Literatures: An Introduction*. Ed. Bruce King. Oxford: Clarendon, 1996: 201-13.
2. Chelva Kanaganayakam in his essay cites Nuruddin Farah's essay in order to state that literature from the margins has separate spaces for those writers who are expatriates and those who are marginalized within their nations.
3. Arundhati Roy, *The God of Small Things*, New Delhi: Penguin, 1997: 31.

WORKS CITED

Ashcroft, Bill, Gareth Griffiths, and Helen Tiffin, eds. *The Post-colonial Studies Reader*. New York: Routledge, 1995.

Desai, Kiran. *The Inheritance of Loss*. New Delhi: Penguin, 2006.

Kanaganayakam, Chelva. "Exiles and Expatriates." *New National and Post-Colonial Literatures: An Introduction*. Ed. Bruce King. Oxford: Clarendon, 1996: 201-13.

Roy, Arundhati. *The God of Small Things*. New Delhi: Penguin, 1997.

23

Booking the Booker: Re-Presenting India to the Western Gaze

Charul Jain

I

The shortlist is ready and anticipations are high.... The Booker Prize will be announced shortly. But this time round, unfortunately, no Indian author has been nominated. But they have been, frequently, in the past. Some have made it to the list, and also to the summit and stayed there for at least a year; some kept coming back, hoping to reach the summit.... Yes I am talking about the fortunate awardees of the Booker Prize and others, not so fortunate nominees for the Prize. If we look back, since the time our nation won its independence, we have been able to keep our nation on the centre stage of global attention, through wars, riots, terrorism and through achievers like, A. Sen, R. Venkataram on the one hand and S. Sen, A. Rai, A. Roy, and A. Adiga on the other.

Why only since Independence, India has held the global attention and imagination since times immemorial? Numerous invaders and colonizers corroborate the fact that India is a much sought after land. India has held the attention of the West too, for centuries. Westerners have adopted it suiting their fancy. Whatever the case may be, it is significant to note that India is a land of fascination for the world and much has been written about it, on it and also by it. Needless to say, the image of India sells. It sells even in fiction. This notion gains credence by the fact that Adiga is the eighth winner of the prestigious award who has written on or about India. "India has been consistently producing award-winning authors or inspiring other writers to base their works on Indian colours, themes and identity" (rediff news, 2008).

There are many Western writers who have won the Booker by situating their works on India: James Gordon Farrell, a British novelist won the award for *The Siege of Krishnapur* (1973). He writes about the incidents that took place during the First Indian war of Independence of 1857 by situating his discourse in an imaginary town of Krishnapur (near Lucknow and Kanpur).

German, Ruth Prawer Jhabvala, views India through the lives of two English women living 50 years apart in India in her novel *Heat and Dust* for which she won the Booker in 1975. V.S. Naipaul, a Caribbean national of Indian ancestry won it (1971) for his collection of short stories that dealt with displacement, *In a Free State* and lately Yenn Martel was awarded the Prize for *The Life of Pi* (2002), set in Pondicherry.

Similarly Indians, diasporic and resident too have been nominated and awarded the prestigious Booker for their re/presentation of India. Anita Desai and Rohinton Mistry, both of Indian origin residing in North America, have been nominated thrice in the last three decades for their works based on India. Salman Rushdie too has been nominated and awarded on several occasions and has been the sole winner of the Booker as well as the most coveted Booker of Bookers Prize for his *Midnight's Children*.

What one notices through an analysis of these works is the trend that seems to be in place of projecting an image of India which is in consonance with the Western view and imagination of India: the bad, the poor, the hopeless and the mysterious India.

This paper would look at the works of two authors who have received the Booker Prize, Roy and Adiga. The former, Arundhati Roy won the Booker Prize for her work, *The God of Small Things* in 1997 and eleven years later, Aravind Adiga won it for his novel *The White Tiger*.

Roy sets the scene of her novel in a quintessential Indian town of Kerala where the lives of its protagonists are shaped by the cultural and social factors of Kerala and result in their unhappiness and despair. Adiga, on the other hand, prefers to situate his work in the shifting locales of rural and urban India. Through the marginalized life and experiences of Balram Halwai, the son of a poor rickshaw puller in a village and later as a driver of a rich businessman in a city, the agony and despair in the lives of rural/urban people as well as poor/rich have been poignantly brought out through *The White Tiger*.

Thus, both the writers manage to capture a criss-cross of Indian topography, culture, lives and ethos of the Indian people. Both these works represent India as a nation that is inscrutable as it is a combination of two opposites:

> Our nation, though it has no drinking water, electricity, sewage system, public transportation, sense of hygiene, discipline, courtesy, or punctuality, (but it) does have entrepreneurs.... (Adiga, 2008)

II

The word 'represent' is defined by *Oxford Advanced Learner's Dictionary* as "to make an image or show; in a picture or play; depict; describe (sb/sthg), often misleadingly, as having certain character or quality". Thus, 'representation' is like an image, more unnatural or unreal than otherwise. Thinkers like Spivak and Said have situated this definition of 'representation' in their works and discussed how imaginative identities are constructed on lines of accepted identities. Any image, to borrow Spivak's terms, can be representation or re-presentation, the former being a 'proxy' (*Vertretung*) and the latter is a 'portrait' (*Darstellung*):

> The relationship between the two kinds of representation brings in; also, the use of essentialism because no representation can take place—no Vertretung, representation—can take place without essentialism. What it has to take into account is that the

"essence" that is being represented is a representation of the other kind, *Darstellung*. (Spivak, 1990)

In both the cases—'proxy' and 'portrait', as explained by Spivak, there is a grave danger of essentialising the objects, persons or even nations that are represented or re-presented. To complicate the matter further, if we go by the semiotic meanings of the word 'representation' it is believed that it is close to reality, it is a 'presence' or a simulation. It is equally unlikely that these simulations can be completely true or real.

Edward Said in the textual representations of the Orient in *Orientalism* highlights the fact that representation of an image can never be natural or real. The book *Orientalism* also brings forth an approach that facilitated the West not only to come to terms with the East but also to (represent) construct the East as a binary opposite to the image of the West. Scholars from various academic disciplines like history, philology, linguistics, and literature created the same image of the Orient, by relying solely on the Eurocentric understanding of the Orient (Said, 1976). The Orient, thus, is a phenomenon constructed by the naturalizing of a wide range of Orientalist assumptions and stereotypes, a representation or an image, which is not a natural or real depiction.

In this age of globalization and multiculturalism, the representation of society through texts may not hold as much value as it used to centuries ago, when texts were primarily the only window to the world. Yet, in the contemporary world, when these representations beget international literary prizes, they invite scrutiny and speculation.

It is deplorable to note that Western imagination still retains the same old image and assumption of the Orient and the Oriental in contemporary world of literature and cinema. The two recent evidences of this credence are—the 2009 Golden Globe award and the Oscar award for the Best Motion Picture to *Slumdog Millionaire* and the 2008 Booker Prize for Literature to Aravind Adiga's *The White Tiger*. Both the works offer a tribute to India by presenting her as a metaphor for the sad, bad and the poor. In both the cases, whoever their creators are, accolades have come from the Western world. These international honours have put us back into—

> our pre-ordained squalor-celebrity slot. We have salvaged our garland of global recognition, but this time it has made up of all the stereotypes we thought we had put in the shredder of Corus, Arcelor, and nine percent growth. (Karkaria, 2009)

Norbert Schurer, in his book *Midnight's Children: A Reader,* gives statistics of how the fortunes of any prize-winning novel soar, by giving *Midnight's Children's* example. He claims that before the Prize, only 650 copies of the first print run of 2,500 books were ordered in advance, whereas, after the announcement of the Prize, the sales rocketed to about one thousand copies in one month (Schurer, 2004).

Another instance, of the impact of an award is in the case of the prize winning novel J.M. Coetzee's *Disgrace* (1999). There was a marked increase in the sales of the work by a whopping thousand per cent plus in an incredibly short time. The Indian author Arundhati Roy's first novel *The God of Small Things* (1997) sold well over a million copies. In 1997, when the list was announced bookshops reported a dramatic increase in the sale of all books in the list, and the trend continued even after the results were announced on October 27 (wisedude, 2008). Even Adiga's novel had earlier failed to grab much attention from the Indian media but with the stamps of approval from the Western world, he experienced exponential growth in book sales in the national as well as international markets.

It is thus surprising then to note that in the long span of a decade, the protagonists in both these novels represent the trite image of the Indian as sad, bad and mysterious Indian. This image, in the ethos of the new millennium, is not the only real image of the Indian. But this image has helped the writers and their works to grab international attention, fame and even awards.

III

The God of Small Things is a tale of zygotic twins and their tragic lives strewn with casteism, religion and patriarchal strives. The tale is set in quintessential Indian town of Kerala, Ayemenem. The author sets the mood of the novel from the page one where she describes the Indian climate and landscape, both complementing each other to create tragic lives of the protagonists.

> May in Ayemenem is a hot, brooding month. The days are long and humid. The river shrinks and black crows gorge on bright mangoes in still, dust green trees. Red bananas ripen. Jackfruits burst. Dissolute bluebottles hum vacuously in the fruity air. Then they stun themselves against clear windowpanes and die, fatly baffled in the sun. The nights are clear, but suffused with sloth and sullen expectation. But by early June the southwest monsoon breaks and there are three months of wind and water with short spells of sharp, glittering sunshine that thrilled children snatch to play with. The countryside turns an immodest green. Boundaries blur as tapioca fences take root and bloom. Brick walls turn moss green. Pepper vines snake up electric poles. Wild creepers burst through laterite banks and spill across the flooded roads. (Roy, 1997: 01)

The story shifts back and forth in time to capture first, the impressions of seven-year-old children about the complex lives led by the older people, their impressions are clear but their understanding of the older world hazy. When these twins grow up and reunite at after thirty-three years of separation, they are able to go back in memory and re-create and re-understand the events of their childhood. Through both these time frames and lenses, issues that influence the lives of Syrian Christians, particularly the women and the children are re-presented.

> He stared at Ammu's breasts as he spoke. He said the police knew all they needed to know and that the Kottayam Police didn't take statements from *veshyas* or their illegitimate children.... When they left the police station Ammu was crying, so Estha and Rahel didn't

> ask her what *Veshya* meant. Or for that matter, illegitimate.... Her face was set like stone, but tears welled up in her eyes and ran down her rigid cheeks.... (Roy, 1997: 08)

But having grown up, the children could very well understand the meanings of those glances as well as the words spoken years ago. The sadness that starts then, envelops the children and lasts with them throughout their lifetime. Estha gradually became quiet and withdrawn from the world, living in his own cocoon, barely connecting with the people and his surroundings,

> Once the quietness arrived, it stayed and spread in Estha. It reached out of his head and enfolded him in its swampy arms.... It stripped his thoughts of the words that described them and left them parted and naked. Unspeakable. Numb.... Slowly, over the years, Estha withdrew from the world.... (Roy, 1997: 12)

Rahel became a rebel and a social misfit. Repeatedly expelled from schools, unable to finish her college, and acquire a degree she is intimidating to other students by "her waywardness almost fierce lack of ambition". Even after she gets married her husband becomes exasperated and "offended by her eyes".

> He didn't know that in some places, like the country that Rahel came from, various kinds of despair competed for primacy. And that personal despair could never be desperate enough. That something happened when personal turmoil dropped by at the wayside shrine of the vast, violent, driving, ridiculous, insane, unfeasible, public turmoil of a nation.... (Roy, 1997: 19)

The men in the novel come out as strongly patriarchal, uncompassionate and inconsiderate towards the sufferings of the women. Ammu's father, Pappachi continually beat his wife Mammachi, Ammu was frequently beaten by her alcoholic husband and later divorced. Chacko too turns Ammu out to die a lonely death.

The world re-presented here is depressing, stifling and "hopelessly practical" where caste and religion play havoc with the lives of the people. Velutha, an untouchable (the lowest caste), a dalit whose family has been working for Chacko's for generations. He is extremely gifted with his hands, an accomplished carpenter and mechanic. Unlike other untouchables, Velutha has a self-assured air. Further, he is a Marxist whose comrades force Baby Kochamma to wave a red flag. And all this combined creates lot of hostility and resentment among the 'touchables'. Yet Ammu falls in love with him, an act unpardonable by the society which ultimately leads to Ammu's misery and Velutha's death.

Religion too plays a significant role in complicating their lives. Ammu, a Syrian Christian marrying a Hindu, baby Kochamma, converting to Catholicism and an English woman marrying Chacko, and again Ammu falling in love with a Marxist—all are time and again derided and despised by the society.

All the characters are hence trapped in their own tragedies, Pappachi, frustrated at his failure to get the moth he discovered, named after him, Chacko after his unsuccessful career and marriage in Oxford, Baby Kochamma after failing to get father Mulligan's attention and love, Ammu and Velutha separated by caste divide yet trapped in their love for each other, Estha and Rahel in their own jinxed destinies. All of them try to escape the Ayemenem old home but all return there to lead and to end their lives in defeated, deserted, desperate, hopeless loneliness.

Thus, Roy recreates the India of the Western imagination which is torn apart by caste divide, and religious strife and is a land inscrutable to the Western imagination, a land of sorrow, agony, loneliness and depression. "*The God of Small Things* is at once exotic and familiar to the Western reader..." (Amazon review).

Adiga's *The White Tiger* studies the contrast between India's rise as a modern global economy and the lead character, Balram, who comes from crushing rural poverty. This novel takes the form of a series of letters to Wen Jiabao, the Chinese premier, from Balram Halwai, the Bangalore businessman who is the self-styled "White Tiger" of the title. Bangalore is the Silicon Valley of the subcontinent, and on the eve of a state visit by Jiabao, our entrepreneur Halwai wishes to impart something of the new India to the Chinese premier—

> out of respect for the love of liberty shown by the Chinese people, and also in the belief that the future of the world lies with the yellow man and the brown man now that our erstwhile master, the white-skinned man, has wasted himself through buggery, mobile phone usage and drug abuse. (Adiga, 2008)

Halwai's lesson about the new India is drawn from the rags-to-riches story of his own life. For Halwai, the son of a rural rickshaw-puller is from the "Darkness":

> Please understand Your Excellency, that India is two countries in one: an India of Light, and an India of Darkness. The ocean brings light to my country. Every place on the map of India near the ocean is well off. But the river brings darkness to India—the black river. The black river is the Ganges, beloved of the sari-and-spices tourist image of India. ("No!—Mr Jiabao, I urge you not to dip in the Ganga, unless you want your mouth full of faeces, straw, soggy parts of human bodies, buffalo carrion, and seven different kinds of industrial acids.) (Adiga, 2008)

Thus, we notice that the two novels, namely Arundhati Roy's *The God of Small Things* and Adiga's *The White Tiger,* portray the image of hopelessness, depression and inscrutability. If Estha and Rahel epitomize isolation and despair, Halwai exemplifies mysticism and enigma. Halwai superficially appears to have a better understanding of the pragmatic world yet his analysis of India is akin to Rahel's understanding of the same.

Mukul Joshi, in his essay, "Illusions and Discoveries: India in the British Imagination" lists out some fictional images of India and the Indians held by the Western people. Among these is a portrayal of Indians in two-dimensional characters—one, as innocent, gullible, found in the likes of loyal servants and sepoys and the second is the middle class or a westernized Indian. In both the cases, characters are 'types' because, as Joshi argues, the writers wanted to avoid complexities. Analyzing the portrayal of Indians in Rudyard Kipling's stories, Joshi affirms that "the illiterate native servant is the most commonly depicted character in Kipling" (Joshi, 2008). What Joshi sees, as a "standardized response", is understood as "exploitation of voyeuristic curiosity of a foreign audience", by others (Thakkar, 2009). Thus, analyzing this kind of lopsided representation of the Indian in so many Booker-nominated novels, one can easily surmise that whether it is the representation of the characters of Uma, Roxana, Coomy and Pi, belonging to the higher strata of society or Balram Halwai, representing the plebs, the image of the Indian as the sad, bad and the mysterious, subsists for rest of the world even today and in a way, this identity has become "age-old claim to fame" (Karkaria, 2009) or a truly prized catch. When one tries to understand India and the Indian through these novels, the understanding often implies essentialised and prejudiced elucidation of the Orient, as had been analyzed by Edward Said in *Orientalism.* Centuries ago, the Western world visualized India as the land of elephants and snake-charmers, and today too, the country, in these novels, remains the land of the 'sad, bad and the mysterious'.

Thus, India is represented in both the works, *The God of Small Things* and *The White Tiger* as a nation that is full of negatives, sadness, agony and desperation yet is attractive to the imagination and in being so is also mysterious and saleable. When one tries to understand India and the Indian through these novels, the understanding often implies essentialized and prejudiced interpretations of Eastern cultures and peoples through the eyes of the West.

REFERENCES

Adiga, Aravind. *The White Tiger*. New Delhi: Harper Collins, 2008: 5-6, 14-15.

Joshi, Mukul. "Illusions and Discoveries: Indian in the British Imagination" in *Asian Quarterly*, Vol. 5, Issue 4, Feb. 2008: 65.

Karkaria, Bachi. "India Inc to India Stink" in the *Times of India*, 16 January 2009.

Macaulay, Thomas Babington. "Indian Education: Minute of the 2nd of February, 1835" in *Macaulay: Prose and Poetry Selected*. ed. G.M. Young. London: Rupert Hart-Davis, 1952: 729.

Roy, Arundhati. *The God of Small Things*. New Delhi: India Ink. 1997.

Said, Edward. "Orientalism" in *Literary Theory: An Anthology* (Revised Ed.) Eds. Julie Rivkin and Michael Ryan. Cornwall: Blackwell, 1998: 873-86.

Schurer, Norbert. *Salman Rushdie's Midnight's Children: A Reader's Guide*. New York: Continuum, 2004: 80-81.

Spivak, G.C. *The Post-Colonial Critic: Interviews, Strategies, Dialogues*. Ed. S. Harasym. London and New York: Routledge, 1990: 108.

Thakkar, Anil. 'Counter View: Amitabh Bachchan Slams Slumdog Millionaire's Success" in the *Times of India*, 17 January 2009: 2.

Internet Sources

http://51stories.wordpress.com/2008/09/06/judging-panels-and-the43 booker-prize

http://www.aseemaa.com/2009/02/adiga-is-a-classic-case-of-brown-skin-thinking-white

http://www.rediff.com/news/2008/oct/16booker.htm

http://www.amazon.com/God-Small-Things-Arundhati-Roy/dp/0060977493

http://www.wisedude.com/art_music/booker_prize.htm

24

Subaltern Voices in 21st Century Indian Fiction: A Study of *The Inheritance of Loss* and *The White Tiger*

Vipin K. Singh

Subaltern voices may be seen to constitute a major part of the concentration of the 21st century Indian fiction in English. Viewing Spivak's idea of subaltern, like women, not being able to speak as a complex critique of the display of human subjectivity in a variety of contexts, the present paper seeks to read subaltern voices in 21st century Indian fiction in English in backdrop of two ground breaking works, *The Inheritance of Loss* and *The White Tiger* which won Man Booker Prizes for their authors in 2006 and 2008 respectively. First published in the journal *Wedges* (1985) and then in *Marxism and the Interpretation of Culture* (1988) Spivak's essay, "Can the Subaltern Speak?", reads in juxtaposition the radical claims of twentieth century French intellectuals like Foucault and Deleuze to speak for the disenfranchised and the claims of the British colonialism to rescue native widows from the practice of self-immolation in nineteenth century India. This Spivak did to bring into light the paradoxical fact that how a kind intellectual impulse to represent the disempowered groups effectively appropriate the voice of the subaltern and thereby silences them. Stephen Morton reads the fact and unearths "how the benevolent, radical western intellectual can paradoxically silence the subaltern by claiming to represent and speak for their experiences in the same way that the benevolent colonialist silenced the voice of the widow who chooses to die on her husband's funeral pyre."[1] One of many objectives of the paper, therefore, is to bring forth the subaltern voices being crushed by the privileged groups (mentally and economically) of society. The paper seeks to compare and contrast the ways Kiran Desai and Aravind Adiga adopted in their Booker winning novels to represent the voices of the disempowered; it has also been attempted to point out whether they adopt the same way to display the voices of the subaltern or differ in their perspectives? The present paper dares to challenge Spivak's qualm "that the postcolonial historians can recover the standpoint of the subaltern",[2] and attempts to find out a ground which Adiga's and Desai's subaltern protagonists seek for. The present study also tries to assess whether subalterns are capable of breaking the ice or they still need/call some of their privileged brothers or sisters to do the job for them. If yes, how they break the silence forms one among the major interests of the paper. Do the authors of the novels adopt the same stand to forward their views or they differ in their standpoints, is also an objective of the present study. Since Kiran Desai stands first in chronology, it will be profitable to discuss her views first.

In *The Inheritance of Loss*, Kiran Desai gives the impression to have found out the subaltern voices either in dreams or in unconscious. She appears to have sought the suppressed voices of the disempowered groups of society either in their frustrated mutterings or in fear of losing life or livelihood. It may be seen either in loneliness or nostalgic remembrance of the past. In *The Inheritance of Loss*, Desai narrates the story of three persons: Jemubhai, the judge, the cook and his son, Biju who is also a cook in America.

Jemubhai is the first person in the novel who represents the subaltern in a foreign land. He is marginalized, humiliated, detested and depressed everywhere and all the time. He tries to speak but could not dare to utter a single word; and all his feelings came as his frustration and depression. Jemubhai's humiliation starts from his expedition to Cambridge for education to his becoming an ICS officer. He could hardly express his experience; it came only through his frustrations. On being ostracized by his cabin mate for his meal given by his mother, he could not restrain his frustration. The novelist depicts his mental condition in such words: "No fruit dies so vile and offensive a death as a banana, but it had been packed just in case. In case of *What*? Jemu shouted silently to his mother.... He was furious that his mother had considered the possibility of his humiliation.... In her attempt to conceal out one humiliation, she had only succeeded in adding another."[3] He went to London that he thought a "Land of Hope and Glory". But he could not find even a room and sufficient food from his landlady to slake the fire of hunger. He wanted to voice his thought but could not; and once again his voice comes choked in his nostalgic recollections of past: "After a spate of nights lying awake listening to the borborygmus of his half-empty stomach, thinking tearfully of his family in Piphit who thought him as worthy of a hot dinner as the queen of England...."[4] In his college, nobody spoke to him, in bus and other public places, no one liked to sit beside him and showed the indignation towards him for being there. As a result, he forgot to laugh, "could barely manage to lift his lips in a smile, and if he ever did, he held his hand over his mouth, because he couldn't bear anyone to see his gums, his teeth".[5]

The only thing Jemubhai could do to prove his erudition and get success is to work hard. He worked eighteen hours a day, over a hundred hours a week. He sits in the "Open Competitive Examination" and clears the written test. But again he could not impress the white examiners in viva voce because he could not be able to break the construction of his race, ethnicity, and skin colour. His examiners chuckled at his peculiar native accent and pronunciation. The novelist describes the why Jemubhai could not impress the examiners: "By the time they stood for the ICS, most of the candidates had crisp-ironed their speech, but Jemubhai had barely opened his mouth for whole years and his English still had the rhythm and form of Gujarati."[6] The result comes, but he could not secure his name in the merit. He got selection only in the second list which was to Indianize the service. Jemubhai could not stop from shedding tears. He weeps because his intelligent is declared his shortcoming. He weeps because he could impress one only through his pen and not his face and voice because no one likes to hear him; and once again his feelings could get their outlet in his tears which no one but he could listen and understand.

Similarly, the cook is another subaltern character who becomes the novelist's spokesman. The cook shows that the voice of a subaltern can only be expressed in unconscious. Jemubhai, the judge hires him when he was a child. Since then, he served the judge with full sense of honesty, truthfulness, devotion and commitment. But the judge who is his master and patron shows no care for him and humiliates him for a dog. The cook is shocked at the judge's behaviour and his humiliation by the latter. His honesty, his duty, his sense of devotion towards his master and his many years service done to him, all is exterminated. He loses his self-respect and is humiliated for a dog. He, out of perturbance, drinks wine, becomes intoxicated and comes to the judge in keif. He knows that he has never been a bit careless in the whole pursuit of his life. He has been fond of Mutt, the dog, has taken her for walks, made toast for her, breakfast with an egg in wintertime, made her stew, called her "Mutty, Ishtu, Ishtoo". Now his guilt begins to grow. Various thoughts strike to his mind at the same time. Had he indeed been negligent? He has failed in his duty, hadn't he? He comes to the judge filled with guilt and remorse. His remorse and sense of guilt displays the picture vividly. Now he speaks, he speaks the subaltern voice in unconscious:

> I have been bad.... I've been drinking I ate the same rice as you not the servant's rice but the Dehradoon rice I ate the meat and lied I ate out of the same pot I stole liquor from the army I made chhang I did the accounts differently for years I have cheated in the accounts each and every day my money was dirty it was false sometimes I kicked Mutt I didn't take her for walks

> just sat by the side of road smoked a bidi and came home I'm, a bad man....[7]

And thus, his voice is suppressed under his intoxication and the beating of the judge. Here it is important to note that a subaltern voice can only be heard in unconscious, dreams, and frustrations.

The same story is repeated with the cook's son, Biju. Biju is a subaltern who bears the lot of both, his father and the judge. He is a cook in America, bearing all the racial and ethnic discriminations. He is exploited everywhere; and no one likes him. If he leaves one restaurant and joins other, his work increases and he has to perform now more duty than earlier. He wants to protest but cannot because he won't be heard; nor does he have any voice also. He could express his experience only through his tearful recollections of childhood that he spent with his uncle. His feelings get expressed only in unsaid dreams.

Kiran Desai, therefore, seems to have searched the subaltern voices in dreams, unexpressed desires, nostalgic recollections of past, unconscious mind, complexes, frustrations and depressions. It was not that, as Desai seems to give the impression, subalterns do not have voice, or they do not want to give voice to their feelings, or they did not try; the fact is that, whenever they try, their voice is either crushed under physical violence or the feelings of disgust and humiliation.

Unlike Desai, Aravind Adiga seems to have adopted a different way to explore the voice of the disempowered sections of society. Adiga's *The White Tiger* seeks succinctly reveal India: India from village to city, from darkness to light, from past to the present and from the deprived to the privileged. It depicts the plight and predicament of most of the Indian subalterns who come from village to city. Aravind Adiga states in an interview: "I tried to tell a very real story about India on the brink of unrest. I tried to challenge the assumptions that many in middle class India hold about the poor: that they are stupid, easily manipulated, excessively bound by caste and family."[8]

The novel starts with Balram Halwai's plight who is a subaltern and becomes able to break the "Rooster Coop" and produce the subaltern voice. The novelist states that the saga of the plight of the poor can be known through the marks of the whips and cuts on their body. They cast seeds, cut weeds, harvest corn and paddy for the privileged sections of the society; but they are devalued and thrown as chaff is separated from the grain. Balram's father yells out of pain the subaltern voice: "My whole life I have been treated like a donkey. All I want is that one son of mine—at least one should live like a man."[9] Here, this is not important that Adiga pointed out the subaltern voice, the significant point is that no one heard him. Similarly, Balram goes to school to usurp his right, but his schooling is discontinued and he is sold to the landlord of the village so that the heavy loan taken from him on his cousin's marriage could be given. After this, he has to work on a sweets' shop; there he can only hear the customers talking and ordering, but he cannot speak. At last, anyhow he learns how to drive a car and searches a job at his landlord's household. Here, the novelist depicts the plight of a subaltern servant in India; how brutally and inhumanly they are treated by masters on very minor mistakes and incidents. On being stolen a son of Buffalo, they suspected the involvement of one of his servants in the act. They tortured the servant like anything and then shot him dead, killed his brother while working in the field, raped his sister and mother and then killed them and finally set his house fire. The reward a servant gets if something wrong happens with his master's family. His innocence is considered a crime, his denial from accepting the charged crime his insolence, and his fear of not facing his master's wrath, his skulking. The novelist states: "I don't know how you organize servants in China. But in India or at in the darkness—the rich don't have drivers, cooks, barbers and tailors. They simply have servants."[10] Balram does not only drive his master's car, but he has also to sweep the floor of the courtyard, make tea, and clean cobwebs.

Adiga has also demonstrated how a subaltern is made silent and sacrifice his life for the welfare of his master. Once Pinky

Ma'am got over drunk and ran the car into a child late at night; the child was dead. On being asked, Balram tells how these people in Darkness live: "they have eight, nine, ten children—sometimes they don't know the names of their own children. Her parents—if they are even in Delhi...—won't go to the police."[11] This is how a subaltern child is brought up in a poor Indian family. If the child defeats and survives the accidental death and fatal diseases; this is only a chance; he is more unfortunate to bear the misfortunes of life like Balram, the driver. Pinky Madam hit the child, but now Balram is there to take all the charges on himself for he is an obedient and loyal servant to his master. With some of the polite words, Balram is shown the legal documents to sign which he reads with shaking hands:

> I, Balram Halwai, son of Vikram Halwai, of Laxmangarh village in the district of Gaya, do make the following statement of my own free will and intention: That I drove the car that hit an unidentified person, or persons, or objects, on the night of January 23rd this year. That I then panicked and to fulfill my obligations to the injured party or parties by taking them to the nearest hospital emergency ward. That there were no other occupants of the car at the time of the accident. That I was alone in the car, and alone responsible for all that happened....[12]

Balram is compelled to take his mistress' crime on himself. He states, he is not the only person to suffer in this way, but the jails of Delhi are full of drivers who are "there behind the bars because they are taking the blame for their good, solid, middle-class masters. We have left the villages, but the masters still own us, body, soul and arse."[13] This is how, according to the novelist, a subaltern is made voiceless and speechless. This is how he is made to suffer and not allowed to speak. He cannot avoid the misfortune. The narrator of the novel says: "I was in terror, and yet not once did the thought of running away cross my mind. Not once did he think, I'll tell the judge the truth, cross my mind. I was trapped in the Rooster Coop."[14] The novelist represents the plight of the subaltern through the metaphor of the Rooster Coop. Roosters see their rooster brothers being slaughtered by the butcher; and they are conscious that they stand next in number to be slain. Yet they do not rebel and they make no venture to get out of the coop.

Balram Halwai, the narrator, attempts to break the coop and is ready to pay anything for that. He murders his master, Ashok, takes his money and runs away with his nephew, Dharm, knowing that rest of his family members will be tortured to death like a beast. He goes to Bangalore and starts a business with his master's money; joins the corrupt system. But he has evolved some of rules his own. He does not treat his subordinates like servants; he does not insult them; he does not make them his friends either because friends are too dangerous. He says that people may be seen talking of revolution in India; but in this country no revolution will take place because no one will dare to initiate and break the rooster coop. He muses that if he is arrested and tortured like anything in jail, he will never say that he had made any mistake that night in Delhi when he slit his master's throat. Rather he will say, "it was all worthwhile to know, just for a day, just for an hour, just for a minute, what it means not to be a servant".[15]

In the conclusion of the study, it may be summarized that Kiran Desai ventured to trace the subaltern voices in dreams, crushed desires, unconscious mind and class and racial discrimination. But she did not make her subaltern heroes to break the rooster coop. Adiga, on the other side, not only finds out the suppressed voices of the disempowered groups of society, but also lets his hero break the rooster coop and butcher the butcher himself. It is noteworthy that Balram speaks throughout the novel and all of us listen to him. Whereas Kiran Desai's protagonist dares to break the silence in an intoxicated state of mind, Aravind Adiga's hero is cognizant when he speaks. Above all significant is the point that Balram speaks subaltern voice not as a subaltern but as a leading figure of the privileged section of society, as a prominent capitalist and an entrepreneur of Indian industry. Equally significant is the fact that Balram does not support the privileged class of society; instead, he is still a subaltern by his heart and temperament and is full of subaltern voices, feelings, experiences, sentiments and plight and predicament.

NOTES

1. Stephen Morton, "Learning From Subaltern", *Gayatri Chakravorty Spivak* (London: Routledge, 2003), 56.
2. Ania Loomba, "Challenging Colonialism", *Colonialism/ Postcolonialism* (London: Routledge, 2001), 234.
3. Kiran Desai, *The Inheritance of Loss* (London: Penguin Books, 2006), 38.
4. *Ibid.*, 39.
5. *Ibid.*, 40.
6. *Ibid.*, 112.
7. *Ibid.*, 320.
8. Aravind Adiga, Interview with *The Times of India* (Oct. 18, 2008), 11.
9. Aravind Adiga, *The White Tiger* (London: Harper Collins Publishers, 2008), 30.
10. *Ibid.*, 69.
11. *Ibid.*, 165.
12. *Ibid.*, 168.
13. *Ibid.*, 170.
14. *Ibid.*, 177.
15. *Ibid.*, 321.

25

Situating Masculinities in Arundhati Roy's *The God of Small Things* and Kiran Desai's *The Inheritance of Loss*

Sunita Sinha

> I view masculinity as a constantly changing collection of meanings that we construct through our relationships with ourselves, with each other, and with our world. Manhood is neither static nor timeless; it is historical. Manhood is not the manifestation of an inner essence; it is socially constricted. Manhood does not bubble upto consciousness from our biological makeup; it is created in culture. Manhood means different things at different times to different people.
>
> —*Michael S. Kimmel*

The critical interrogation of men and masculinities is a relatively recent phenomenon. 'Masculinity' is composed of many masculinities, for, while all men have the male body in common, there are various forms and expressions of gender, of "being masculine" and "being feminine". The pluralization of masculinity highlights that there is not a single masculinity, but rather multiple masculinities, which vary within and across time, space, and cultures (Connell, 1995). Further, these masculinities are arranged in a hierarchy, with the culturally dominant masculinity, or hegemonic masculinity, at the top. R.W. Connell defines hegemonic masculinity, "as the configuration of gender practice...which guarantees...the dominant position of men and the subordination of women" (Connell, 71).

Men are not born with masculinity as part of their genetic make-up; rather it is something into which they are acculturated and which is composed of social codes of behaviour which they learn to reproduce in culturally appropriate ways. It is indexical of class, subculture, age and ethnicity, among other factors. It is hardly surprising that when first encountered, the plural form surprises because it contradicts the widely held, commonsensical assumption that masculinity is a standardized container, fixed by biology, into which all 'normal' men are placed, something 'natural' that can even be measured in terms of psychological traits and physical attributes. But when we link masculinity to culture (itself, obviously, hugely varied) masculinity appears as a diverse, mobile, even unstable, construction. I am adopting what is best termed a 'culturalist' approach to masculinity. Like its primary source feminism, the sociology of masculinity is ultimately concerned with the possibilities of men to change and hopefully dismantle what Connell calls 'gender order'. Manhood in the novel is "defined by the degree of control men exercise over women and the degree of passivity of women of the caste" (Kannabiran, 254). New directions in feminist studies have begun to take up this problem of rethinking masculinity. In today's scenario, Indian masculinities have been approached and studied from a variety of perspectives. This paper endeavours to focus on the various trajectories of masculinities that the two eminent Indian Booker winner women novelists Arundhati Roy and Kiran Desai present in their respective Booker winning novels.

Firstly, I propose to consider Desai's treatment of the terrain of Postcolonial Indian Masculinities in her Man Booker Prize winning novel, *The Inheritance of Loss.* I am using the term 'Postcolonial' not only in the sense of historical time, but also to mean that Desai's novel subtly and subversively scrutinizes the colonial relationship. This paper shall highlight that in the Postcolonial age Indian Masculinities are more akin to Homi Bhabha's concept of the Mimic man and Mrinalini Sinha's concept of Effeminate man rather than to Radhika Chopra's concept of Alpha man or to the Kshatriya model of Masculinity. In England, with the onset of Renaissance, MAN suddenly came into focus. The glorification of manhood received a fillip when the British naval forces under Sir Francis Drake defeated the so-called invincible Spanish Armada in 1588. The famous 16th century surgeon Ambroise Pare suggested that men were more perfect creation of Nature than women and hence it was impossible to change from a man to woman, though the reverse is acceptable: "Nature tends always toward what is most perfect and not, on the contrary, to perform in such a way that what is perfect should become imperfect" (Glover and Kaplan, xiii-xiv).

The Augustan age ushered in the concept of *homo economicus*—men, and not women, were at the fountain head of trade and commerce—and the Rousseauvean concept of the Noble Savage was an exaltation of masculinity. The Industrial Revolution of the 18th century led to a meteoric rise in England's capital formation. This sudden increase in capital made it necessary for the English people to set up colonies in order to channelize their capital. Naturally, their colonial quests were underlined by a sense of manly masculinity. Tales of adventure and heroism were abundantly produced and Robert Baden Powell went so far as to base, as Elleke Boehmer points out, "...the ethos of the Scout Movement on the belief that colonial frontier life was guaranteed to train boys to be *manly* men" (Boehmer, 71). In the colonies the English people upheld their superior position over the natives. Arthur C. Danto aptly points out: "The superiority of Western civilization was never doubted, and one of the premises of Victorian anthropology was in effect that there is a moral direction in history as there is in evolution, that societies and species evolve toward optimality, and that Western Europe was history's masterpiece just as *Homo sapiens* was [sic]

Nature's" (Danto, 338). As far as India was concerned, the infamous Macaulay Minute of February 2, 1835, declared the superiority of colonial education over native education. The target of colonial education was the males and it aimed to create a sort of inaccurate doubling of the colonized as a reflection of the colonizers. The venture is directed upon creation of the construct colonial stereotype as desirable through a colonial discourse. This often resulted in, what Homi Bhabha terms, "metonymy of presence" (Bhabha, 384). The "metonymy of presence", as Homi Bhabha suggests, refers to the mimicry by the colonized of the colonizers. As Bhabha elucidates his concept of the "metonymy of presence"—"Those inappropriate signifiers of colonial discourse—the difference between being English and being Anglicized; the identity between stereotypes which, through repetition, also become different; the discriminatory identities constructed across traditional cultural norms and classification, the Simian Black, the Lying Asiatic—all these are metonymies of presence" (Bhabha, 384). The coloured colonized in their desperate bid to imitate the white colonizers become impoverished specimens of humanity who are almost the same as the colonial masters, but not the same—what Bhabha calls "almost the same but not white" (Bhabha, 384). These Mimic men, living within the interfaces of two cultures, develop split identities. They hate to imitate, but cannot help imitating. This flawed mimetic effort obviously results in the creation of frustrated men who cannot come to terms with themselves as well as with the society at large.

The central male character in the novel, Jemubhai Patel, finds himself languishing on the interface of English and Indian cultures. Educated at Bishop Cotton School and having developed a profound veneration for the portrait of Queen Victoria that stood at the school's entrance, Jemubhai had developed a fondness for the colonial masters. Such was his proclivity for the English life that he married for the purpose of going to England with the dowry, leaving behind the scope of a happy conjugal life at home. Once he boarded the SS Strathnaver, he began hating everything related to the indigenous culture. His father's instruction to throw the coconut overboard as an auspicious prologue to the voyage only gave rise to a sense of pity and shame in his heart—"Jemubhai looked at his father, a barely educated man venturing where he should not be, and the love in Jemubhai's heart mingled with pity, the pity with shame" (*IOL*, 37). A sense of humiliation gripped him when he felt that the food that his mother had packed for him—the profundity of a mother's love was quite lost on him—did not meet the norms of food that the colonizers consumed. So, in order to save himself from being belittled in the eyes of the colonial masters, Jemubhai threw the entire food packet overboard. Desai brings out, in graphic manner, Jemubhai's desperate attempt to eschew his Indian affiliations—"Jemu picked up the package, fled to the deck, and threw it overboard. Didn't his mother think of the inappropriateness of her gesture? Undignified love, Indian love, stinking, unaesthetic love—the monsters of the ocean could have what she had so bravely packed getting up in that predawn mush" (*IOL*, 38). The passage is not only a clear indicator to the locus of the author's sympathies, but also a lucid exploration of Jemubhai's psychic myopia. Jemubhai's refusal of his hearth and home is caused by his intense desire to ape the English to perfection. The colonizers' effort to create an image of their own selves among the colonized, as already mentioned, led to a stunted growth of masculinity. His predilection for all that the English life and culture presented to his imagination makes him a close kin to Ralph Singh in V.S. Naipaul's *The Mimic Men*, "We pretended to be real, to be learning, to be preparing ourselves for life, we mimic men of the New World, one unknown corner of it, with all its reminders of the corruption that came so quickly to the new" (Naipaul, 146).

Hardly had his disenchantment set in than he felt the brunt of being an alien in the land of his dream. The attitude of indifference and insult that was cast on him made him eschew society and hide himself in a shell of loneliness, "He worked twelve hours at a stretch, late into the night, and in thus withdrawing, he failed to make a courageous gesture outward at a crucial moment and found, instead, that his *pusillanimity* and his loneliness had found fertile soil. He retreated into a solitude that grew in weight day by day. The solitude became a habit, the habit became the man, and it crushed him into a shadow" (*IOL*, 39) [italic mine]. Jemubhai felt in his heart that he was a mimic man—almost white, but not quite—and he lacked the courage and conviction of the normative masculine characterised by strength, virility and courage to break through his shell. The noun "pusillanimity" shows that under the influence of the colonial culture, Jemubhai had become a specimen of mimic Indian Masculinity. Jemubhai realizes that in trying to learn a foreign way of life he had become the mimic man, but he would not acknowledge it. When, after retiring from his job, he meets his friend Bose who scathingly criticizes the British, he decides to remain silent. He would not acknowledge that his exalted concept of the British had bitten the dust—"He wouldn't tumble his pride to melodrama at the end of his life and he knew the danger of confession—it would cancel any hope of dignity forever" (*IOL*, 208).

So he decides to buy Cho Oyu, a house made by a Scotsman and tucked in the lap of the north-eastern Himalayas. He felt that the location of the house would give him a shelter where he could hide not only from the eyes of his fellow men, but also from himself—"The judge [Jemubhai] could live here, in this shell, this skull, with the solace of being a foreigner in his own country, for this time he would not learn a new language" (*IOL*, 29). The decision is definitely an indicator of the erosion of masculinity. In fact, after he had come back from England as an ICS officer, he had a realisation of his failed masculinity. Jemubhai comprehended that he had become a stranger to his own people and culture—more distant that anybody else—a non-White carrying out the 'white man's burden' in his own country where he himself is contextualised as a cultural alien, "[h]e had been recruited to bring his countrymen into the modern age, but he could only make it himself by cutting them off entirely, or they would show up reproachful, pointing out to him the lie he had become" (*IOL*, 306).

The character of the cook is a paradigm of failed masculinity. He is weak, both physically and mentally. His superstitions and his acceptance of the fact that he has failed to play the socially sanctioned masculine roles of protector and provider reveal that he is a far cry from the traditional concept of masculinity. However, he does not become an "ogre" like Jemubhai. It is his sterling love for his son, Biju that redeems his feeble masculinity. Both the Boss and the cook represent impoverished specimens of humanity: the former standing for a type of people in whom a decadent slavery to colonial values has displaced the heart from its right place; the latter representing spineless, weak, and cringing individuals who enjoy a shadowy existence. Thus, Desai reveals interestingly, how the defined roles of "male" and "female" approach each other, and how these affect gender issues. Desai's novel also affirms that definitions based on physical or genetic sex alone are therefore not always sufficient when discussing the traditional roles of men and women.

I next propose to consider *The God of Small Things*—a saga of three generations which amply demonstrates how the hegemonic masculinity is constructed in relation to various subordinated masculinities as well as in relation to women. In *The God of Small Things*—a lyrical and poetic evocation of post-independence India, Arundhati Roy captures a segment of life in a small Indian town where male hegemony as well as andocentric power relations are prevailing—where we observe identities rooted in traditional gender definitions like Pappachi and Chacko, as well as identities challenging the traditional gender definitions like Estha, Rahel, and the divorced progressive daughter, Ammu.

Pappachi's tyrannical attitude at home is not a form of cultural or nationalist assertion, as he has already rejected Indian culture. He seems to revere British, but, as a man, he feels "disenfranchised and excluded" assimilating racial disempowerment as a form of castration. Thus, Pappachi, the mega Anglophile, is totally frustrated with his Indian, colonised identity that he becomes such a despot at home, making of the female bodies at hand (Mammachi and Ammu) the means to compensate for his "effeminate"/powerless position. By beating his women, he is asserting his masculinity in the only way left for him. For the colonised subject, the violent subjugation of women becomes perversely important as mimicry of a display of colonial power and in *The God of Small Things,* Pappachi struggles to display colonial power through the violent subjugation of women. Mammachi is portrayed as the stereotypical woman, defenseless against her husband's violence. She makes no attempt to defend herself and constantly lives in fear. She accepts the discontinuance of her violin classes, the beatings with a brass flower vase and the slashing of her daughter, Ammu. Pappachi thus asserts his masculinity by disciplining the bodies of Mammachi and Ammu by violent humiliation. According to Ania Loomba "Colonialism intensified patriarchal relations in colonised lands, often because native men, increasingly disenfranchised and excluded from the public sphere, became more tyrannical at home. They seized upon the home and the women as emblems of their culture and nationality" (Loomba, Ania: 168).

Pappachi seems to tolerate Mammachi's role as a business woman as it deals with the preparation of traditional Indian food—a venture which engages with the traditional feminine role of woman as nurturer and guardian of authentic tradition. Still, Pappachi views the business venture as some sort of threat, and weaves "sullen circles around the mounds of red chilies and freshly powdered yellow turmeric" (*GST*, 46-47). His manly pride is hurt watching his wife running her own career successfully—"Late at night he went into his study and brought out his favorite mahogany rocking chair. He put it down in the middle of the driveway and smashed it into little bits with a plumber's monkey wrench.... He never touched Mammachi again. But he never spoke to her either as long as he lived.... In the evenings, when he knew visitors were expected, he would sit on the verandah and sew buttons that weren't missing onto his shirts, to create the impression that Mammachi neglected him" (*GST*, 47).

Chacko, product of the culture that has a fixation on masculinity, concealed the reality that he was unable to procure the job by taking over Mammachi's pickle factory, even though he had legally claimed ownership of all the family's properties. "My Factory, My pineapples, My pickles", Chacko spoke loud like a roaring lion (*GST*, 56). Chacko creates an image of a well-educated dignified man by ceasing Pappachi's domestic violence. This way he easily manages to take his father's position. Ammu call's him "a Male Chauvinistic Pig" (*GST*, 144). He assigns easily Mammachi the title of "sleeping Partner" (*GST*, 55) in the Pickle Factory. As a successor to Pappachi, Chacko becomes a new patriarch of the Ipe family. Pappachi recedes back to, "his favorite mahogany chair which is reduced to a heap of varnished wicker and splintered wood" (*GST*, 47). "Mammachi packed her wifely luggage and committed it to Chacko's care. From then onwards he became the repository of all her womanly feelings" (*GST*, 160).

Love Laws often become flexible for men. Dube comments, "In the case of inter-caste sexual relations a man incurs external pollution which can be washed off easily but a woman incurs internal pollution which pollutes her permanently" (Dube, 231). When Chacko was discovered having sexual activities with the women in the pickle factory, the act was justified. Mammachi said, "he can't help having a Man's Needs" (*GST*, 160). Mammachi, who herself has been the victims of injustice and has endured her husband's abusive attitude, ignores Chacko's sexual exploitation of the female workers, and thus perpetrates the injustice, she is however, intolerant to her daughter's love affair with a Paravan.

Coming to identities challenging the traditional gender definitions we can begin with Estha, whose blurred gendered identity is revealed on various occasions. First, by his twin status, followed up in the chapter titled, "Mrs Pillai, Mrs Eapan, Mrs Rajgopalan", in which all three children dress up as Hindu ladies complete with saris and bindis but where Estha is the acknowledged 'draping expert'. This playful feminization of Estha can be contrasted with the more traumatic one enacted in his assault at Abhilash Talkies. Further, he is pictured as a junior Julie Andrews with a "nun's voice, as clear as clean water" set against his assailant's 'grovelley' voice. Estha's response is marked by a retreat into invisibility and silence so that he is "Estha Alone and Estha the Quiet". In his father's house he refuses both, the traditional privileges of masculinity and the public life of men and takes a role of a family servant much to the initial embarrassment of his father and stepmother. Until Rahel returns, he remains a ghostly figure whose presence barely registers.

Ammu and Rahel also confound the inherited models of feminity. Having married outside her community, Ammu, leaves and subsequently divorces her husband. She initiates an affair across caste boundaries with Velutha in which she is the sexual teacher. Through Ammu's deeds, Roy shakes the phallocentric boundaries on the societal expectations concerning gender and sexuality and Velutha's socio-religious casteist boundaries. Rahel's character is also marked by subversion of gender identities while Estha mimics Julie Andrews, Rahel aligns himself with Christopher Plummer, *The Sound of Music's* Captain von Trapp. Because of her refusal to conform, she is even blacklisted by her teachers in school for her incendiary behaviour.

Thus, both men and women in Roy's novel refuse bounded gendered identities and the set roles that go with them.

REFERENCES

Bhabha, Homi. "Of Mimicry and Man: The Ambivalence of Colonial Discourse" in Philip Rice and Patricia Waugh (eds.), *Modern Literary Theory,* New York: Arnold, 1967.

Boehmer, Elleke. *Colonial and Postcolonial Literature.* Oxford: O.U.P., 2005.

Connell, R.W. *Masculinities.* Oxford: Polity Press, 1995.

Danto, Arthur C. "The Shape of Artistic Pasts, East and West" in Eliot Deutsch (ed.), *Culture and Modernity: East-West Philosophic Perspectives.* Delhi: Motilal Banarasidass, 1991.

Desai, Kiran. *The Inheritance of Loss.* Penguin Books India, 2006. (Abbreviated as *IOL* in the text.)

Dube Leela. "Caste and Women" *Gender and Caste,* Ed. Anupama Rao. London: Zed Books, 2005.

Ganapathy, Maitreyee S. "Never-ending Narratives", *The Hindu,* Online Edition, Sunday, Feb. 05, 2006.

Glover, David and Cora Kaplan. *Genders.* New York: Routledge, 2008.

Kannabiran, Vasanth and Kalpana Kannabiran. "Violence and Sexuality." *Gender and Caste.* Ed. Anupama Rao. London: Zed Books, 2000.

Loomba, Ania. *Colonialism/Postcolonialism.* London: Routledge, 1998.

Moore, Henrietta. "The Problem of Explaining Violence in the Social Sciences", Eds. Penelope Harvey Peter. *Sex and Violence: Issues in Representation and Experience:* Routledge, 1994.

Naipaul, V.S. *The Mimic Men.* London: Penguin, 2010.

Roy, Arundhati. *The God of Small Things.* New York: Random, 1997. (Abbreviated as *GST* in the text.)

Scott-James, R.A. *The Making of Literature.* New Delhi: Allied Publishers Ltd., 1948.

26

The Failed God of Small Things: Political Aspects in *The God of Small Things*

Jaya Kapoor

Arundhati Roy has so far not come up with a second novel but seems to be devoting all her energies in supporting the underdog wherever her conviction leads her. When asked whether she will write another one in near future, she replied "I'll have to find a language to tell the story I want to tell. By language I don't mean English, Hindi, Urdu, Malayalam, of course. I mean something else. A way of binding together worlds that have been ripped apart" (Guernica, 2011). The interesting thing to note here is that as a commentator and activist in the past few years her language has been her strongest weapon. The greatest strength of her first novel was its language which effectively conveyed that there was a crisis about to happen, that something had become tense and on a short leash. The socio-political atmosphere of Ayemenem reflected the difficult and sad times that lay ahead. Its background based on the period of communist rule and party domination conveyed an age-long anxiety of the powerful class of losing their hold over system. It conspires and makes every effort to remove the first sign of empowerment of the subaltern. The anxiety is not only on the part of those owning the resources but also those who benefit from these resourceful people. Roy's rejection of the usual narrative patterns is a reflection of the inability of such patterns to tell the stories of people who are struggling to find a foothold in their own lives since till now the terms on which they are to live are being dictated by others. The novel might at one level be a social and psychological study but the environment in which the story evolves gives the right background to the events. She has not focused on the Communist rule in Kerala in the novel but if we take a look at the trajectory of her development subsequently, we will realize that we need to take a really serious cognizance of the political undertones of the novel. The present paper focuses on her understanding of the influence of the communist party in Kerala and how a system that is supposed to empower the weak and deprived, when controlled by the historically powerful groups becomes another big god in legion of the other big gods instead of a herald of a new world order. The proposed area of exploration of this paper is not an analysis of the book from the communist or the anti communist perspective. The reason why I take up the issue of her handling of the Communist system owes a lot to her public stance subsequently on issues where she has spoken for the underdogs. For her observation of the strengths and moreover the evils that crept into the system and led to its downfall we can use it as a document.

Kerala is a unique state. Christianity came here earlier than in most of Europe and a lot of its population depends on jobs in the highly Islamic Middle East countries for their livelihood. The Muslims and Christians form more than 40% of its population. The Hindu community there is a highly traditional society with deeply trenched idea of untouchability that spread even into the Christian and Muslim populace. Amidst such a strong religious presence, if a system that stands on the opposite pole of faith succeeds in winning a democratic election, it does make an interesting study. What probably went in its favour was the class of people who had been exploited and ostracized by both the Hindus and the Christians. These poor and marginalized sections of society took up the Communist system for staking their claims and asserting their rights, erected as a sort of god by the small. The Communist system's vision of a classless society led to the rise of the Communist Party in Kerala strongly supported by the marginalized subaltern classes. But slowly somewhere down the line the system failed to fulfil the promise made and seemed to adopt the influences of the social atmosphere of discrimination and unbridled power leading to a corruption of its ranks. It failed to stand up to the ideals and dreams of an equitable society. When the subaltern start staking their claims on their land, they are targeted and victimized by the larger forces controlling history—the big god coming to claim the small god. The story that Roy tells has the Communist Party as one such God of the small people. Roy's own agitation in support of farmers and tribals is her attempt to come to the defense of the small god when their own government starts acting like an extension of the multinational capitalist conglomerate hell bent on grabbing even the right to exist with dignity of these people. When she wrote her novel, in making the child as the narrator, she was already confessing to a breakdown of the traditional forms of narrative and language. So now when she says that needs to find language to express the breakdown that she can see, she probably indicates that the breakdown she is talking about in *The God of Small Things* has grown deeper and now there can be no holding back of the new forces of history which cannot be defined within the extent of our language today.

Aijaz Ahmed is critical of Roy's handling of the issues of communism and caste structure in her novel. He says her novel fails on three counts "far too much is anxiously written, and therefore overwritten"; "the book panders to the prevailing anti-Communist sentiment which damages it both ideologically and formally...she has neither a feel for Communist politics nor a rudimentary knowledge of it", and, "the way it depicts and resolves the issues of caste and sexuality, especially female sexuality...since the novel does stake its transgressive and radical claim precisely on issues of caste and bodily love" (*Frontline*, 1997). In fact, the novel was harshly received by the then critics with a communist leaning of views. Coming from critics like Ahmed such criticism can be held up and explored for validity. It certainly cannot be simply brushed aside. As far as writing style is concerned, probably there is an element of overdoing but then that is probably the tool the writer uses to make the reader sit up and take note. But the fact remains that on the issue of communist ideology, what Roy projected was closer to reality than most of these critics would like to accept. The claim is validated by the course that history followed and the communist regime ended in Kerala. Aijaz Ahmed differentiated between the picture of communist system drawn up by Roy and the caste issue. First on the subject of the communist system, the cadre of the communist party and its leadership along with the think tank of intelligentsia work at a different level from those who have elected the party to power—the voters on the grassroot level. And the writer need not always write from the intellectual's perspective. Since she is talking about an ideology that captured power through popular elections, it is necessary to know how the system works in reality. But the fact is that anywhere in India, the issue of caste never leaves the arena politics—even if it is a communist set up we are talking about. At the level of a few, a select few intellectuals, probably the issue of caste might give way to the issues of class, but in a country where caste is almost always synonymous with class, it is not feasible at the grassroot level. In an interview with Emily Guntheinz, Arundhati Roy observes about caste: It's the defining consideration in all Indian politics, in all Indian marriages.... The lines are blurring. India exists in several centuries. simultaneously. So there are those of us like me, or people that I know for instance, to whom it means nothing.... It's a very strange situation where there's sort of a gap between... sometimes it's urban and rural, but it's really a time warp.

The point that Roy probably wants to emphasize is that though the communists began as a movement and a promise to change the oppressive and discriminating system where caste and class were synonymous and used as instruments for exploitation of the weak. First Roy refers to the failure of Christianity to uplift the Paravans. There were widespread conversions from the untouchables to Christianity with the hope of getting rid of the tag of untouchability but the result is still the same. The discrimination does not end. They become outcaste Christians with their own churches and even their own Bishop. And to add to their tragedy, they are deprived of the government programmes for the upliftment of the untouchables, "It was like having to sweep away your footprints without a broom. Or worse, not being allowed to leave footprints at all" (Roy, 1997: 74).

And then there was hope again in the form of the Communists who promised to empower the downtrodden. But as it turned out, even the communist system at the grass-root level was engaged in the caste discrimination. Like the flag fluttering over the party office, the vision that formed the base of the communist system had faded, paled and withered. Historically Communism had replaced the Churches by the ideology and challenged the existence of a God. It had turned into a faith and a religion for the underprivileged, as I would like to put it, 'a god of small things'—a god for the small people with small needs and even smaller expectations—people who as Roy always puts it 'leave small footprints on this earth'. It promised a life of dignity—something that no other religion had been able to deliver. And when its leaders like Pillai sold out to people like Chako—the symbol of the bourgeois, it was the capitalist forces claiming the communist vision with a promise of profit and prosperity that it ultimately fails to deliver. The ideological bankruptcy comes as a result of leaders aiming to win the next elections and devoting their energies to that end. Dedicated party cadre like Velutha who can be made role model case of what the success of the communist system could do for the people is sacrificed at the altar of next elections. It is a story that is heard for leaders of every corrupted and decaying system—whether political or religious. And Roy's novel epitomizes the tragedy of this betrayal. Pillai does try to justify his desertion to Velutha in high ideological rhetoric (Roy, 1997: 287) but the fact is that the priest has sold the God for profit booking. She said in an interview "Capital requires the coercive powers of the nation state to contain the revolt in the servants' quarters. But it ensures that individual countries cannot stand up to the project of corporate globalization alone, which is why you have even people like Lula Inacio da Silva of Brazil or Nelson Mandela of South Africa, who were giants in the opposition but reduced to dwarfs on the global stage, blackmailed by the threat of capital flight" (*ISR*, 2004). She is referring to the larger picture here, but it applies to the situation in Ayemenem just as well. Only in Ayemenem the leaders probably did not have the honesty of intention that the leaders she mentions here had. It is not the ideology that is at fault. It is the intention with which it was used and the resulting impact it had on society that is wrong.

If implemented with honest intention, the communist ideology would have been an instrument of the weakest sections of society. It had the power of people behind it and when such a power as has the strength of people behind it, rises in support of a cause, none have the strength to oppose it. Gandhi's Civil Disobedience was one such movement that made the people realize the political strength that even a non-violent movement agitation possessed. In Ayemenem too, at the level of the organization the upper castes were not willing to ruffle the feathers of the party. Baby Kochamma's humiliation when the party workers' demonstration forced her to shout slogans and wave the party flag lay pent up inside her. She could not vocally condemn the incident or the abrasive behaviour of the workers, but as an aftermath of the incident her attitude towards Velutha as a symbol of the incident, changed. Her falsely charging Velutha with attempted rape was an attempt to get even with a petty Paravan for daring to challenge the established order of society. But nobody dared to say anything to him knowing that he had the power of organization behind him. Even when Chako approached Pillai, he had never expected Pillai to speak against Velutha. And it is only when he discovers that the party does not support him, that he can find the courage to harm him. In fact, he is quite shocked when Pillai speaks against Velutha (Roy, 1997: 277). Inspector Mathew prefers to cross check with Pillai whether the party is supporting Velutha or not before he goes out to search for Velutha and hounds the Paravan on the complaint of an upper caste which he realizes is false. Even when he sets out to search for Velutha it is simply because Velutha in spite of being a Paravan had the guts to defy his caste and think and feel like an uppercaste. And at each of these points it is the party and the organization that could have saved him but that betrays him for the simple reason that he is a Paravan. Inspector Thomas Mathew as the guardian did not escape the caste stigma and without making even a token effort to find out the other side of the story, hounded Velutha like a hardened criminal.

It has been more than twelve years since the book appeared and if the Supreme Court of India is now expressing its concern over the police making fake encounters and killing like hired killers, Roy could not have been totally ignorant and living in an ivory tower. So if Aijaz Ahmed says that she has no understanding of the ideology he may be right but her insight about the ground reality is not off the mark. At another point of time in another interview she said "It happens all the time. You say something and it sounds extreme and outrageous, and a few years down the line it's pretty much accepted as the norm." In 1997 it might have seemed off the mark to think of the communist system as rotten and the communist regime as a failure but in 2011 we know it was a very close reading of the situation. A creative writer who is not very clear about the nitty gritty of ideology but writes with an ear to the ground, able to hear the footsteps of the approaching times much, able to look at the world and see what is going wrong with it earlier than most is a better writer than one who ends up sounding like a mouthpiece for ideology.

What the novel reveals as its story gradually unfolds is that even a system like the communist rule which should be or at least aim to be free from caste politics in order to pursue the vision of a classless society, cannot do much about it and fails to protect the underdog. Velutha is a grassroot level worker for the party and can expect the party to stand by him in his hour of crisis but when the need comes the corrupted system cannot support its own people let alone protect. If anything, the local leader betrays him and virtually hands him over to the enemy. Comrade Pillai tells Chako "That Paravan is going to cause trouble for you...take it from me...get him a job somewhere else. Send him off" (Roy, 1997: 278). A few lines later the reason for the betrayal revealed "He may be very well ok as a person. But other workers are not happy with him. Already they are coming to me with complaints.... You see, Comrade, from local standpoint, these caste issues are very deep-rooted" (Roy, 1997: 278).

Velutha transgresses the established order and norms in two symbolic ways before finally literally breaching the social order. First through his extensive technical expertise even while lacking a formal training he exhibits signs of intelligence, and more importantly, the quiet and self-assured way in which he conducts himself show presence of self-respect—a crime more heinous than anything since the society has not given people like him the freedom to possess either is a crisis. Both these qualities are manifested in his behaviour when he joins the Communist Party and actively participates in its agitations and in his personal life, falls in love and has a physical relationship with an upper caste woman who is from the family of his masters.

He can symbolically be seen as staking his claims to the land for the factory is an overt symbol of the land and the woman as a covert symbol of land. He was not the brash and shallow person who when empowered forgets the responsibility that comes with it. His character has a depth that makes him fully aware and responsible in the power that he has garnered as a result. That is why he is so shocked when he is not even given a chance to put his case forward let alone defend himself. The very ideas that had groomed his self-confidence and given him identity give way and he is left a petty game to the cruel forces of history. "And there it was again. Another religion turned against itself. Another edifice constructed by the human mind, decimated by human nature...his feet walked to the river. As though they were the leash and he were the dog. History walking the dog" (Roy, 1997: 288).

Velutha's attempt to seek protection from elements in the social order that seemingly stood by his side was futile. He stood lonely on a rainy night betrayed and victimized for what he was and for what he thought of becoming.

REFERENCES

Ahmed, Aijaz, "Reading Arundhati Roy Politically". *Frontline*, Aug. 8, 1997.

Caste in India, http://english.emory.edu/Bahri/caste.html.

International Socialist Review, Issue 38, Nov. Dec. 2004.

Roy, Arundhati. *The God of Small Things*. 1997.

The Un-victim, Amitava Kumar interviews Arundhati Roy www.guernicamag.com. Feb2011.

List of Contributors

A.S. Rao, Associate Professor, MITS University, Lakshmangarh, Rajasthan.

Anita Bhela, Associate Professor, College of Arts and Commerce, University of Delhi, New Delhi.

Anjita Singh, Associate Professor, Department of English, AND College, Kanpur.

Ansul Chandra, Assistant Professor, Ch. C.S.P.G. College, Heonra, Etawah.

Bhupendra Chauhan, Assistant Professor, VGMPG College, Auraiya, Uttar Pradesh.

Charul Jain, Assistant Professor, Maharaja Sayajirao University of Baroda, Vadodara.

Chhaya Jain, Associate Professor, Department of English, VSSD College, Kanpur.

G.K. Das, Former Vice Chancellor, Utkal University, Odisha.

Jaya Kapoor, Assistant Professor, Department of English, University of Allahabad.

Keki N. Daruwalla, Renowned Poet, Novelist and Critic.

Krishna Singh, Associate Professor, Govt. P.G. College, Shahdol, Madhya Pradesh.

Manisha Mathur, Assistant Professor, Department of English, Mata Sundri College for Women, University of Delhi, New Delhi.

N.M. Nigam, Convenor, Board of Studies CSJM University, Kanpur, Principal MMVPG College, Kanpur.

Neeraj Kumar, Associate Professor, Magadh University, Bodh Gaya, Bihar.

Neeru Tandon, Writer, Critic, Feminist, Chief Editor Illuminati, Associate Professor, VSSD College, Kanpur.

P.C. Pradhan, Associate Professor, Dept. of English, B.H.U., Varanasi.

Pawan Kumar, Department of English, MITS University, Lakshmangarh, Rajasthan.

R.N. Rai, Head, Dept. of English, Banaras Hindu University, Varanasi.

R.P. Pradhan, Assistant Professor, Department of English, VSSD College, Kanpur.

Reena Mitra, Associate Professor, Department of English, Christ Church College, Kanpur.

Sarvajit Mukherji, Associate Professor, Dept. of English, University of Allahabad.

Smita Verghese, Associate Professor, Department of English, JNU, New Delhi.

Soumen Mukherjee, Assistant Professor, Institute of Management Studies, Ghaziabad.

Sudhir Arora, Assistant Professor, Department of English, Maharaja Harishchandra P.G. College, Moradabad.

Sunita Sinha, Writer, Editor, Critic, Dept. of English, Women's College, Samastipur, Bihar.

Supriya Shukla, Head, Dept. of English, VSSD College, Kanpur.

Vipin K. Singh, Assistant Professor and Editor Mekal Insights, Dept. of English and Foreign Languages, I.G.N. Tribal University, Amarkantak.